# POLITICS TODAY

Series editor: Bill Jones

# BRITISH POLITICAL PARTIES TODAY

Robert Garner
*and*
Richard Kelly

Manchester University Press
Manchester and New York
*Distributed exclusively in the USA and Canada by St. Martin's Press*

*Published by* Manchester University Press
Oxford Road, Manchester M13 9PL, UK
*and* Room 400, 175 Fifth Avenue, New York, NY 10010, USA

*Distributed exclusively in the USA and Canada*
*by* St. Martin's Press, Inc., 175 Fifth Avenue, New York,
NY 10010, USA

*British Library Cataloguing-in-Publication Data*
A catalogue record for this book is available from the British Library

*Library of Congress Cataloging-in-Publication Data*
Garner, Robert, 1960–
    British political parties today / Robert Garner and Richard Kelly.
        p.   cm — (Politics today)
    ISBN 0-7190-3047-1 (hard). — ISBN 0-7190 3048-X (paper)
    1. Political parties—Great Britain—History—20th century.
I. Kelly, Richard N.   II. Title III. Series: Politics today
(Manchester, England)
JN1121.G37   1993
324.241′009′04—dc20                                    93-79

ISBN 0 7190 3047 1 *hardback*
ISBN 0 7190 3048 X *paperback*

Photoset in Great Britain
by Northern Phototypesetting Co. Ltd, Bolton
Printed in Great Britain
by Bell & Bain Limited, Glasgow

# CONTENTS

# TABLES

# PREFACE

Had this textbook on British political parties been written twenty-five years ago, we might still have been able to offer the following synopsis:

British politics is dominated by two parties, each dependent upon the instinctive support of most blue collar and white collar workers respectively, each capable of attracting substantial support in all parts of the country and each therefore capable of winning a handsome majority in the House of Commons. Although the two parties differ considerably in origins and history, the distribution of power and authority inside them is – in practice if not theory – remarkably similar. Partly as a result of this, the policies each party presents to the general public are also broadly similar, although anxious supporters of electoral reform – and hopeful radicals in either party – believe this consensus is not unassailable, with each party having the potential in government to effect major changes in society. For this reason alone, the two main parties remain the most important channels of popular participation in contemporary British politics.

As Harold Wilson famously remarked, even a week is a long time in politics, so it should not be so surprising that a quarter of a century should have made questionable about ten of the (formerly commonplace) assumptions contained in the above paragraph. Yet one need not go back to the 1960s to uncover signs of substantial change. Even during the period of Conservative Government since 1979, scholars have been obliged to re-examine, then re-examine again, the axioms of modern party politics.

In the early 1980s, for example, it seemed as if the new Social

vii

Democratic Party, fired by a new public mood of 'classlessness' and scepticism towards the 'old politics', augured a new age of multi-party politics and inter-party co-operation. Yet the demise of the Alliance after 1987, and a further slippage of centre party support in 1992, were to make such claims seems facile as the Tories embarked upon their fourth successive term in office. Conversely, Labour's fourth successive defeat – and its failure again to secure more votes in southern England (excluding London) than any other opposition party – punctured any idea that, since 1989, British politics had reverted to a two-dimensional 'reality' with Her Majesty's Opposition at last poised to take its rightful turn in office. Moreover, Labour's inability to regain power raises questions with enormous implications for the future of British party politics. Is a single party alternative to Conservative rule any longer feasible? And does Labour's string of defeats undermine the very *rationale* of one of Britain's major parties? Labour's dwindling membership already betrays a belief on the centre-left that the various 'progressive' pressure groups which emerged in the 1980s (such as Charter 88) now offer a more satisfying means of political participation – at least for those with specific interests and concerns.

In other areas too there was fluctuation in the course of a single decade. The 'Butskellite' consensus, which bound the parties together for much of the post-war era, was plainly ripped apart during Mrs Thatcher's first Government. Yet Neil Kinnock's leadership of the Labour party after 1983 (and especially after 1987) and John Major's premiership after 1990 were widely thought to have steered the country to a new age of consensus politics. On the other hand, the differences that were revealed during the 1992 campaign were, in certain areas, unprecedented and perhaps more fundamental than those seen in any other post-war election. As with the electoral structure of the party system, the policy relationships within it were, by the end of 1992, far from clear-cut.

In terms of internal party structures, the 1980s gave additional cause for fresh thinking. The organisational changes inside the Labour party between 1980 and 1981 were a direct challenge to the 'oligarchic' theories offered in R. T. McKenzie's seminal study of 1955. After 1983, however, there were further changes inside the Labour Party which seemed to revive the McKenzie thesis. Following Labour's subsequent defeats in 1987 and 1992, many of these later changes are now themselves likely to be revoked as decentralisation again becomes a popular theme: in short, Labour's organisational flux seems set to continue. Inside the Conservative Party, Thatcher's charismatic leadership seemed to strengthen the conventional theories of 'hierarchy' and 'deference'. Yet, at the same time there were new and often concealed trends at work among both backbenchers and grass roots activists which were to be exemplified by Thatcher's downfall and its aftermath. Friction inside the party after the 1992 election, conspicuously in respect of Europe, implied that these iconoclastic forces were not simply by-products of huge Parliamentary majorities; as in the Labour Party, academic debate about power in the party looked set to survive well into the 1990s.

The impact of parties in government has also been subjected to intense reappraisal since 1979. The crusading spirit of the Thatcher ministries, and the bold reforms they instigated, all appeared to vindicate the capacity and utility of determined governing parties in a dynamic liberal democracy (something which also underlined growing demands for constitutional reform by those alarmed at some of the policies initiated by a government without majority support from voters). Yet, when recalling the circumstances of the late 1970s, how could we be sure that the Thatcher Governments were not the symptom, rather than the cause, of profound socio-economic change? It was also ironic that a government associated with ambitious and controversial reform should have taken two historic steps (the passage of the Single European Act 1986 and entry into the European Exchange Rate Mechanism in 1990) which arguably limited not only the likelihood of serious party differences in future but also the scope for any future government with similarly radical intentions. Have these developments (when allied to the continued internationalism of commerce and industry) finally brushed aside the idea that British general elections, and by implication British political parties, are somehow important? Or should events since the 1992 election, particularly the delayed Conservative reaction to the Maastricht Treaty, make us wary of any deterministic 'end of history' approach? Do the vicissitudes of British politics since the 1992 election merely present a whole new range of challenging questions for students of party politics?

Having illuminated such questions, we must stress that this textbook is a diagnosis rather than a prognosis, an analysis and not a prescription. We do aim, however, at least to clarify and explain the most important areas of discontinuity and uncertainty that have arisen in party politics during the lifetime of most sixth-formers and undergraduates – and, by doing so, provoke a more informed and measured debate in lessons, seminars and tutorials.

In the chapters which follow, we have tried to examine those same areas in a way that is comprehensible and accessible to those studying politics at A Level and beyond, taking full account of recent changes in examination content and syllabus development. We have also tried to inspect Britain's major parties not as autonomous entities but as interdependent units whose behaviour cannot be understood without some reference to broader trends in society, the economy and overseas (not to mention other political parties!). Again, this particular approach reflects the changing focus of political study in both further and higher education.

This textbook, of course, takes on board fully the 1992 election result and its consequences. In view of the Conservative Party's epoch-making victory, and the undoubted electoral superiority it now enjoys over its rivals, we have decided to devote slightly more attention than originally planned to its evolution, ideas and organisation. Indeed, the internal workings of this phenomenally effective party have remained a curiously ignored area of political science, and we believe that the treatment afforded by this textbook is the most detailed – and radical – to appear since the party took office in 1979.

Although we are entirely responsible for the contents and structure of this book, we would still like to thank Ray Offord and Richard Purslow at MUP for their patience and encouragement, and our colleagues at the University of Buckingham and The Manchester Grammar School for their advice and helpful criticism. The book is dedicated to Maria, Cheryl and Zoë.

RWG
RNK
August 1992

# 1

# WHY DO PARTIES EXIST?

As teachers, we regularly stress to our students the importance of defining the terms they use. At the beginning of this book we should practice what we preach and define what we mean by political parties. As James Jupp pointed out, the idea of a party 'rests on the acceptance of uniformity and co-operation by those engaged in collective deliberation'.[1] Defined in such a way, a party can exist in many spheres of social life from a church to a trade union. What distinguishes a *political* party from the more general use of the term is its aim, realistic or not, to take control of the political institutions of a particular society. Thus, Madgwick defines a political party as an 'organised group seeking political power . . . and aiming to form, or form part of, a government'.[2]

There are two additional points that need to be made here. In the first place, the definition does not distinguish between the types of system within which parties are operating. For some political scientists this is a crucial omission. Sigmund Neumann, for instance, limits the title political party to the competitive systems of the West. As he points out, 'the very definition of party presupposes a democratic climate' since to 'become a "party" to something always means identification with one group and differentiation from another'.[3]

Clearly there are important differences between the one-party systems which have existed in Eastern Europe for much of the post-war period and the competitive party systems found in the West. Indeed, the very notion of choice inherent in the latter

1

ensures that political élites remain responsive to the electorate.[4] However, to deny that the former type of party can properly be called a political party is a stifling limitation which restricts our ability to compare and contrast different types of parties effectively.

The second point is that some commentators seek to limit the definition to include only those parties that have a mass organisation in addition to a recognisable grouping within a legislature. This has important implications since it determines the point at which parties can be said to have emerged. Hague and Harrop, for instance, claim that parties were created as 'a response to the extension of the suffrage and the need imposed on parliamentary caucuses to develop extra-parliamentary organisation'.[5] Again, it is not clear why this artificial limitation has been introduced. In Britain, the stimulus for the creation of mass party organisations was provided by the extension of the franchise in the nineteenth century. After the 1832 Reform Act, local registration societies and national bodies such as the Tory Carlton Club and the Whig Reform Club were created to organise the parties' efforts to attract votes. Modern mass party organisations, however, did not appear until after the Second Reform Act in 1867. Local Liberal organisations, most notably in Birmingham, were the first to emerge in order to attract the newly enfranchised working-class voters and these were followed by national organisations, the National Union of Conservative Associations in 1867, Conservative Central Office in 1870 and the National Liberal Federation in 1877.[6]

It would be wrong, however, to regard this as the beginning of political parties in Britain as opposed to the emergence of a *different* kind of party system. Groups had existed in Parliament at least as far back as the seventeenth century and, although they were not particularly coherent or well organised, the labels Tory and Whig were in common usage by the beginning of the nineteenth century. Indeed, the party labels 'Liberal' and 'Conservative' preceded the creation of extra-Parliamentary organisations. The Tory Party became generally known as the Conservative Party in the 1830s following Peel's declaration to his constituents that Tory policy was to 'conserve' all that was good in existing institutions. The Liberal Party, likewise, emerged in the 1860s as an amalgam of those Conservatives who split from the party over the issue of the Corn Laws, a group of radicals and the old Whigs.[7]

## Functions

Political parties exist because they perform a number of crucial functions in the political system. Surprisingly, their important role is often not appreciated. They are not, for instance, mentioned in the American Constitution and, despite its former hegemonic role, the Communist Party of the Soviet Union got only a fleeting mention in the Soviet Constitution. In Britain, likewise, only recently have party labels appeared on ballot papers; and in Hansard, the official record of Parliamentary proceedings, the constituency – but not the party – of MPs is recorded. Despite this, it would be difficult to imagine the British political system without them. Their importance quickly becomes apparent when we consider the functions they perform.

### *The Articulation of Demands*

Political parties, together with pressure groups, provide the mechanism by which issues of public concern find their way on to the political agenda. Different demands, of course, may be articulated by different parties. In Britain, the demands of trade unions, for instance, are more likely to be a priority for the Labour Party than the Conservatives who are more closely associated with business interests. Some demands, on the other hand, may, for a variety of reasons, never or rarely be articulated. Nevertheless, the need for parties to maximise votes in liberal democracies ensures that they will take great care to listen to what the electorate is saying – a factor evident in Labour's policy reversals since 1983 and the Conservatives' recognition that the poll tax was massively unpopular.

## *The Aggregation of Interests*

The key difference between political parties and pressure groups is that parties are responsible for forming order out of chaos by converting the demands of a wide-ranging set of interests into a manageable set of policies for the electorate's consideration. Thus, they develop programmes which are then further refined into election manifestos. By aggregating interests in this way parties simplify elections and provide the voters with a choice – a key characteristic of the party system in liberal democracies. In terms of the choice offered, it would be correct to label Britain as a multi-party system since the choice is considerable. Of greater explanatory validity, however, is an examination of the electoral strength of the parties.

In this respect, Britain for most of the post-war period had a classic two-party system (see Chapter 2). Since 1970, this system has come under persistent pressure, with the growth of support for a wider range of political parties; the impact of centre parties like the Liberals will be considered separately in Chapter 8. Yet it has not been just the centre parties that have benefited from the fragmentation of party support. The Scottish Nationalist Party has commanded between 11 and 30 per cent of votes in Scotland at the last seven general elections, winning eleven seats and more votes than the Conservative in October 1974. In Wales, Plaid Cymru has secured on average 8 per cent of the votes at elections since 1970 and has become a veritable force in 'Welsh-speaking' constituencies (gaining one from the Liberal Democrats as recently as 1992). The Green Party achieved almost 15 per cent of the votes in Britain at the 1989 European elections, a performance reflected and often bettered by many of its members contesting local elections in the late 1980s. In the late 1970s, there was even increased support for the National Front, which came third in three by-elections in 1976 and 1977 while polling up to 17 per cent in certain local elections.

The emergence of such parties prompts some reassessment of party functions in British politics today. As pointed out at the start of this chapter, all parties could be credited with the pursuit of governmental power. It was also pointed out, however, that in many cases this aim is not wholly realistic, with many parties accepting (and not always tacitly) that their 'real' aim is to shape the policies of other, stronger parties. As indicated in the preceding paragraph, a considerable number of high-profile parties in Britain now fall into this category – and their effect has been far from negligible.

Both main parties, for example, began to examine seriously the prospect of devolution following the success of nationalist candidates at by-elections in the late 1960s, Labour's interest becoming even more urgent as the threat to its electoral heartlands became more obvious. (Indeed, as parties like the SNP contest only a limited number of seats, it is quite clear that 'moral' influence, rather than office, is their immediate objective.) The hardening of Tory policy on immigration in 1978, along with Mrs Thatcher's comments about British culture being 'swamped', were also encouraged by electoral developments concerning smaller parties, in this case the National Front. More recently, the progress made by the Green Party forced environmental issues to the forefront of the main parties' agendas, even though the Greens (like the NF) achieved no representation at all at Westminster.

It should be added that the increased likelihood of hung parliaments (and even electoral reform) offer a more direct prospect for such parties to attain 'influence without power', thereby giving further reason and motive for their activities. In such circumstances, the wishes of the Northern Ireland parties (whose influence has hitherto been constrained by the failure of British parties to compete for votes in Ulster) might also acquire a new dimension of influence, their functions no longer confined to territorial representation.

What all parties have in common is an urge to maximise support. This in turn, can have a unifying and stabilising effect upon society. The accommodation of divergent interests prevents powerful groups being alienated from the political process and thereby becoming a source of instability. Furthermore, it requires parties to forge a compromise between competing demands, thus promoting consensus and unity. The Conservative Party's electoral success, for instance, has been based on their appeal to members of different social, economic and regional sections of British society, all of whom have been offered something they valued.[8] Equally, parties can reflect irreconcilable divisions within society. Thus, the parties in Northern Ireland are a direct result of the permanent Protestant majority and Catholic minority.

### The setting of ideological goals for society

All parties have some principles, although their coherence and the extent to which they guide the work of the party vary. Ideology in one-party totalitarian states plays a vital role, justifying the party's elevated position and providing aims for the society as a whole. Obviously, mainstream British parties are more pragmatic than this but the extent of the pragmatism is a matter of dispute. It may be, for instance, that the demands of electoral competition require parties to tone down their ideological convictions or that, alternatively, parties in government may be forced to abandon their principles in the face of mounting opposition or evidence that the convictions are misplaced. These issues are discussed further throughout this book but particularly in Chapters 4 and 6.

The principles a party promote are likely to be linked with the interests represented. Labour's traditional socialism, for instance, with its emphasis on equality and the general improvement of working-class living standards, obviously reflects the party's close ties with the trade union movement and its reliance on working-class votes. Similarly, the Conservative emphasis on the efficacy of the free market and private enterprise reflects the party's links with business and financial interests. Having said that, for much of the period since 1945, as Chapter 3 will show, there was a consensus on methods and goals which belied the divergent origins of the two main parties. It was only in the 1970s that this consensus began to break down and fundamental differences between the two main parties began to emerge.

### Political communication, education and mobilisation

Political parties seek to educate the people politically and get them involved in politics. In Britain, this means canvassing at elections to make sure people turn out and vote, using the media and producing their own literature to instruct the public of what they stand for and trying to persuade people to join them as members. In some political systems, political mobilisation is and has been far more extensive. Hitler's National Socialist Party, for instance, held mass rallies, provided uniforms for its members and organised an active youth movement. In one-party states, political communication is uni-directional – from the top down – whereas in competitive party systems the process is two-way, with considerable emphasis placed upon the communication of the wants of the people to their political leaders.

British parties, therefore, provide a link between the rulers and the ruled, whereby the interests of the latter are represented in the political system. Thus, as Jupp points out, parties 'must remain until either no one or everyone is prepared to take part in the political process'.[9] The picture is somewhat more complicated, however, since we need to distinguish between a party's leadership, its rank and file and its supporters or potential supporters. The primary aim of mainstream British parties is to attract enough votes to win a majority of seats in the House of Commons. Given its importance, it is not surprising that political scientists have devoted much of their time to examining the nature of the parties' electoral support – a task which is undertaken in Chapter 9 of this book. Equally important is the recognition that, because modern parties require a mass organisation in order to attract support from the wider electorate, they have complex internal structures which are worthy of study.

One key question is the ideological and organisational relationship between the ordinary party member and the leadership. One possibility is that the party's leadership is prevented from effectively representing the interests of the wider electorate because of the pressure applied by the rank and file or even a small group within the rank and file. This was exactly the fear expressed by Ostrogorski in his major study *Democracy and the Organisation of Political Parties*. Writing at the turn of the century, Ostrogorski noted with concern the emergence of mass extra-parliamentary party organisations. He saw in this development the danger that party leaderships in Parliament would become the servants of the powerful party bosses outside Parliament. Thus, MPs would lose their independence and become the delegates of unaccountable forces in political parties.[10]

Writing partly in response to Ostrogorski, Robert Michels strongly argued that he had nothing to fear.[11] Michels proposed a hypothetical law governing all complex social organisations including political parties. This 'Iron Law of Oligarchy' postulated that all organisations, of any size or complexity, are characterised by oligarchic tendencies. That is, power in organisations comes to reside within a small élite group at the apex. These leaders, for organisational and psychological reasons, cannot be controlled by the rank and file and therefore democracy is impossible in these organisations.

The classic work on the organisation of British parties was written in the mid-1950s by Robert McKenzie.[12] McKenzie's main aim was to assess the relevance of Michels's theory to the distribution of power within the two main British parties. He concludes, in line with Michels, that authority in both parties rests with the Parliamentary party and its leadership and that the role of the party outside Parliament is limited to vote-getting rather than policy-making. Thus, McKenzie seeks to dispel what he sees as the myth that the Labour Party, unlike the Conservative Party, is internally democratic. McKenzie argues that both parties have a similar power structure because they both accept the rules and conventions which govern the British political system. Thus, both parties accept that party leaders must exercise absolute power in the choice of their Cabinet colleagues and that MPs must be responsible to the electorate and not the extra-Parliamentary party.

The organisations of the two main British parties are examined in Chapters 5 and 7. It is strongly suggested, in particular, that McKenzie may well have overestimated the power of the Parliamentarians. Taking into account Labour's democratic ethos and the recent attempts to 'democratise' the party of which McKenzie, of course, was not aware, this is not a particularly novel conclusion. It is argued in addition, however, that McKenzie may well have also underestimated the influence of the rank and file in the

Conservative Party, a political grouping which has traditionally been seen as the classic example of an oligarchical organisation.

### *Political recruitment*

By dominating the political process, British parties provide political leaders from within their ranks. In the first place, *parties organise elections*. To become an MP it is necessary to be selected by a political party, since independents are very rarely elected to the House of Commons. As a result, strict party discipline ensures that parties *organise the legislature*. This, in turn, produces *strong party government* since, with very few exceptions, one party controls the executive by virtue of its majority of seats in the Commons. Thus, we distinguish between governments by referring to the party in charge at that particular time.

Parties do not have such a pervasive influence in all political systems. In the United States, for instance, parties are relatively weak. The introduction of primaries (elections in which voters may help determine a party's presidential candidate) has meant that parties have lost control of the nomination process. Furthermore, the vast diversity of the USA, symbolised by the federal system of government, militates against the development of a coherent party line. Finally, the separation of powers prevents the President from exercising the patronage available to a British Prime Minister which acts as a crucial instrument of party unity. The result, in the United States, is a legislature where the members owe little to their parties, where constituency interests are a priority and where executive office for Congressmen is not on the agenda.

Despite the central position of parties in British government, it would be wrong to assume automatically that they are the dominant, or even the most important, influence on government outputs. Indeed, as the final chapter of this book illustrates, there are many constraints acting upon party governments. It is at least a possibility that their intentions are dwarfed by on-going policy commitments, the influence of an experienced, permanent civil service (which provides an alternative route into the political élite), and the demands of powerful groups in society. Finally, there are the limitations imposed by Britain's increasing absorption into Europe, a factor which threatens to undermine many of the commonplace assumptions about British parties and, indeed, British politics in general.

### Notes

1   J. Jupp, *Political Parties*, London, 1968, p. ix.
2   P. J. Madgwick, *Introduction to British Politics*, London, 1984, p. 254.
3   S. Neumann, 'Toward a comparative study of political parties', in J. Blondel (ed), *Comparative Government: A Reader*, London, 1969, p. 69.
4   See M. Harrop & W. L. Miller, *Elections and Voters*, London, 1987.
5   R. Hague & M. Harrop, *Comparative Government and Politics. An Introduction*, London, 1987, p. 139.
6   A. R. Ball, *British Political Parties*, London, 1987, pp. 26–51.
7   See J. Vincent, *The Formation of the British Liberal Party 1857–68*, London, 1966.
8   A. R. Ball, *Modern Politics and Government*, London, 1977, pp. 77–8.
9   Jupp, *Political Parties*, p. 109.
10  M. Ostrogorski, *Democracy and the Organisation of Political Parties*, Vol. 1, Chicago, 1964.
11  R. Michels, *Political Parties*, New York, 1954 (first edition published in 1915).
12  R. T. McKenzie, *British Political Parties*, London, 1955.

# 2

# BRITAIN'S PARTY SYSTEM: A TWO-PARTY AFFAIR?

In recent years, there has been a great deal of argument and confusion concerning the true character of Britain's party system. This represents a sharp contrast with the situation obtaining for most of the post-war period, when Britain's party system was widely considered a supreme example of the two-party model. Writing in 1962, Ivor Jennings suggested that there was a 'natural' tendency for Britain to have a two-party system,[1] while in 1968 R. M. Punnett agreed that such a system was the logical outcome of both the Westminster model of Parliamentary democracy and the pattern of political debate in Britain.[2]

Since 1974, however, this type of certainty – and unanimity – has disappeared. Drucker's study of 1977 suggested that Britain's party system had become 'multi-party' in character, citing the 1974 general elections as evidence.[3] Three years later, an introductory chapter by S. E. Finer implied that the 1979 election had highlighted that Britain's was, in essence, 'still a two party system'.[4] The emergence of the SDP–Liberal Alliance in 1981 prompted further conflicting speculation. By 1985, for instance, Berrington saw fit to publish articles entitled 'Enter the three party system' and following the 1987 election, Benyon cited the existence of 'two two-party systems', on account of the Alliance having displaced Labour as the major opposition to the Conservatives in the south of England.[5] In early 1988, however, Crewe suggested that 'the three-party system Britain has known since 1981 is dead', while Alderman's study of 1989 contemplated the possibility that Britain now had a 'one-party system' similar to that of Japan.[6]

To make sense of this confusion, and to examine the extent to which Britain's party system has changed, it is necessary to clarify the nature of the 'old' two-party system, as acknowledged by most scholars of British politics prior to 1974.

## Features of the two party system (1945–74)

(i) To begin with, there was a *duopoly of support* among voters for the two major parties. The vast majority of electors supported either the Labour or Conservative parties at a general election – as in 1951 when the combined two-party vote was as high as 96.8 per cent. Until 1974, the two parties' share of the vote was never much below 90 per cent, while the third party vote never exceeded the Liberals' 11.2 per cent in 1964 (see table 2.1).

(ii) There was also a *duopoly of Parliamentary representation*, with well over 90 per cent of seats in the House of Commons being occupied by Labour or Conservative MPs (not yet ten in 1955). Indeed, it has been suggested that the rectangular shape of the House, in contrast to the circular appearance of most other European legislatures, reflected its confrontational, two-party nature.[7] The Commons was widely considered to be less a debating chamber than a battleground, accommodating two disciplined and coherent political armies (see table 2.2).[8]

(iii) The two parties were, in addition, supported and sustained by *two huge blocks of reliable voters*, giving rise to the psephological phenomenon of *partisan stability*.[9] The vast majority of voters were habitual supporters of either the Labour or Conservative parties, whose views on most political issues were informed by party allegiance, rather than *vice versa*.[10] Elections were therefore determined by a small portion of the electorate (usually 10–15 per cent) who were 'floating voters', those without any firm commitment to either party. This situation naturally made it exceedingly difficult for third or fourth parties to break the two-party stranglehold and thereby establish themselves as viable alternatives at elections.

*Table 2.1* Main parties' share of votes cast in UK general elections 1945–92 (%)

| | Con. | Lab. | Combined Con-Lab vote | Lib.[a] | Others[b] |
|---|---|---|---|---|---|
| 1945 | 39·8 | 47·8 | 87·6 | 9·0 | 3·4 |
| 1950 | 43·5 | 46·0 | 89·5 | 9·1 | 1·4 |
| 1951 | 48·0 | 48·8 | 96·8 | 2·5 | 0·7 |
| 1955 | 49·7 | 46·4 | 96·1 | 2·7 | 1·2 |
| 1959 | 49·4 | 43·8 | 93·2 | 5·9 | 0·9 |
| 1964 | 43·4 | 44·1 | 87·5 | 11·2 | 1·3 |
| 1966 | 41·9 | 48·0 | 89·9 | 8·5 | 2·6 |
| 1970 | 46·4 | 43·0 | 89·4 | 7·5 | 3·1 |
| 1974 (Feb.) | 37·9 | 37·1 | 75·0 | 19·3 | 5·7 |
| 1974 (Oct.) | 35·9 | 39·2 | 75·1 | 18·5 | 6·4 |
| 1979 | 43·9 | 36·9 | 80·8 | 13·8 | 5·4 |
| 1983 | 42·4 | 27·6 | 70·0 | 25·4 | 4·6 |
| 1987 | 42·3 | 30·8 | 73·1 | 22·6 | 4·3 |
| 1992 | 41·9 | 34·4 | 76·3 | 17·8 | 5·9 |

*Notes*

[a] The Liberal Party vote becomes the Liberal/SDP Alliance vote in 1983 and 1987 and the Liberal Democratic vote in 1992.

[b] Since 1974, the votes of the 'other' parties have included those of the Ulster Unionists which until then had been incorporated into the Conservatives' total.

(iv) These two large blocks of 'aligned' voters provided the parties with *roughly equal levels of support* at elections. In the eight elections prior to 1974, for example, the average gap between the parties was a mere 4 per cent. This, in turn, provided each of the parties with roughly equal periods in office (a factor assisted by the relatively high number of 'marginal' constituencies which then existed). It would be careless to state that, until 1979, the two parties alternated in government as the Conservatives won three consecutive elections in the 1950s and were in power for a period of thirteen years (1951–64). Nevertheless, it is remarkable that in the period of thirty-four years between 1945 and 1979, each of the two parties governed for roughly seventeen years.

(v) The two party battle had a *nationwide pattern*. Throughout the country, the main constituency contest involved Labour and Conservative candidates. In no more than 10 per cent of all British

*Table 2.2*   Main parties' Parliamentary representation after UK general elections 1945–92

|  | Con. | Lab. | Lib.[a] | Others[b] |
|---|---|---|---|---|
| 1945 | 213 | 393 | 12 | 22 |
| 1950 | 298 | 315 | 9 | 3 |
| 1951 | 321 | 295 | 6 | 3 |
| 1955 | 344 | 277 | 6 | 3 |
| 1959 | 365 | 258 | 9 | 1 |
| 1964 | 304 | 317 | 9 | – |
| 1966 | 253 | 363 | 12 | 2 |
| 1970 | 330 | 287 | 6 | 7 |
| 1974 (Feb.) | 297 | 301 | 14 | 23 |
| 1974 (Oct.) | 277 | 319 | 12 | 26 |
| 1979 | 339 | 268 | 11 | 17 |
| 1983 | 397 | 209 | 23 | 21 |
| 1987 | 375 | 229 | 22 | 24 |
| 1992 | 336 | 271 | 20 | 24 |

*Notes*
[a]  The Liberals' total becomes that of the Liberal/SDP Alliance in 1983 and 1987 and the Liberal Democrats in 1992.
[b]  Until 1974, the Conservatives' total included Ulster Unionists.

constituencies could a candidate of any other party expect to achieve even second place when the votes had been counted. This state of affairs was reflected in the fact that both parties, though obviously stronger in some areas of the country than others, each had *substantial levels of support nationwide.* At the 1959 election, for example, Labour returned fifty-four MPs from the south of England, while in Scotland the Tories won only seven fewer seats than Labour (see table 9.7). In the major cities, such as London, Manchester, Liverpool and Glasgow, it was common to find similar numbers of Conservative and Labour MPs.

(vi) Finally, the above factors helped to produce a *two-party culture* in British political life. Political arguments inside and outside Parliament and – for that matter – outside the two parties themselves were normally a reflection of the Labour or Tory standpoint. On television and radio current affairs programmes, it was customary to pit Labour and Conservative spokesmen against each other, with little interest being shown in representatives of any other parties.[11] Likewise, at Labour and Tory meetings or conferences, criticism and calumny were inevitably directed at the other party, with third or fourth parties considered unworthy of attention. Until 1979, the two parties' manifestos did not even acknowledge the existence of any other parties, while from an academic angle it is interesting that McKenzie's exhaustive study of British parties in 1955 relegated any assessment of the Liberal Party to its appendix.

### The foundations of the two-party system

The two-party system was founded upon a number of factors which are in themselves essential to any understanding of British politics in the post-war era. The first, and most important, of these was a *class alignment* – the sociological phenomenon whereby most voters felt a strong and lasting affinity with one of the two major social classes in society: the working class (those in manual, 'blue collar' occupations) and middle class (those in non-manual, 'white collar' occupations). As a result, about two-thirds of manual workers identified with and voted for the Labour Party – a party rooted in urbanised, trade unionist politics – while about three-quarters of non-manual workers identified with and voted for the Conservatives – a party long associated with wealth, property and status (this phenomenon is examined further in Chapter 9).

Although social class was the main foundation of the two-party system, it was nevertheless fortified by the *consensus* which characterised the parties' relationship for much of the post-war period (see Chapter 3). Following the economic traumas of the inter-war years and the apparently successful way in which the economy and society were 'planned' between 1939 and 1945, public opinion at the end of the war was increasingly sympathetic towards 'centre-left' or social democratic ideals (economic planning, public ownership, greater public spending, greater equality etc.). Labour's landslide victory at the 1945 election demonstrated the party's success in articulating this new mood and the reforms it subsequently effected in government enjoyed widespread approval. The Conservatives' recognition of Labour's success provoked a number of key changes in Tory policy and philosophy, paving the way for a new, social democratic consensus that endured for nearly thirty years. In short, by 1951 the two main parties were firmly encamped in the new middle ground occupied by most of the electorate. This compounded the problems of those parties, like the Liberals, who sought to resist the Labour–Tory duopoly. The Liberals' hoped-for revival had already been hampered by their 'classless' image at a time when voters' loyalties were determined largely by the class alignment; as a 'centre' party as well, they now had the added problem that their political 'market' had been cornered by their two major rivals. With hindsight, it is remarkable that the Liberals managed even to survive. Indeed, after the election of 1951 (when they attained only 2.5 per cent of the votes), their leader was invited to consider the prospect of being merged into the Conservative Party (see Chapter 8).

Finally, this consensus – and the two-party system – were upheld by the relative health of the British economy, and the continual rise in living standards for most of the 1950s and 1960s (an epoch immortalised, perhaps, by Harold Macmillan's claim, in 1958, that most people had 'never had it so good'). Election results suggest that many voters shared Macmillan's view, while those who were more circumspect seemed to believe that any problems could be remedied by voting the 'other' party into office. This confidence in the ability of at least one of the two parties to guarantee prosperity again hampered the prospects of third and fourth parties.

### Effects of the two-party system

The most significant consequence of two-party dominance was that one of the parties was usually able to achieve a comfortable overall majority in the House of Commons and thereby form a government without the assistance of other parties. *Single party government* was therefore the norm in British politics, in stark contrast to most other European democracies where coalition government was usual. Of course, this was partly a product of

Britain's non-proportional electoral system, which tended to exaggerate a winning party's number of seats. Yet it must be recalled that first-past-the-post does not, in itself, guarantee a two-party system and therefore single-party government. It does so only if the two parties are alone in having concentrated support. That the Labour and Tory parties fulfilled this condition owed everything to the class basis of their support and to the fact that the demographic map of Britain consisted largely of working-class and middle-class areas.

Single-party governments were to have a profound impact upon the nature of British politics. The situation whereby Her Majesty's Government consisted solely of one party's representatives, with Her Majesty's Opposition consisting solely of the other's, discouraged serious co-operation between the parties and fostered what became known as *adversary politics*; the party in government would instinctively reject anything proposed by the Opposition, which would likewise oppose anything the Government said or did. For many liberal academics and observers, adversary politics had a deleterious effect not just upon the conduct of government but upon the tenor of society. As Bogdanor asserted, 'it overstates what divided us and understates the strong national desire for consensus'.[12]

This adversarial system certainly had a strong effect upon the atmosphere of the House of Commons; its debates took place in a mainly gladiatorial and acrimonious fashion peculiar by European standards, also contrasting with the United States Congress which was also dominated by the representatives of two parties. Perhaps the most telling consequence, however, of single-party government was that it spawned the *doctrine of the mandate*, a concept which has been crucial to the evolution of Parliament and the development of modern party politics. Having won an overall majority and formed a single-party government, the leaders of that party were bold enough to claim a 'mandate' or licence to implement the policies on which they had fought and won the election – that is, those policies enshrined in the party's manifesto (regardless of the fact that no post-war government had ever secured an electoral majority and that there was no evidence for the party's voters having positively affirmed every manifesto policy). The importance of this doctrine was underlined by the increased content of manifestos in the post-war era, a result of the 'statist' or social democratic consensus which decreed that 'enlightened' governments should legislate and interfere in most areas of social, economic and industrial life (see Chapter 3). The doctrine could not, of course, have been applied in a multi-party system resulting in post-election deals and coalition governments, as in such circumstances any 'programme for government' (as manifestos were often called) could be formed only after the electorate had voted and would have to reflect a combination of manifestos – for which nobody could have voted.

The doctrine of the mandate was to have a serious effect upon those MPs belonging to the majority party in government and, *ipso facto*, the behaviour of the House of Commons. The two hundred or so MPs who belonged to the governing party without being part of the government became susceptible to the argument, often springing from government whips but mainly from their own conscience, that they had been elected not as independent legislators whose duty was to scrutinise the executive but as *party representatives* whose role was to ensure the implementation of those manifesto promises upon which they and the party leadership fought the election. As a result, governments were seen to have little trouble in imposing their will upon Parliament. Backbench MPs were widely regarded as 'lobby fodder' for the frontbenchers and the House of Commons was seen increasingly as a 'rubber stamp' for governments.[13] In brief, single-party government and the doctrine of the mandate were thought to have rendered Parliament impotent and to have left Britain without any efficient, institutional check upon the actions of government – an 'elective dictatorship' was one of the more memorable descriptions used.[14] The two-party system, and its concomitant of single-party government, may therefore be held largely responsible for the wide-ranging debate about *constitutional reform* (select committees, Bill of Rights, the future of the House of Lords, electoral reform, referenda etc.) which has played a central part in the study of British politics during the last thirty years. As the latter stages of this chapter suggest, much of the urgency surrounding such debates could well be rendered irrelevant by a series of hung parliaments which tend to undermine traditional constitutional assumptions.

## The eclipse of the two-party system (1974–89)

As explained at the start of this chapter, the nature of Britain's party system was at the heart of many academic debates that occurred in the fifteen years following the 1974 general elections. The debate had its origins in a widespread belief that the two-party system just described had been eroded and that the term itself was no longer relevant to the modern party contest. A number of factors supported this belief:

(i) *The bulk of the electorate was no longer firmly wedded to one of the two parties* and the number of floating voters had increased dramatically. Whereas 43 per cent of the electorate 'strongly identified' with either the Labour or Conservative Party in 1964, this figure had fallen to less than 19 per cent by 1987.[15] This development, variously described by psephologists as 'partisan instability', 'volatility' and 'partisan dealignment', meant that the two parties could no longer rely on the huge, dependable blocks of supporters so vital to the two-party system.

(ii) This new volatility produced a *marked increase in support for other parties*. In February 1974, the Liberals achieved nearly a fifth of the votes cast with a notable increase in support for nationalist parties in Scotland and Wales (the SNP polling more votes than the Scottish Conservatives in October 1974). This trend was continued in the 1980s with the emergence of the SDP–Liberal Alliance (the SDP being partly a response to a growing public interest in an 'alternative' approach to politics). After recording some spectacular by-election victories within its first year (as at Crosby, where it overturned a 19,000 Tory majority – itself a splendid example of electoral volatility), the Alliance achieved over a quarter of the votes cast at the 1983 general election – only 2.2 per cent fewer than the Labour Party and the best third party performance since 1923. Between 1983 and 1987, the Alliance

19

retained a comparable level of support in opinion polls (occasionally scoring higher than one of the two main parties), came first or second in all but one of the sixteen by-elections and achieved over a quarter of the votes in the various local authority elections. Its 22.6 per cent of the vote in 1987 was a disappointment to Alliance leaders, yet was still remarkably high by post-war standards (see Chapter 8). The demise of the Alliance after 1987 was matched by the meteoric rise of another new party, the Greens, which after 1988 recruited 15,000 members and gained almost 15 per cent of the votes in the 1989 European elections. These voting figures from the 1980s stand in sharp contrast to those of the 1950s, for example, when the combined two-party vote (as low as 70 per cent by 1983) was well over 90 per cent.

(iii) Increased support for third parties, especially the Alliance, put *an end to the nationwide two-party contest*. In the south of England, the Alliance came second in over two-thirds of Tory-held seats in 1983 and 1987, with Labour's vote sinking as low as 17 per cent outside London. Likewise, in certain by-elections after 1987 (Glasgow Govan in 1988, Glasgow Central and Pontypridd in 1989) it was clear that the essential contest was between Labour and the nationalist parties. This regionalisation of the party battle reflected the growing regionalisation of party support. Far from still being national class parties, the Conservatives owed their landslide victories of 1983 and 1987 to their hegemony of southern constituencies, while Labour was forced back into its urban heartlands in Scotland, Wales and the north of England. In 1987, Labour won only three seats in the south of England and East Anglia (excluding London), while the Conservtives won only ten of the seventy seats in Scotland and returned no MPs from such northern cities as Manchester, Liverpool and Sheffield. This distribution of two-party support was hardly consistent with a national two-party system.

(iv) Given that a two-party system involves two parties with comparable support and a roughly equal chance of gaining power, it is significant that *the 1980s witnessed a widening gap between the parties' shares of the vote at elections, and a growing scepticism about the ability of one of them to seize power from the other*. Labour's loss of three consecutive elections was not unprecedented, as the elections of the 1950s show, yet never in the post-war era has the Opposition lagged so far behind the victors. In 1983, the Government and Opposition were separated by nearly 15 per cent of votes cast – the biggest difference since 1935 when the Labour opposition was confronted by a coalition government – with the gap narrowing only marginally by 1987. This naturally provoked discussion about the two-party system being superseded by a one-party system similar to that in Japan.[16] It has been argued, of course, that this enormous gap, and the apparent invincibility of the Tories, was artificial and ephemeral – a product of increased support for other parties which thereby split and depressed the non-Conservative vote. Yet electoral surveys do not uphold this view entirely. Crewe, for example, estimated that had the Alliance not existed in 1987, as many of its voters would have gone to the Tories as to Labour. In other words, far from preventing a Tory defeat, the Alliance instead prevented a Tory victory of perhaps even greater proportions.[17]

(v) Accompanying these changes was an inevitable *change in the tone and atmosphere of British party politics*. That television and radio programmes such as 'Question Time' now invariably included a spokesman from 'another' party signalled an acceptance that political debate was no longer a purely two-dimensional affair; a recognition, in short, that the views of the Conservative and Labour parties no longer echoed those held by the vast majority of electors. This change of tone even extended into the counsels of the two parties themselves. After the 1974 and 1987 elections, the Scottish Labour Party was preoccupied with a struggle against the SNP rather than the Tories, while a study of Conservative conferences held in 1986 found that, on many occasions, the Alliance and not Labour was the prime target of activists' venom.[18] As the nature of party conflict changes, so does the rhetoric.

The changes in the nature of Britain's party system can be attributed to a mixture of sociological, economic and political developments which have also conspired to alter the nature of British politics in general. Sociological change, in the form of *class dealignment*, has had a critical impact upon British party politics. The class basis of society, whereby most people felt a strong sense of identity with one of the two social classes (distinguished by a uniformity of economic conditions and cultural perspectives) has steadily diminished. An increased number of voters do not define their interests within the context of a particular class, and express their ambitions in a more individualistic, diverse fashion (the reasons for this crucial development receive a more detailed examination in Chapter 9).

If the causes of class dealignment are somewhat complex, its effects upon the party system are quite straightforward. As voters feel less affinity with either of the two social classes, so they are less enthusiastic about voting for the two class-based parties and more prepared to vote for 'classless' parties like the nationalists and the Alliance. Yet class dealignment does not explain entirely the contraction of support for the two main parties since 1970. Fewer voters may have felt inclined to vote Labour or Conservative out of habit, yet this does not explain why fewer voters were even prepared to vote for either of the parties on even a short-term, conditional basis.

The explanation probably derives° from the disappointing record of successive Labour and Conservative Governments. That is, the effects of class dealignment (which would inevitably threaten Labour and Tory support) coincided with a period – arguably between 1959 and 1979 – when British Governments were unable to fulfil the economic expectations of their voters. Neither party in office proved capable of maintaining earlier rates of increase in voters' standard of living, a problem compounded by later failures to prevent industrial unrest and the subsequent disruption of essential services like power supplies and refuse collection. By the mid-1970s, these failures had occasioned clear evidence of 'plague on both your houses' in the public's attitude towards the main parties, translating itself into voting behaviour at the 1974 elections when the combined two-party vote fell from its 1970 figure of 89.4 per cent to 75 per cent.

The parties themselves were, of course, aware that their disappointing performances in office had cost them much support, yet the course of action both parties took, between 1975 and 1983, to remedy the problem merely enhanced the prospects of other parties – especially the parties of the supposed centre. The radical analyses of both major parties, which led them to reject much of the old social democratic consensus (see Chapter 3), gave rise to a theory that British party politics had 'polarised' between Bennite socialism on the left and Thatcherism on the right. The related theory that the centre ground had become vacant hastened the birth of the SDP in 1981 and largely explains the astonishing levels of support it achieved during its early life (on the day of its launch, opinion polls gave it over 50 per cent and a 15 per cent lead over other parties). Clearly, just as consensus politics had thwarted the chances of 'centre' parties like the Liberals in the 1950s and 1960s, so the breakdown of consensus in the 1970s and early 1980s allowed them to claim a distinctive political image and thereby attract greater public interest.

## Consequences

The collapse of the traditional two-party system after 1974 has already had important consequences for British government and politics, although they could have been – and could still be – much graver.

(i) Those who oppose the Conservative party were inclined to argue that the most severe effect of increased third party voting has been *a split in the anti-Tory vote which allowed the re-election of an 'extremist' government in both 1983 and 1987.*[19] Although this argument has been dismissed by Crewe, it is nevertheless interesting that Mrs Thatcher's Governments – arguably the most radical since the war – were elected with shares of the vote that would have spelt certain defeat in the heyday of the two-party system. However, the argument that third party voting has allowed 'extremist' and 'unrepresentative' government is not peculiar to left-wing circles. After 1974, it was common to hear Conservatives claim that Liberal voters had permitted the election of a radical Labour Government which, on less than 40 per cent of the vote, proceeded to enact its most left-wing manifesto since 1945 (involving further nationalisation and the extension of trade union immunities). Nevertheless, the fact that an 'unrepresentative' Tory Government succeeded in getting re-elected with ease meant that this line of argument has gained most currency in non-Tory areas.[20]

(ii) Although both the main parties have lost support since the 1950s, *the Labour Party's loss has been especially severe, from a peak of 48.8 per cent in 1951 to a nadir of 27.6 per cent in 1983*. As readers may have already inferred from this chapter, it is debatable whether the growth of third party voting has been a cause or effect of Labour's decline. Yet the consequences of that decline have been clear enough – one of which was a decade of internal examination into its ideals, strategy and organisation, the nature and effects of which will be considered in Chapters 6 and 7. Suffice to say here that while its re-examination prior to 1983 seemed to accelerate its electoral decline, promote the interests of other parties and assist the re-election of the Thatcher Government, after 1983 (and especially after 1987) it played no small part in Labour's revival as a credible challenger to the Conservatives.

(iii) The election of the radical Thatcher Government on such a comparatively low share of the vote also stimulated *much wider interest in electoral reform and, in particular, proportional representation*, reinforced by the fact that the Alliance's creditable levels of support in 1983 and 1987 were rewarded by only 3 per cent of Parliamentary seats. Perhaps the most urgent development, however, in the debate about electoral reform is the growing interest within the Labour Party. Prompted by three consecutive defeats, an expanding number of Labour supporters (especially in the south, where the 'winner takes all' aspect of first-past-the-post is felt acutely) and Labour MPs noted that the party had no vested interest in the present electoral system. Even more striking was the belief of certain Labour MPs, like Frank Field and Austen Mitchell, that in order to deny the Tories an overall majority and instigate PR, Labour should undertake pre-electoral deals with other parties, thus uniting the anti-Tory vote in most constituencies.

The prospect of electoral reform being embraced by one of

Britain's major parties naturally made the likelihood of PR being introduced much more urgent – and duly focused the mind on the enormous constitutional consequences this would have. Labour's burgeoning interest in electoral reform was reflected in its own official investigation of the subject, chaired by Professor Raymond Plant between 1991 and 1992. Indeed, by 1992, Labour had already lent support for PR in the elections to its proposed regional assemblies and reformed second chamber.

(iv) If one accepts that the survival of the Thatcher Governments was a product of the growth of the third party vote and its effects upon the anti-Tory vote, then the weakening of the two-party system may also be held responsible for the *widening interest in other areas of constitutional reform*. The argument that a government elected on less than 44 per cent has used its Parliamentary majority ruthlessly, 'steamrolling' a series of controversial reforms, has focused further attention upon Britain's lack of a codified constitution, a modern Bill of Rights and an 'adequate' second chamber (a critique articulated by the pressure group Charter 88, formed to advocate fundamental constitutional change). Although the collapse of overall Tory support has not been as spectacular as Labour's, its loss of confidence among Scottish voters was just as severe, the party obtaining less than 25 per cent in 1987. This undermined the Government's legitimacy in pushing through in Scotland such contentious measures as the poll tax, and when coupled with Labour's clear victory in Scotland making no difference to the outcome of the 1987 election, reawakened interest in devolution and put serious strains upon the unitary character of the British state. The failure of Scotland's major party to collect substantial support nationwide not only altered the nature of Britain's party system but also made many Scottish voters question the relevance of Westminster elections.

(v) The debate about constitutional reform was made all the more intense after 1974 by the *increased possibility of hung parliaments*, itself a reflection of the growth in third and fourth party support. The three-way split in many constituency contests had helped to reduce considerably the number of marginal seats. This, in turn, meant that one party needed a much larger lead (in terms of overall votes) over its nearest rival if that lead were to be translated into a Commons majority; for example, the 0.7 per cent Labour lead which gave Wilson victory in 1964 – even perhaps the 3.4 per cent lead which gave victory to Heath in 1970 – might now produce only a hung parliament. It is striking that the Conservative lead over Labour in 1992 (over 7 per cent) produced an overall majority of only twenty-one – the smallest Tory majority since 1951 when they polled *fewer* votes (but more seats) than Labour. The difference in votes between the parties in 1992 was almost identical to that which existed in 1945, but which then produced the largest single-party majority seen in the post-war era. Furthermore, it has been calculated that whenever a third party secures over 20 per cent of votes cast in a general election, one of the other two parties must have an overall lead of at least 6 per cent if a hung Parliament is to be averted.[21]

As a result of the 1974-79 period, students of modern British politics were not unfamiliar with the consequences of hung parliaments and the absence of single-party governments with comfortable Commons majorities. For most of the 1974-79 period, the customary rhythms of a two-party Parliament and single-party executive were disturbed largely as a result of Liberal and nationalist support in the 1974 elections. A hung parliament after the February election meant that a government was not formed, as is usually the case, within twenty-four hours, with the possibility even arising that it would not even consist of the party with the most seats (Heath had offered the Liberals the chance to join a 'Con–Lib' coalition government). After 1977, when the Labour Government lost the tiny overall majority secured in October 1974, the Liberals were given some influence in government decision-making in return for their Commons support. Later, in return for similar support from nationalist MPs, the Government was compelled to devote much time and energy to a complicated and unpopular devolution Bill. The anomolous Parliamentary arithmetic also revived the capability of backbenchers, with a number of important Government Bills having to be drastically revised, even dropped, after failing to get the Commons majority normally taken for granted by ministers (in 1977, the Government even failed to secure Commons approval for its Budget in the first instance). Eventually, in March 1979, the Government was brought down by a Commons vote of no-confidence, the first occasion since 1924.

Such events would not seem extraordinary in many of those countries where proportional representation and multi-party politics are customary. They seemed remarkable in Britain only because the two-party sytem usually guaranteed single-party governments with solid Parliamentary majorities. As already indicated, the possibility of further hung parliaments brought into question many assumptions concerning the workings of Britain's parliamentary democracy. Parties would be forced to enter a less adversarial dialogue for governments to be formed and sustained; backbench opinion would have to be courted much more assiduously, with the idea that most MPs were 'lobby fodder' rendered obsolete – along with the idea that the Commons was a mere 'rubber stamp' for the executive; the notion that an unelected second chamber had no right to obstruct the government's programme would also be weakened if that programme were seen to be the product of post-election deals between the parties in the Commons. In fact, much of the reasoning behind constitutional reform would lose its force if minority (or coalition) governments were obviously unable to act in the 'arrogant' or 'bombastic' fashion often cited by those in favour of constitutional change.

## The 'restoration' of a two-party system (1989–92)

Hugo Young wrote in June 1989: 'Recently, for the first time in years, the Conservatives have looked as if they might lose and Labour as if they might govern . . . We seem to be moving ever more swiftly back to two party politics.'[22] Young's speculations were prompted by the European election results that had just been announced, in which Labour had achieved over 40 per cent of the vote compared to the Tories' 34.7 per cent. This represented Labour's best performance in a nationwide election since 1970 and was the sort of result that would return Labour to power in a general election – the indispensable condition of any revival of a two-party system. Even before the European elections, there had been definite signs of a recovery in Labour's electoral fortunes. In May 1989, Labour had taken the Vale of Glamorgan from the Conservatives in a by-election, polling 49 per cent and fending off an energetic challenge from both the centre and Plaid Cymru. This was the biggest swing from Tory to Labour in any by-election since 1935 and was the first relatively safe Tory seat lost during the Thatcher years to the official Opposition.

Labour's fortunes continued to improve in 1990. At the Mid-Staffs by-election in March, Labour recorded one of the most remarkable by-election feats in its history, toppling a 14,654 Tory majority and more than doubling its 1987 share of the vote. Such results seemed to obviate claims that Labour had little chance of obtaining an overall majority at the next election. That the Mid-Staffs result was no flash in the pan was later highlighted by a series of opinion polls offering enormous cheer to Labour supporters. A Gallup poll in April 1990 showed Labour with 52 per cent, with its lead of 23 per cent being the highest since Gallup began polling in 1938.[23] Of particular importance to those contesting a revival of the two-party system was the statistic showing that 75 per cent of those who had voted Alliance in 1987 now intended to vote Labour.

The decline of centre party support between 1987 and 1990 was both a cause and effect of Labour's revival as a 'respectable' centre-left party. The aforementioned Gallup poll found that centre party support was no higher than 11 per cent, a figure consistent with recent by-election and local election performances. Following the SDP's lost deposit at the Bootle by-election in May 1990 the SDP's National Committee effectively shut down the party's formal organisation and therefore the party itself – a far cry from its exceptional year of 1981, where some polls projected 50 per cent support for the SDP alone.[24] For David Owen, the SDP's demise was inextricably linked to Labour's readoption of social democratic values, claiming moreover that this had been hastened by the electoral success of the Alliance.

Many of the centre parties' problems after 1987, however, were self-inflicted. The decision by the bulk of SDP and Liberal members to seek a merger after the 1987 election was directly responsible for the estrangement of Owen and his 'rump' of Social Democrats, who frustrated the new party's efforts at both the Epping (1988) and Richmond (1989) by-elections. This 'muddle in the middle' was compounded by the failure of the new merged party even to agree on its name – 'Liberal Democrats' not being finally agreed upon until the autumn of 1989 (see Chapter 8).

Despite these developments, there were a number of signs that the electorate remained extremely fickle and that, as a result, another upsurge of third and fourth party support could not be ruled out. As mentioned earlier in this chapter, the Greens achieved a surprisingly high level of support in the European elections of 1989, while the Liberal Democrats – having finally acquired a measure of confidence, unity and purpose – went on to score notable by-election victories in Eastbourne (1990) and Ribble Valley (1991). The by-election contest in Kincardine and Deeside (1991) also demonstrated that, in Scotland, many voters faced not just a three but a four-party contest. As the 1992 election approached, the reasonable level of Liberal Democrat support (15–20 per cent) and the narrow gap between the two main parties all pointed to a hung parliament in which the Liberal Democrats would play a pivotal part. The 1992 campaign, perforce, turned out to be a far from two-dimensional affair; opinion polls amplified the possibility of third (and fourth) parties having an influence upon – even a place within – future British governments, their position perhaps being copper-fastened by the implementation of electoral reform (the 1992 election being the first in which the subject played a central role). Furthermore, the Tories during the second half of the campaign found themselves fighting on two fronts, having been obliged to confront the Liberal Democrat challenge to many of its traditional supporters.

## Conclusion: a one-party system?

In the event, the 1992 result substantiated the theory offered by some commentators after 1987 – that Britain was moving towards the Japanese model of 'democratic one-party government', where only one party seemed capable of attracting enough public confidence to govern a modern, pluralist, capitalist society.[25] Instead of heralding the continued existence of two governing parties, the progress made by Labour in 1992 (3.6 per cent) was little more than that made in 1987; the gap between the two main parties (7.5 per cent) was still much wider than that seen during the 1950s and 1960s, and Labour's vote remained lower than when it lost power in 1979. By the next general election, it seems likely that thirty years will have elapsed since Labour last won an emphatic general election victory and over a quarter of a century since it obtained even 40 per cent of the votes cast.

Such realities scarcely accord with the principles of a two-party system; as Anthony King wrote, 'the pendulum has simply ceased to swing'.[26] In addition, the decline of third party support at a second consecutive election suggests that Britain's three-party system, anticipated with such confidence ten years ago, still lacks a secure foundation – even though a third party, for the third successive election, polled more votes than Labour in southern England (excluding London), while in Scotland the Conservatives' meagre 26 per cent was only 4 per cent greater than support for the SNP. Labour's belated interest in electoral reform and its concomitant – a partnership of some kind with other centre-left parties – betray a suspicion not only that 1945-style Labour victories may now be chimeric but also that the modern electorate is now too diverse (or sceptical) to deliver working majorities in Parliament to a single anti-Conservative party. If Britain's one-party system is to be destroyed, it may have to be replaced by a pattern of party politics quite unique to post-war Britain. The fact that the 1992 election – according to Rallings and Thrasher[27] – was only four thousand votes off producing a hung parliament (despite the Tories' enormous lead in votes) shows that, under modern electoral conditions, such a transformation is far from improbable.

## Notes

1 I. Jennings, *The British Constitution*, Cambridge, 1962, p. 62.
2 R. M. Punnett, *British Government and Politics*, London, 1968, p. 101.
3 H. Drucker (ed.), *Multi-Party Britain*, London, 1977.
4 S. E. Finer, *The Changing British Party System*, New York, 1980, pp. 3–4.
5 H. Berrington, *Sunday Telegraph*, 5 May 1985; J. Benyon, 'The enduring two-party system', *Social Studies Review*, November 1988.
6 G. Alderman, *Britain: A One Party State?*, London, 1989; I. Crewe, 'Politics after the Alliance', *New Society*, 22 January 1988.
7 I Gilmour, *The Body Politic*, London, 1969, p. 25.
8 J. P. Mackintosh, *The Government and Politics of Britain*, London, 1977, chapter ten.
9 See D. Denver, *Elections and Voting Behaviour in Britain*, Hemel Hempstead, 1989, chapter two.
10 Denver, *Elections and Voting Behaviour*, chapter two.
11 D. Butler, *British General Elections Since 1945*, Oxford, 1989, chapter ten.
12 V. Bogdanor, *The People and the Party System*, Cambridge, 1981, p. 41.
13 See B. Crick, *The Reform of Parliament*, London, 1964.
14 Lord Hailsham, *The Elective Dictatorship*, London, 1976.
15 Denver, *Elections and Voting Behaviour*, chapter two.
16 S. Jenkins, 'A one-party system', *Sunday Times*, 14 June 1987.
17 Crewe, 'Politics after the Alliance'.
18 R. N. Kelly, *Conservative Party Conferences*, Manchester, 1989.
19 See, for example, M. Foot, *Another Heart and Other Pulses*, London, 1984.
20 J. Curtice, 'Must Labour lose?', *New Society*, 19 June 1987.
21 M. Harrop & A. Shaw, *Can Labour Win?*, London, 1990, chapter two.
22 *Guardian*, 20 June 1989.
23 *Daily Telegraph*, 4 April 1990.
24 G. & A. Lee-Williams, *Labour's Decline and the Social Democrats' Fall*, London, 1989, p. 119.
25 Alderman, *One Party State?*.
26 *Daily Telegraph*, 11 April 1992.
27 *Sunday Times*, 12 April 1992.

# 3

# BRITAIN'S PARTY SYSTEM:
# CONSENSUS OR DISUNITY?

As the previous chapter revealed, the structure or shape of Britain's party system has been the cause of much academic debate since 1974, largely because the old certainties concerning the two-party system have disappeared. Likewise, the 'atmosphere' or 'spirit' of party politics in Britain have also occasioned discussion, again largely because significant changes have been perceived in recent years. The extent to which these changes are the *cause* or *effect* of the old two-party system's breakdown is itself a matter of dispute; suffice to say at this stage that developments in the relationship between the parties have been both responsible for, and a reaction to, declining support for the two major parties after 1970.

During the 1980s, a great deal of literature was produced arguing that the tone of Britain's party system (or the policy relationship between the major parties) had undergone a profound change and that the main agency of these changes was the Thatcher Governments – thereby challenging the much aired theories of both Marxists (such as Ralph Miliband)[1] and non-Marxists (such as Richard Rose)[2] that parties could not make a crucial difference to the nature of politics and society in Britain. Peter Jenkins's survey of politics in the 1980s was revealingly entitled *Mrs Thatcher's Revolution*;[3] John Cole's study similarly proclaimed on its front cover *The Thatcher Years: A Decade of Revolution in British Politics*;[4] Kavanagh's exhaustive study of *Thatcherism and British Politics* respected the trend by granting it the sub-title *The End of Consensus?*.[5]

Kavanagh's sub-title is illuminating for absolute beginners in the study of British party politics, as it indicates that for many years the old two-party system described in the last chapter was underpinned by a large measure of agreement. For all the observations about 'adversary politics' in Britain, and for all the noisy disagreements in the House of Commons, it was widely recognised that what united the two parties was much more important than what divided them.[6] This theme was supported by McKenzie's famous treatment of the two parties' internal structures, which argued that their differences were contained by the demands of government and the need to adhere to the consensual views of the crucial floating voter.[7]

This consensus, which many believe to have collapsed since the 1970s, is often referred to as the 'Butskellite' consensus – 'Butskellism' being a tongue-in-cheek word coined in the 1950s to illustrate the close similarity between the views of R. A. Butler, the then *de facto* deputy leader of the Conservatives, and Hugh Gaitskell, leader of the Labour Party from 1955 to 1963. From an academic angle, it is perhaps more respectable to describe it as a social democratic consensus, as its features and assumptions approximate to the various 'social democratic' theories of politics and society expounded between 1945 and 1979.[8] Just as Disraeli once criticised the Tory Government of Sir Robert Peel for embodying 'Tory men and Whig measures', it became commonplace to hear 'Thatcherites' condemning the Tory Governments of the 1950s as 'Conservative men, social democratic measures'. However, though we should be wary of oversimplifying a complex subject, it may be pointed out that recent social democratic theorists have argued that social democracy was only *attempted*, and not *achieved*.[9] Notwithstanding these 'revisionist' sentiments, this chapter (in common with most previous accounts) will refer to this period in post-war British history as the 'social democratic consensus', mindful of the inevitable gap which exists in politics between aspiration and achievement!

## Features of the social democratic consensus

(i) The most important feature of the social democratic consensus was that *both Conservative and Labour Governments up until the late 1970s adopted (in varying degrees) a Keynesian approach to the economy*; that is, their diagnoses of and cures for Britain's economic problems owed much to the theories of John Maynard Keynes – a senior Treasury official during the 1930s and 1940s. As Butler said of Gaitskell (his predecessor as Chancellor), 'We both spoke the language of Keynes but with different accents.'[10] It is, perhaps, odd that Keynes should have contributed so much to the evolution of a 'social democratic' consensus as he would have most certainly rejected any claim that he was a social democrat, protesting instead that his politics were impeccably liberal.[11] Yet as Foote points out, Keynes's views were closely related to the 'New Liberalism' pioneered at the end of the nineteenth century by Hobhouse, Hobson, Ritchie *et al.* and which proved a vital foundation in the development of what later passed for social democratic doctrine (see Chapter 8).[12]

The best guide to Keynesian theory is to be found in Keynes's own seminal study, the *General Theory of Unemployment* (1936). In contrast to what was then economic orthodoxy, Keynes attached prime importance to *demand* rather than *supply*. A depressed economy was usually one in which demand for goods was low, when consumption did not match the potential for production in a country's economy. At that time it was considered sensible for governments to react to rising unemployment by deflating the economy, namely, reducing public spending, raising taxation and interest rates and generally slackening the level of activity within the economy. Keynes argued that this merely exacerbated the problem by crippling demand even further. It should be stressed, therefore, that Keynes – and his disciples who governed Britain for much of the post-war era – regarded *full employment* as an economic as well as a moral imperative. An economy in which unemployment was high was also one in which demand for products was low, a state of affairs inimical to any hopes of economic recovery. This belief was echoed by a future Tory Prime Minister,

Harold Macmillan, in his book *The Middle Way*, published two years after Keynes's *General Theory* and later applied in a fateful dispute with his Chancellor of the Exchequer (Peter Thorneycroft) in 1958. According to Macmillan's biographer, his fervent opposition to Thorneycroft's prescriptions were not simply that they would, in his view, create further unemployment but that such a rise would seriously damage the nation's economy in the future – an analysis perfectly consistent with that of Keynes.[13]

Keynes had proposed that the proper response to rising unemployment was reflation or expansion – stimulating demand for products by raising government expenditure and increasing opportunities for private individuals to borrow and spend money ('spend and prosper' was a favourite Keynesian aphorism), the overall effect being to rejuvenate economic activity and growth. *High public spending* was thus a key feature of the Keynesian project, which was to allure a series of Chancellors grappling with economic difficulties in general and rising unemployment in particular (one of the most spectacular examples being the Chancellor in the 1970–74 Conservative Government, Anthony Barber, whose response to one million unemployed in 1971 was to 'go for growth' by unleashing the 'Barber Boom' involving cuts in personal taxation and a huge monetary expansion). It should be recalled, however, that Keynes was not wholly opposed to deflationary policies; they would still be necessary in the event of demand outstripping supply or production, thus creating a rise in imports and a resulting balance of payments deficit.

Keynes's prescriptions implied a much more interventionist role for government economic policy than had hitherto been thought tolerable. Politicians and senior civil servants would be required to engage in 'demand management', encouraging and discouraging demand through a mixture of policies related to taxation, borrowing and spending. Keynesianism, in other words, highlighted the 'need' for *economic planning*, often referred to as *managerial capitalism*, which a series of governments after 1960 acknowleged. This was reflected in the various agencies set up by both Labour and Conservative administrations with a view to establishing greater government control over the market economy – for example, the National Economic Development Council created in 1961, the Department of Economic Affairs created in 1964 and a series of bodies designed to encourage investment and specific commercial development, such as the Industrial Reorganisation Corporation (1966–70) and the Industrial Development Executive (1972–74).

The belief that government could and should regulate the economy extended into a belief that governments should regulate the level of incomes, stemming from an analysis which linked the health of the economy to the rate of increase in wages (an analysis widely regarded as 'neo-Keynesian', as Keynes' own writings only gave it *implicit*, and not *explicit*, support). The idea that 'economic planning' and 'managerial capitalism' required governments to accommodate the major economic interest groups (such as the trade unions and the employers' associations) into the decision-making process had already given the Keynesian consensus a *corporatist* dimension, exemplified by the creation of the NEDC in 1961. This corporatist trend was now reinforced by politicians' belief in the efficacy of *incomes policies*, which found its bureaucratic expression in the foundation of such bodies as the National Incomes Commission after 1962, the National Board for Prices and Incomes after 1964 and the Pay Board after 1972. The importance of the trade unions to the effectiveness of these bodies, allied to the 'social contract' of 1975–79 which formalised their input into economic policy making, naturally enhanced the institutional power of organised labour in Britain and gave rise to the view that the unions had too much political power – a major factor behind the retreat from corporatist (or perhaps more precisely, *neo-corporatist* as the corporatist model was never realised to the extent it was in other European democracies) economies after 1979.

(ii) The Keynesian element of the social democratic consensus was complemented by a *bipartisan acceptance of a mixed economy, a supposedly judicious balance between private enterprise (regulated in the manner described above) and public or state-owned enterprise.* The Conservatives after 1945 accepted that the major utilities, such as gas, water and electricity, should be run by public corporations, containing ministerial appointees expected to respect the general themes of government policy.[14] Even more significant was the Conservatives' acceptance that such a principle should apply to 'heavy' industries such as coal. The only major denationalisation pursued by the Tory Governments of the 1950s and 1960s was that of iron and steel. Indeed, one of the crucial aims underlying nationalisation – that commercial criteria must be tempered by 'social' considerations – was actually applied by a Conservative Government after February 1971 when it nationalised the ailing Rolls Royce industry, which threatened another embarrassing rise in unemployment figures.

Having completed an extensive nationalisation programme by 1950, the Labour Party's leadership also expressed its faith in the mixed economy by showing a reluctance to diminish further the size of the private sector, arguing that the 'management', rather than the curtailment, of private industry was the most prudent course. Anthony Crosland, one of the party's leading theoreticians in the post-war era, suggested in his book *The Future of Socialism* (1956) that further nationalisation was now irrelevant to achieving the basic socialist aim of an egalitarian society. In brief, Crosland stated that Clause IV of the party's Constitution (which many party activists then took to mean the party's commitment to wholesale nationalisation) had been rendered bankrupt by the possibilities inherent to the Keynesian-based mixed economy. This argument was given greater urgency after Labour's third successive election defeat in 1959, which the party leader Hugh Gaitskell attributed largely to the public's distaste for further nationalisation. Although Gaitskell failed to expunge Clause IV from Labour's Constitution (after a stormy debate at Labour's 1959 conference), Labour's successful 1964 manifesto reflected the Crosland–Gaitskell analysis by proposing no significant change in the balance between the public and private sectors (see Chapter 6).

(iii) The support of social democrats like Crosland and Gaitskell for the new status quo owed much to the importance it attached to *the government's provision of extensive and expensive*

*welfare benefits – a situation generally referred to as the welfare state.*
Both parties in government were eager to boast about the extra
money they had spent in such areas as public health (with both
parties proclaiming their zeal for the new National Health
Service), education, pensions, disability and sickness benefits and
housing. The 1950 Tory conference, in what was then considered
a rare display of dissent towards the party leadership, actually
demanded that a future Tory Government set itself the target of
building 300,000 new 'homes for the people'. The main argument
over housing at the 1950 election was, accordingly, over which
party would spend the most money on council house construction
projects. Both parties, in short, were agreed that the state should
be the provider of most social needs and both were agreed on the
desirability of even greater public spending to service the state's
welfare facilities. The belief of 'moderate' Labour politicians (like
Gaitskell) that Clause IV was superflous was premised on an
assumption that greater equality could be achieved within the new
framework of society, through the allocation of increasingly
effective welfare benefits financed by an ever-growing Keynesian
economy.

(iv) The consensus, though mainly social and economic in
character, was not entirely confined to domestic matters. On
defence, for example, *both party leaderships were fervently Atlanticist
in that they had a clear commitment to collective nuclear deterrence under
the aegis of NATO*. Although the Labour conference of 1960
passed a motion calling for unilateral nuclear disarmament, the
party leader Hugh Gaitskell promised to 'fight, fight and fight
again' to reverse the decision and the conference of 1961 duly
passed a motion accepting Britain's possession of nuclear
weapons and endorsed NATO membership (it may also be
recalled that Britain's first nuclear weapons were manufactured
during the post-war Attlee Government). Although the new
Labour Government in 1964 installed a 'Minister for Disarmament', its commitment proved to be more rhetorical than
practical and Defence Secretary Denis Healey was later praised
by defence chiefs-of-staff for the 'continuity of policy' guaranteed
by his stewardship.[15]

The parties' leaders also demonstrated a *similarity of objectives concerning the European Community*. The first attempt to join the Community under the Macmillan Government, and the eventual success of the Heath Government in securing entry (under the European Communities Act 1972) were loudly criticised by the Labour opposition. Nevertheless, the Labour Government of 1966–70 also tried – and failed – to gain admission, and when Labour was re-elected in 1974, Wilson defied the party's left by refusing to negotiate Britain's withdrawal before the result of a national referendum in 1975 (in which Wilson and most of the Labour Cabinet advocated continued membership).

Any summary of the social democratic consensus may usefully conclude by recalling that its basic characteristics were egalitarian, collectivist and statist. The leading politicians of both major parties appeared to accept (albeit implicitly in the case of the Conservatives) that society should be made more equal, more classless, more 'compassionate' and somehow more 'fair'. The language of politics during the thirty years or so after the War seemed to suggest that the gap between rich and poor, strong and weak, should be narrowed, with emphasis placed upon a better society for 'the people' *en bloc* rather than for a collection of diverse individuals (an idea strengthened by the fact that about two-thirds of the population were classified as 'manual occupation/working class' and therefore relied heavily upon state provision). The means by which this predominantly blue collar society was to be improved was to be the state; it was deemed appropriate that enlightened governments, with the help of expanding, benevolent bureaucracies, should seek to effect a solution to most of the problems and difficulties attending an advanced capitalist society. For a generation of politicians who came of age either during or after the First World War, when it was widely felt that governments had 'not done enough' for 'the people', and had thereby engendered deep and almost fatal divisions in society, the ideals embodied in the post-war consensus represented an almost irresistible logic. This latter point prompts a more careful examination of the origins of the social democratic agreement.

### The foundations of the social democratic consensus

Many students of British politics seem to assume that the post-war consensus has its roots in the radical post-war Labour Government led by Clement Attlee. There can be no doubt that Labour's six years in office after 1945 made an enormous contribution to the social democratic climate which was to prevail in British politics until the late 1970s. The welfare state, to which a succession of governments were apparently devoted, was largely shaped by legislation imposed by the Attlee Governments – the National Insurance Act and National Health Service Act (1946) being the outstanding examples. Similarly, the existence of the mixed economy owed much to the nationalisation of the Bank of England, the coal industry and civil aviation (1946), electricity (1947), railways and gas (1948) and iron and steel (1949). Indeed, it is common for historians to refer to the social democratic consensus as the 'Attlee Settlement'.[16] Furthermore, it takes two parties to form consensus politics, and it is clear that during the years of the Attlee Governments the Conservative Party made several key changes in politics and philosophy in recognition of the Government's achievements. Under the direction of R. A. Butler, whose aim was to create 'Conservativism with a human face . . . to give the party a facelift', the Tories in opposition adopted policies and priorities which acknowledged Labour's reforms in respect of welfare and the economy.[17]

Nevertheless, if one accepts that the essence of the social democratic state was a belief that governments had a duty (on the grounds of both humanity and efficiency) to interfere actively in the areas of welfare and the economy, then its roots go further than 1945. It is interesting that R. A. Butler justified the Tories' post-war 'facelift' not mainly on the basis of electoral necessity but on the basis of Tory philosophy and tradition.[18] Butler stated that the party's acceptance of Labour's welfare reforms represented not a break but a continuation with the record of previous Tory Governments acting on the 'One Nation' principle. In later life, Butler made the arresting claim that the post-war consensus was merely a development of traditional Tory paternalism; the notion that the strong and powerful had an obligation to help the weak and powerless was simply being given bureaucratic and legislative expression – a process he claimed had been set in motion by the Tory Government of Disraeli as long ago as the 1870s, whose legislative achievements included the Factory Act (1874), the Public Health and Artisans' Dwellings Act (1875) and the Education Act (1876), all designed (to use Disraeli's famous phrase) to 'elevate the conditions of the people'.[19] Likewise, the Conservatives' acceptance of the mixed economy was breezily justified by recalling the party's historical character. Anthony Eden, who led the party from 1955 until 1957, remarked: 'we are not a party of unbridled capitalism and never have been . . . we are not the political children of the *laissez-faire* school. We opposed them decade after decade.'[20]

The Liberal Party's contribution to the ideals of the post-war consensus was arguably more important than that of the Tory paternalists. No account of the evolution of Britain's welfare state would be complete without some consideration of the reforms instigated by Asquith's Liberal Government between 1906 and 1911. Lloyd George's 'People's Budget' of 1909 established the principle of welfare benefits financed by progressive taxation, while the National Insurance Act (1911) underlined the state's responsibility for helping with the personal costs of sickness and unemployment. In short, the social policy of the last Liberal Government was 'at variance with past practices of *laissez-faire* and an anticipation of radical changes in the future'.[21]

The inter-war years were also crucial to the development of social democracy as the economic slump and the rise of mass unemployment highlighted the shortcomings of any *laissez-faire* approach to social and economic policy (i.e. one that insisted that government involvement should be minimal or non-existent). It would be wrong to regard the inter-war years (and especially the depressed 1930s) as a period when governments dogmatically resisted all forms of state assistance in the social and economic sphere. By 1937 the National (Coalition) Government led by Neville Chamberlain who, as Mayor of Birmingham, had initiated many interventionist policies which many considered to represent 'municipal socialism', had encouraged the reorganisation of many basic industries and had supported a policy of regional revival embodied in the Special Areas Acts (1935–37). None the less, that traumatic era convinced many of the politicians who were to play a leading part in the post-war years – such as Macmillan who was MP for the depressed constituency of Stockton-on-Tees – that the state would have to play a more central role in social and economic policy if the structure of society was to be maintained and similar crises were to be averted.

The trend towards a more interventionist state was intensified by the Second World War. A large measure of economic planning was administered with apparent success; prices, incomes, production and industrial relations were all rigorously controlled by the wartime Coalition Government. In addition, a number of official reports appeared which were to have a vital influence upon the conduct of politics after 1945. The *Beveridge Report* of December 1942 recommended a comprehensive system of social insurance and the foundation of a national health service. The *Employment White Paper* of 1944 set the priority of 'maintaining a high and stable level of employment after the war'. The War years were also important in that the tribulations they involved fuelled a general vision of an altogether 'better' and 'fairer' society once peace had been attained. This goal was almost universally believed to be synonomous with the expansion of government provision and activity, that a bureaucracy which could be effectively extended for wartime purposes should also be extended to 'win the peace'. The public's reaction to the *Beveridge Report*, for example, was so enthusiastic that it promptly 'established a national consensus on the future development of the social services . . . to believe in Beveridge was to have faith in a successful outcome to the war'.[22] The landslide Labour victory at the 1945 election may be attributed to Labour's success in articulating the pro-reform, pro-statist sentiments of the bulk of the electors – an observation which strengthens the hand of those who argue that political parties merely react to, rather than create, new developments in British politics and society (see Chapter 10).

To summarise, the post-war social democratic consensus – or

the agreement concerning the relationship of the state to society and the economy – was not based simply upon the achievements of a government lasting less than seven years; it was the product of trends extant in British politics since the end of the nineteenth century, a gradual acceptance that the scope of government should grow if modern society was to be efficient, cohesive and stable. While the political determination and political success of Attlee's Government should not be diminished in any way, the fact remains that it accelerated many of the trends already in place. In the years which followed 1951, the new consensus was reinforced by the apparent success of the economy, reflected in the emphatic re-election of Conservative Governments in 1955 and 1959. Throughout the 1950s, it appeared that Keynesian techniques of economic management could guarantee steady economic growth and avoid the 'downward spirals' to which pre-Keynesian capitalist economies had been vulnerable. As far as many on the left were concerned, economic growth ensured ever increasing levels of public spending on the various welfare facilities designed to produce a more equal society, while obviating the need for any further substantial reductions in the private sector of the economy. For many of those on the right, economic growth indicated that an expansive welfare state and public sector could be maintained without prohibitive levels of personal taxation or threats to the existence of a 'property owning democracy', a view strengthened by the electoral success of Conservative Governments pursuing social democratic policies. In other words, the case for an alternative approach to social democracy seemed dubious on both ideological and political grounds.

## The collapse of the social democratic consensus: the causes

Many students seem to assume that the attack on social democratic ideals, and the subsequent collapse of the post-war consensus, have been the result of the Thatcher Governments since 1979. Superficially, this idea has received support from many of the detailed studies of the Thatcher era; as the beginning of this chapter pointed out, some of the titles of these studies are them-

43

selves revealing in this respect. Kavanagh and Morris's study *The Making and Unmaking of Consensus Politics*, for instance, argued that the Attlee and Thatcher Governments mark 'the book-ends of British politics, one making the post-war consensus, the other presiding over its abandonment'.[23]

However, as such authors would readily acknowledge, the weakening of the consensus – and therefore the roots of Thatcherism – predate 1979. One of the earliest attacks on Keynesian orthodoxy came in 1958 when Macmillan's trio of Treasury Ministers (Peter Thorneycroft, Enoch Powell and Nigel Birch) resigned in protest against rising levels of public expenditure, claiming a link between monetary growth and inflation (thereby underwriting their claim to be the post-war Tory Party's first monetarists. Many thought it poignant that Thorneycroft was recalled to the political limelight in 1975 as the first Tory Party Chairman under Margaret Thatcher's leadership). In addition, Mrs Thatcher was not the first post-war Tory leader to question social democratic and Keynesian assumptions. After becoming leader in 1965, Edward Heath promoted a range of policies emphasising lower public spending, lower taxation, the reduction of trade union influence in government and a much less interventionist role for government in the economy. The Tory manifesto of 1970 was accordingly seen as the most radical since the war, claiming to herald a 'quiet revolution' in British politics. Heath's 'revolution' was short-lived. By the end of 1971 inflation had risen by 3 per cent in one year with unemployment rising to one million, prompting the Government into a conspicious 'U-Turn' involving increased public spending, a strict prices and incomes policy and a new phase of *dirigisme*, or state direction in industry.

Heath's 'U-Turn', however, and his Government's displacement by Labour in 1974, did not represent a renaissance for traditional, consensus-style policies. By 1975, Anthony Crosland – one of the chief intellectual exponents of social democracy in the 1950s – told local authority chiefs that, for the time being at least, 'the party's over', a pointer to the Labour Government's recognition that public expenditure could not (as had once been assumed in the heyday of Keynesianism) rise inexorably and that modern economic policy demanded its containment rather than expansion. It has also been argued that monetarism – supposedly a key component in the 'Thatcher Revolution' – has its roots in the Labour Government led by James Callaghan. Tony Benn, for example, alleges that Denis Healey was the first and most effective monetarist Chancellor of the Exchequer between 1976 and 1979.[24] Such claims should be treated cautiously as Healey and Callaghan also tried to follow a 'neo-Keynesian' incomes policy which monetarists reject. Nevertheless, Healey announced monetary targets in 1975 and refused to stimulate demand through reflation in the face of rising unemployment. At the 1976 Labour conference, Callaghan made a statement which seemed to deny the essence of Keynesianism: 'We used to think you could spend your way out of recession and increase employment by boosting spending . . . That option no longer exists and it only ever existed by injecting a bigger dose of inflation into the system.'[25] Later, in 1976 (in return for a massive loan from the International Monetary Fund), further controls on public spending were imposed, the first time since the War that monetary targets were used as a main instrument of economic policy. By this time, the ideals of economic planning enshrined in Labour's 1974 manifestos and its new National Enterprise Board had also been virtually abandoned (see Chapter 6).

Such developments were vital to the outcome of the 1979 election, as they seemed to vindicate the economic policies being advanced by the Conservative opposition under Mrs Thatcher, making any argument that they were 'extreme' or 'adventurist' seem otiose. It therefore seems reasonable to conclude that the Conservative election victory in 1979, far from *presaging* the end of an era, merely *confirmed* it.

Mrs Thatcher would not have been able to attack the social democratic approach to politics so vigorously had there not been plenty of evidence that such an approach was failing to produce desirable results. Neither should it be assumed that this 'failure' was a phenomenon of just the 1970s. Since the early 1960s, politicians of both parties had been worried by the relatively slow rates of growth in the British economy and the resulting failure of living standards to match the high public expectations generated by the 'never had it so good' period of the mid-to-late 1950s. The Labour Governments of 1964–70 were bedevilled by economic problems, having to resort to 'freezes' on public spending and wage rises in 1966 and devaluation in 1967. During the 1970s, economic problems intensified, leaving politicians perplexed by the apparent failure of traditional Keynesian–*dirigiste* techniques. Inflation had risen steadily between 1964 and 1971 and the Keynesian-inspired ideas applied in the four years that followed only seemed to boost inflation from about 6 per cent in 1971 to over 25 per cent in 1975. Likewise, unemployment rose steadily throughout the 1960s and early 1970s, from 1.6 per cent in 1964 to 4 per cent in 1976. The combination of rising unemployment *and* rising inflation served to undermine the theoretical basis of Keynesian economics. Keynes assumed that unemployment rose only when the balance of payments was relatively healthy and that balance of payments deficits could not occur when there was a shortage of jobs. By 1974/75, with unemployment, inflation and the balance of payments deficit standing at record levels (and rising) this reasoning was exposed as erroneous, with the term 'stagflation' (coined to describe this constellation of problems) standing as a serious indictment to the Keynesian consensus.

These problems were compounded by the failure of 'neo-corporatism' to contain and appease trade union pressure. Both the Heath Government after 1971 and the Labour Government elected in 1974 attached enormous importance to the restriction of wage rises through incomes policies and tried to reach some kind of 'solemn and binding' accord with the major trade unions. Yet both Governments were subsequently weakened by trade union strike action leading to power shortages and a 'three day week' in the case of the Heath Government, and paralysing stoppages among key public sector workers and a 'Winter of Discontent' in the case of the Callaghan Government. The election of February 1974 was actually called by the Heath Government on the premise of 'Who governs – government or unions?' (the electorate's failure to give any party an overall majority may have indicated that they were no longer sure of the answer). If the fall of the Heath Government could be attributed to the unions' hostility to Conservative Governments, especially those adopting a 'confrontationalist' posture, no such excuse could be made in the case of the 'Winter of Discontent' (1978–79) which all but destroyed the credibility of the then Labour Government. The *débâcles* of 1973/74 and 1978/79 naturally lent weight to the view that incomes policies and the paraphernalia of neo-corporatism were neither desirable nor workable; it also bolstered the idea that the attempt to incorporate large economic interest groups into the decision-making arena had only fuelled trade union 'militancy' and that governments now had a duty not to accommodate but to 'reform' the trade union movement (in such a way as to diminish its political influence).

Finally, and mainly as a result of the difficulties just described, faith in social democratic politics was gravely weakened by the failure of social democratic governments to get re-elected. After 1959, no government, serving what might be regarded as a normal term of office and pursuing policies consonant with the post-war consensus, managed to obtain a fresh mandate from the voters. The Labour Government lost office in 1970 as a result of what was then a record swing of 4.7 per cent against it. The Heath Government lost power in 1974 with less than 38 per cent of the vote, arguably the party's worst ever electoral performance. The Labour Government lost office in 1979 on a record swing of 5.2 per cent, polling what was then its lowest share of the vote (36.9 per cent) since 1931. Plainly, these statistics encouraged politicians in both parties, simply on the grounds of electoral self-interest, to reappraise traditional policies and objectives.

## The collapse of the social democratic consensus: the consequences

The collapse of the social democratic consensus in the 1970s has had two broad consequences for the conduct of party politics in Britain. First, a period of 'polarisation', when it appeared that the two major parties were drifting even further apart in their analyses of Britain's problems and in terms of what needed to be done. Secondly, as a result of fresh electoral calculations, there was an alleged re-emergence of consensus politics, though largely different in character to the social democratic model.

## Polarisation (1975–83)

During the late 1970s and early 1980s, it became fashionable to suggest that the principles and aims which had once united the Labour and Tory parties had been weakened, that the differences between the parties were now concerned with fundamentals rather than details and that British politics was afflicted by dangerous centrifugal forces.[26] It was also widely believed that the main agent of these trends has been the Conservative Party, which had undertaken a major reassessment of its ideas and strategy after losing office so ignominiously in 1974. There is an unquestionable logic behind such an argument. The old social democratic consensus arguably reflected 'centre-left' analyses of society, with its implicit distrust of unfettered capitalism and individualism, combined with its stress upon collective welfare provision to alleviate inequality. In addition, as has been shown earlier in this chapter, a great deal of the post-war consensus had its origins in the reforms of a radical Labour Government. Consequently, it might have been expected that any serious assault on its ideals would come from a party of the right.

### The development of Thatcherism

As explained earlier, the Conservative Party had not waited until 1975 to question some of the nostrums of social democracy. The party, when led by 'Heath Mark I' (1965–71), had emphasised less state involvement in the economy and the encouragement of a more *laissez-faire* society. This initiative came to grief, of course, less than two years into the Heath Government when economic pressures precipitated a 'U-Turn' in which many of the ideas colouring the 1970 Tory manifesto were jettisoned in favour of a more traditional Keynesian–statist approach – an apostasy which had much to do with the then lack of broad 'intellectual' support

48

for Heath's original strategy. By 1975, however, the party had fewer reservations about challenging the social democratic analysis. It was believed that Heath's 'U-Turn' had merely compounded the ever more acute problems of the economy and society, while making it more difficult for voters to discern the 'real' nature of Conservatism and what distinguished it from the views of other parties. The fact that the Conservative vote in both 1974 elections fell below 40 per cent confirmed the opinion of many Conservatives that the party should 'get back to basics', by redefining exactly what the party stood for and by offering a genuinely alternative view of what was wrong and what should be done – and a view which, next time, would not be deflected by 'short-term' pressures once applied in government.

The dethronment of Heath as party leader in early 1975, and his replacement by the relatively unknown Margaret Thatcher, is rightly considered a key moment in the history of recent party politics – not because she was a determined ideologue with a clear idea of how to reform the Conservative Party but because she shared the view of many Tory thinkers that the Heath Government had made a number of serious mistakes and that the ideals of the party had become obscured.[27] Furthermore, although no 'intellectual' herself, she was genuinely interested in new ideas and was eager to listen to those who were keen to give the party a clear (and fresh) intellectual basis.

In the years that followed 1975, the term 'New Right' entered the currency of British political debate. The term was coined to describe the collection of politicians, academics, economists and writers who sought to 'feed' (and to a large extent succeeded in feeding) the new Tory leader with a series of radical ideas which questioned the aims and assumptions of post-war British politics. Interestingly, this collection included many (such as the economist Alfred Sherman and journalist Paul Johnson) who had once been considered doctrinaire socialists, thus raising the idea that they had ditched one discredited ideology in favour of one yet to be applied. The most influential sections of the New Right included the 'right-wing' think tank, the Institute of Economic Affairs (though its devotees would certainly object to the term 'right-wing', preferring instead 'classical liberal'). Under the guidance of economist Ralph Harris, the Institute had since the late 1950s fought a lonely battle against the Keynesian orthodoxy, only for it to find that it was now being taken seriously by the Tory leadership. The IEA was complemented in 1974 by the creation of another 'think tank' with a similar ethos – the Centre for Policy Studies – set up by Sir Keith Joseph and Sherman to provide a regular flow of anti-social-democratic initiatives to the party leadership. It is, indeed, difficult to exaggerate Sir Keith's contribution to the development of Conservative policy in the late 1970s and therefore the subsequent changes in the atmosphere of British party politics. A prominent member of the Macmillan–Home and Heath Governments (with responsibility for Housing and Social Services), Joseph had upheld many of the consensual ideas regarding state intervention and welfare. Yet the traumatic years following Heath's 'U-Turn' convinced him that the social democratic approach was flawed on both economic and moral grounds, a view Mrs Thatcher willingly shared. So great was Sir Keith's influence in the early years of Mrs Thatcher's leadership that it became quite common for Tory MPs to regard her as a mere mouthpiece for a man who would have been a leadership contender in 1975 himself but for some injudicious comments about population growth made shortly beforehand.[28]

The developments in Conservative policy after 1975 were crystallised in a party document entitled *The Right Approach*, published in 1976. Implicit to the document was a rejection of the Keynesian stress upon demand management and an alternative emphasis upon 'supply-side' or 'neo-liberal' economics, which implied a much less interventionist role for the state and an altogether more individualistic view of a healthy society. Echoing the erstwhile opinions of the IEA, *The Right Approach* asserted the importance of the free market and entrepreneurial individuals in avoiding stagnation and encouraging economic growth. The social democratic idea that enlightened governments could plan or manage the economy to good effect was scorned; the 1960s and early 1970s, it was claimed, showed that such an approach led merely to bureaucratic excess which stifled the entrepreneurs' initiative, impeded market forces and thereby vitiated capitalism's potential to enrich society. Put simply, it was argued that governments could do little to inspire a successful economy, save create an appropriate *laissez-faire* climate in which individuals and private businesses could flourish. There was nothing especially novel about this line of argument; it recalled the ideas of nineteenth-century 'classical liberal' economists and owed much to economic theories first propounded in 1776 by Adam Smith's seminal study *The Wealth of Nations* (one New Right think tank, the Adam Smith Institute, quite plainly acknowledged the traditions inherent to its free market ideology). It was, nevertheless, a line of argument which brazenly challenged the benevolent view of statist economic policies which was central to Keynesianism and a series of post-war British governments.

*The Right Approach* also gave added importance to a relatively new word in the vocabulary of British politics – *monetarism* – for it seemed to reflect the economic analyses of Professor Milton Friedman of Chicago University, widely recognised as the high priest of monetarist economics and the author of such influential works as *Capitalism and Freedom* (1962), which assailed the basic assumptions of Keynesian orthodoxy. Friedman and his disciples contested that the critical feature of a thriving economy was low inflation, the parent of secure employment and international competitiveness. The key to low inflation was said to be the containment of the money supply, or the amount of money circulating within the economy (known in Treasury circles as M3). Monetarism is not necessarily synonomous with the free market ideas associated with the IEA; monetarists may or may not believe that the money supply can be controlled only through a limitation upon the size of the public sector and the active encouragement of market economies. Similarly, monetarists do not automatically share the free marketeers' concern with the size of public sector borrowing (known in Britain as the PSBR) as such, only the means of financing it. It was Friedman himself who harnessed the ideas of the IEA to theories of the money supply, based upon his own energetic support for free market economics. So it was *Friedmanism* rather than *monetarism* which the Tory party under Mrs Thatcher seemed to endorse.

Friedmanism brought into question the very character of post-war British politics. Not only did it confront the Keynesian belief in the possibility and desirability of steadily increased public spending and the extent to which the state should aim to harness market forces, it also challenged the mixed economy to which successive governments had deferred, as its stress upon the minimalisation of state spending presupposed a drastic reduction in state ownership of industry; many social democratic observers also inferred an attack on the notion of a welfare state if public expenditure was to be reduced to a level conducive to the 'enterprise culture' Friedman, and now the Tories, were promoting.[29] Furthermore, monetarism and *The Right Approach* seemed to undermine the primacy of *full employment* which successive governments had upheld, albeit rhetorically, since the famous White Paper of 1944. Friedman had asserted that there was a long-term equilibrium between supply and demand and a natural wage level at which workers would find jobs. He acknowledged that trade unions were inclined to distort this balance by demanding, and often securing, higher wages; yet if governments were to keep a firm control of the money supply, this rapacity on the part of the unions and capitulation on the part of management would result merely in higher costs of production, a loss of competitiveness and eventually a loss of jobs. Monetarists therefore seemed to regard as inevitable a certain amount (or natural level) of unemployment for the foreseeable future, but considered it a salutary *deterrent* to other workers in their pay demands, thereby strengthening the long-term monetarist strategy. Of course, such an approach would have been anathema to trade union leaders and, together with the dogmatic rejection of state planning along post-war lines, implied a reappraisal of the state's relationship with the major economic interest groups and trade unions in particular; in other words, an end to social democratic neo-corporatism.

If the social democratic policies of the 1950s and 1960s were underpinned by a philosophical commitment to greater equality, then the economic ideas enshrined in *The Right Approach* may be said to have been underpinned by a philosophical commitment to greater individual liberty. It must be stated that these two philosophical concepts are not always deemed mutually exclusive or antipathetic; most Labour Party politicians, for example, would maintain that equality is the means by which 'real' liberty and individualism are achieved.[30] Yet for those on the New Right, whose influence upon the Tory leadership was now becoming pronounced, the desire for a more equal society – and the way it was being pursued (tacitly or otherwise) by post-war governments – posed a menacing threat to the survival of individual freedom.

In this respect, the 'New Conservatism' appeared to draw heavily upon the philosophy of the Austrian professor Friedrich Hayek, whose work *The Road to Serfdom* (1949) was given almost biblical status by many devotees of the New Right. Hayek had argued that liberty and collectivism were incompatible and that the growth of the state's responsibilities (based as it might be upon noble humanitarian intentions) jeopardised individual freedom. The expansion of the state's industrial ownership and welfare provisions – a feature of most post-war democracies in Western Europe – threatened to turn their citizens into people who were economically and socially dependent upon the beneficence of governments and bureaucrats. Social democracy, in short, was the road to slavery and serfdom; such a destiny could be avoided only by preserving free market capitalism and by encouraging thrift, enterprise and self-reliance. These ideas struck a chord with Conservatives such as Margaret Thatcher, for they echoed the petit-bourgeois principles attending her corner-shop upbringing, principles which she and others believed to have been obfuscated during the era when social-democratic–welfarist values prevailed. Yet it is interesting that these ideas were more redolent of traditional Gladstonian liberalism than traditional Toryism, where the notion of individualism had been tempered by the paternalist ethos of 'noblesse oblige' and 'One Nation' (with the collectivist implications they carried). It is, indeed, remarkable that Hayek himself derided Conservatism on the grounds that it had 'regularly compromised with socialism and stolen its thunder'.[31] The final chapter of *The Road to Serfdom* was appropriately entitled

'Why I am not a Conservative'.

On the basis of what has been described above, it may seem reasonable to conclude that the New Conservatism which appeared in the mid-to-late 1970s was libertarian in character and was an attempt to transform Conservatism into an updated version of nineteenth-century liberalism; such a claim has in fact been made by 'traditional' Tories dismayed at the party's 'ideological drift' under Mrs Thatcher's leadership.[32] Such a conclusion would be reinforced by the fact that the New Conservatism claimed to be a direct assault upon the old social democratic consensus which, as explained earlier, was essentially statist and collectivist in terms of aims and methods. Yet it should be pointed out that the New Conservatism also had another (though perhaps less important) strand which was more authoritarian in character and arguably more consistent with the Tory tradition. Certainly, New Right luminaries, such as Roger Scruton and John Casey, argued that the crisis which enveloped Britain in the 1970s arose not from an erosion of liberty and an expanding oppressive state but from a surfeit of individual freedom and a corresponding loss of authority.[33] It was asserted that the main problem stemming from the extension of the state's role was not that it had become too strong but that it had overstretched itself and had become too weak. This problem had been compounded by the supposedly permissive, self-indulgent mood of the 1960s which had conspired to undermine respect for authority, discipline and traditional codes of conduct, a problem to which the state – now overburdened with a plethora of social, economic and industrial duties to perform – had been ill equipped to respond. Pursuing this theme in 1978, Peregrine Worsthorne insisted that the main priority was: 'for the state to regain control over the people, to re-exert its authority, and it is useless to imagine that this will be helped by some libertarian mish-mash drawn from the writings of Adam Smith and John Stuart Mill'. The central task for the next Conservative Government, Worsthorne continued, was 'not so much a splendid libertarian crusade as an ugly battle to restore some minimum of public order'.[34]

The rejection of social democracy by these types of Conservative writers included a much greater stress upon law and order and greater powers for the police, the diminution of trade unions (although this complemented the economic aims of the monetarists), the restoration of 'traditional' standards and values in education and tighter laws regarding immigration and nationality (an objective encouraged by the apparent rise in support for racist parties like the National Front between 1976 and 1978) – supplemented by a belief in a 'stronger' defence policy and a more combative attitude towards Soviet communism.

This twin-pronged attack on the old consensus, by those with both libertarian and authoritarian analyses, was synthesised in the personal philosophy of Margaret Thatcher, who blended an emphasis upon economic individualism and free market capitalism with a belief in the need for greater public order, discipline and respect for traditional norms and morals.[35] Such a synthesis was not especially novel, as the career of Enoch Powell demonstrates – his well known views on nationhood, race and the importance of tradition being accompanied by a long-standing belief in the primacy of controlling inflation through controlling the money supply. It has, indeed, been argued that 'Thatcherism' was merely a plagiarisation of 'Powellism', with Powell himself claiming to be the father of the 'revolution' inside the Conservative Party after 1975.[36] The belief that the state should be 'rolled back' in the economic and industrial spheres, while pushed forward in others, was not seen by its exponents as contradictory. They claimed that by releasing the energies of society's entrepreneurs, the state would be able to consolidate and concentrate its grip on its 'truly essential' functions such as law and order and the reassertion of 'public morality', a process resulting in what has been called 'The Free Economy and the Strong State', which a number of authors consider the essence of Thatcherism.[37]

The idea that *The Right Approach* and the New Conservatism marked the Tory Party's departure from the traditional centre of British politics was substantiated to a large extent by the performance of the first Thatcher Government elected in 1979. Between 1979 and 1982 the Government appeared to respect the diagnoses of monetarist economics by raising interest rates to a record

C

level of 17 per cent and by producing a 'crisis' budget (in 1981) which slashed an unprecedented £3.5 million from public expenditure, a move which reflected the advice of the Government's monetarist adviser, Professor Alan Walters. Such deflationary measures (ostensibly designed to create a 'leaner and fitter' economy), coupled with the Government's insistence that it would not assist 'lame duck' industries, resulted in the closure of 20 per cent of Britain's manufacturing industry and a doubling of unemployment to over three million. Such drastic 'medicine' was seen by many as a means of 'softening up' the trade unions in readiness for new trade union laws passed in 1980 and 1982, which imposed new restrictions concerning the closed shop, secondary picketing and union immunities during strike action – all of which could be regarded as consonant with the monetarist demand for an end to trade unionism's restrictive practices which distorted the free flow of the market. At the same time, the Government acted to alter the balance of the mixed economy by starting its privatisation programme, admitting private finance and varying measures of market discipline to no fewer than sixteen public industries. The doctrinaire thrust of the first Thatcher Government, allied to the fact that its success was not immediately apparent, served to give the impression to many voters that the Government was extreme and insensitive to 'moderate' opinion. This was manifested in the low standing of the Government in opinion polls throughout 1980 and 1981 (with Mrs Thatcher being seen as the most unpopular Prime Minister since polling began) and contributed to the loss of several safe Tory seats in by-elections – including Crosby (November 1981) with a majority of 19,000 – to the new SDP–Liberal Alliance.

## Labour's leftward lurch

The theory of polarisation was bolstered by concurrent developments in the Labour Party. After 1979, there was a widespread feeling within the constituency Labour parties that the party had lost office because the previous Labour Government had 'betrayed socialism', a view powerfully articulated by the Campaign for Labour Party Democracy. This idea was particularly evident at the 1980 Labour conference which seemed receptive to the view that in order to win next time, the party would have to put forward a 'purer' and more radical brand of left-wing politics. As such, delegates accepted much of Benn's Alternative Economic Strategy (involving the spread of nationalisation, state direction of industry and import controls) as well as voting for unilateral nuclear disarmament, and withdrawal from the EEC. Furthermore, in order to ensure that these measures were implemented by a future Labour Government, the party accepted a series of constitutional reforms intended to strengthen the power of the rank and file and weaken the autonomy of Labour's Parliamentary leadership (see Chapters 6 and 7). All these changes proved anathema to a number of leading Labour moderates, who, following a change in Labour's leadership election process in early 1981, formed a new Social Democratic Party out of a belief that the Labour party was no longer a vehicle for the 'Butskellite' ideals they held dear. That the new party stimulated such phenomenal public interest during its first year, and accomplished such remarkable feats in a string of by-elections, suggested that a sizeable body of the electorate shared the opinion that the middle ground of British politics was now vacant.

The 1983 general election offered the voters one of the starkest choices ever witnessed in modern British politics. On the one hand, the Conservatives (somewhat rejuvenated by the triumphant Falklands campaign and signs of an economic recovery) proposed a continuation of the *laissez-faire* economic policies pursued since 1979 and a renewed emphasis upon the 'individualistic' society, while on the other, Labour (now under the leadership of veteran left-winger Michael Foot) advanced a programme involving reflation and a massive extension of state interference in most areas of society and the economy, in addition to iconoclastic policies in respect of defence, Europe, Northern Ireland and the House of Lords. Although the Conservative Party won a share of the vote lower than in 1964 when they lost, they were nevertheless re-elected with a landslide majority, while Labour (with a meagre 27.6 per cent) plunged to the most shameful defeat in its history. The fact that Labour's alternative left-wing approach had palpably failed, accompanied by evidence that two-thirds of the centrist Alliance's vote had come from disenchanted Labour supporters, was to prompt a reordering of the party political agenda in the years that followed.

## Towards a new consensus? (1983–90)

Some Labour supporters singled out certain ephemeral factors when trying to explain Labour's calamitous defeat. These included Foot's lacklustre leadership, mistakes made during the campaign, the novelty and apostasy of the SDP, media distortion and the 'jingoism' generated by the Falklands conflict a year earlier. Yet many Labour politicians, including Neil Kinnock (elected leader shortly after the 1983 election), took a less sanguine view and suspected that there had been something essentially inappropriate about the fundamentalist, Bennite approach with which the party had been associated from 1980 to 1983. The fact that the Tories had secured a plurality of skilled and southern working-class voters, for example, seemed to suggest important social and economic changes which Labour had yet to comprehend. It was also by now clear that the working class, Labour's traditional constituency, was shrinking inexorably and that society in general was becoming more diverse and white collar. That being so, Labour would now have to adapt in order to appeal to those who were not its natural supporters in much the same way that the Tories had been forced to adapt for most of the twentieth century. The failure of the miners' strike in 1984–85, arguably the final chapter in the annals of traditional class struggle and industrial militancy, merely confirmed the belief of leading Labour politicians that political assumptions which held sway only ten years previously were now redundant.

Between 1983 and 1987, Labour's leadership thereby resolved to steer the party away from its image of left-wing extremism and towards an implicit recognition that significant and irreversible changes had occurred since the Tories took office in 1979. This strategy involved a purge against the Trotskyite Militant Tendency within the party, Kinnock's spirited denunciation of left-wing Labour councillors at the 1985 conference, the 'Freedom and Fairness' campaign launched in 1986 designed to identify Labour more closely with the growing emphasis upon individual liberty and consumer choice, and the publication of books by the leader and deputy leader in early 1987 which downgraded the importance of nationalisation as well as hinting at an acceptance of the centrality of market economics.[38] These centripetal tendencies were reflected in the party's 1987 manifesto, a much blander and vaguer document than its predecessor, with few specifically controversial pledges save a continued commitment to unilateral nuclear disarmament.

Despite these moderating forces, and a campaign which was almost universally acclaimed as 'slick' and professional, Labour's share of the votes in 1987 (30.8 per cent) was little better than 1983. Furthermore, the excuses that were to hand in 1983 (Falklands, Foot, novelty of the Alliance etc.) were no longer tenable. All this provoked the leadership to take an even more urgent look at the nature of contemporary society and the relevance of the Labour Party to it. It was widely felt that the party would either have to adapt at a much more vigorous pace or face extinction as a contender for government. The outcome of this analysis was a 'Labour Listens' campaign, designed to give the impression that the party was now making a serious attempt to espouse modern values and priorities, and a Policy Review undertaken (largely as a 'top down' exercise) between 1987 and 1989. The results of the Review were said to involve the 'wholesale abandonment of Labour's 1983 and 1987 programmes', representing 'the least socialist policy statement ever to be published by the party' (see Chapter 6).[39] This view was given added credibility shortly afterwards by the formation of a new party pressure group calling itself 'Labour Party Socialists' to protest against the dilution of 'traditional' socialist ideals and the capitulation to many 'Thatcherite' values. The Policy Review shifted the party away from unilateral nuclear disarmament, committed it to closer involvement with the EEC, and ruled out any return to the pre-1979 position regarding trade union laws.

Such developments naturally encouraged talk of a new consensus in British politics. Yet this was not inspired solely by changes inside the Labour Party. Even prior to Mrs Thatcher's resignation as Tory leader, there had been suggestions that the policy differences between the parties might not be as great as the leaders' speeches and personalities implied. Radicals of the New Right had been complaining since 1983 about the disappointing reality of government performance. *Whither Monetarism?*, a pamphlet published in 1985 by the Thatcherite Centre for Policy Studies, argued that the Government had abandoned the Friedmanite experiment earmarked after 1979 and had manifestly failed to reduce the burden of public expenditure (a claim borne out by figures released by the Government itself during the 1987 campaign!).[40] Chancellor Lawson's response to the alarming balance of payments deficit after 1987 (and the expansionist policies which seemed to precipitate it) also prompted a number of previously sympathetic commentators – like Alfred Sherman – to argue that the Government had forsaken its previously anti-Keynesian analysis in favour of traditional demand management techniques.[41] It should also be recalled that one of the last crucial economic policy decisions made by the Thatcher Governments was that of entering the European Exchange Rate Mechanism in October 1990 – one which eliminated overnight what had been one of the starkest differences between the economic pre-scriptions of Britain's two major parties.

## Majokism? (1990–92)

Any centripetal tendencies during Mrs Thatcher's premiership were obscured by her bombastic defence of certain controversial policies – the poll tax being the obvious example. Yet this same bombastic style was to play no small part in her failure to secure re-election as Conservative leader in November 1990, when a large section of Tory MPs (with a clear eye to electoral realities) began to crave a more cordial style of leadership. This was high-lighted, of course, by her replacement by John Major, described by colleagues as a 'social liberal', who was to promise 'a nation at ease with itself' rather than any continuation of 'conviction politics'. All three contestants in the second round of the leadership contest had promised a revision of the poll tax and this was, indeed, the first significant policy decision instigated by the new Prime Minister.

In the sixteen months that ensued between Major's accession and the 1992 election, the notion of a new 'Majokite' consensus was fuelled by a series of changes in both the style and the substance of the Conservative Government, changes which served to narrow the differences between it and the Labour Opposition. In stylistic terms, there was a clear movement towards something much less adversarial than was common during the Thatcher years. As Marquand observed: 'It's no longer a case of government saying "Right, here's our agenda, now we're going to smash it through", but instead saying "We've got some thoughts, please tell us what yours are, let's thrash them out and see if we can find some common ground." '[42] Likewise, the ideal of a 'leaner and fitter' society – based upon rugged individualistic competition – was downgraded in favour of the 'social market', with a continued emphasis upon private enterprise and capitalism now being accompanied by a renewed stress upon collective provision and greater public expenditure. As the new Party Chairman (Chris Patten) admitted, it represented a rhetorical shift from 'the ideals of Chicago to those of Christian democracy' (Chicago being the professorial home of monetarist guru Milton Friedman).[43]

These rhetorical changes were to be substantiated by a number of policy developments between 1991 and 1992. The Government's 'citizen's charters' aimed to improve, rather than privatise, such key public services as British Rail, education and the National Health Service – which Major described as 'uniting us all as members of the same national family. Our hearts revolt against the idea that one child with leukaemia should be treated and another not because of the luck of the economic draw.'[44] Such policy initiatives were later described by one shadow minister as 'only the most spectacular piece of our clothing which the Prime Minister is now trying on for size.'[45] This change was repeated after Lamont's 1992 Budget doubled the level of government borrowing – another clear break, it seemed, with the Thatcher era.

By 'accommodating much of the modern social democratic agenda' (to quote Riddell), Major was not simply expressing whatever philosophical bias he favoured.[46] The various surveys of electors' attitudes undertaken since 1987 all indicated that his policy changes had a strong electoral imperative. As Worcester and Jacobs revealed in 1990, a decade of Thatcherism had failed to convince voters that state intervention in the economy, high public expenditure and expanding state welfare were outdated objectives.[47] Indeed, as the 1980s progressed, the signs were that the electorate was as wedded as ever to such centre-left ideals.

The changes in party policy wrought by Kinnock after 1987 and by Major after 1990 appeared to vindicate Richard Rose's seminal thesis that if more than one party attempts to reflect the evidence of opinion polls, then the choice offered to voters would become marginal.[48] In other words, a clear and compelling choice – that is, the breakdown of consensus – would occur only when (as in 1983) one of the major parties so completely misread public thinking as to render itself hopeless in the race for power. By the 1992 general election, it seemed as if the polarisation illustrated in 1983 was proving the exception to the rule, while at the same time showing that the re-emergence of consensus was vital to the prospect of more than one party exercising power in government.

## Conclusion

The publication of the main parties' manifestos in March 1992 seemed to confirm that the choice facing voters was one not of competing ideologies but of alternative managerial strategies.[49] Although it was never suggested that the parties' policies were identical, the arguments that raged during the 1992 campaign were often redolent of the 'ferocious debates over mere technicalities' that marked the general elections of the 1950s.[50] Indeed, the embittered tone of much of the 1992 campaign, and the personalised nature of many of its debates, were often depicted as a substitute for genuine philosophical disgreement.

There was some dispute over the true character of the 'new consensus'. Some Conservative supporters argued that it is a 'by-product of the Thatcher years . . . with both parties accepting the main part of her agenda'.[51] On the other hand, it has been suggested that British politics has witnessed the revival of social democracy as the 'all-embracing credo of mainstream politicians'.[52] Neither of these propositions was wholly satisfactory. Despite Labour's concessions to many of the changes effected by the Thatcher Governments, the party remains opposed to a free enterprise culture, believes in the regulation of the market and favours a quasi-corporatist partnership between the two sides of industry. Similarly, the Major Government's emphasis on the value of the public services seemed to put a brake on Thatcherism's influence inside the Conservative Party. Yet to argue merely that the spirit of Keynes and Beveridge had been resurrected would also be facile. The Major Government pressed ahead with the market-inspired reforms of health and education started under Thatcher while Labour's recognition of the privatisation reforms means that today's mixed economy is a very different compound to that obtaining in the early 1960s. Furthermore, both parties in 1992 stressed the primacy of controlling inflation and public expenditure, thereby suggesting that the Keynesian goal of full employment had been jettisoned and differences over macro-economic policy diluted (something largely brought about by Britain's membership of the ERM).

'Post-Thatcherite' seemed to some a fair way of describing the consensus that had arguably emerged by 1992, one that fused the popular elements of Thatcherism (low inflation, relatively low direct taxation, wider house and share ownership, less public ownership of the economy) with the enduringly popular features of social democracy (extensive state health and welfare services, relatively high levels of public expenditure). It might also be argued that this new consensus was underpinned by a European dimension, with the Conservatives drawing increasingly from the traditions of Christian democracy with Labour and the Liberal Democrats remodelling themselves on those electorally effective centre-left parties on the continent.

With regard to an argument made in Chapter 1, it is also worth recounting the role that the minor parties (those without any serious aspiration to govern) have played in the recent evolution of the main parties' ideas, a role that perhaps vindicates their utility in the British party system. The revived interest of both parties in ecological matters, for example, was activated to a large degree by the electoral impact of the Greens in 1989, while the principles of the 'social market' (upon which both now seem agreed) were at least advertised by Owen's SDP. Of course, the 'success' of such parties does not necessarily produce, among other things, a consensus between the two main parties. Much plainly depends upon the extent of the electoral threat posed by the minor party concerned, a proviso neatly demonstrated by the main parties' differing response to the advances made by the SNP after 1987.

Following on from this, it is rather easy for the similarity between many of the major parties' policies to blind us to the survival of many key differences – differences which imply that the term 'consensus' may be a misnomer. The arguments that raged during the 1992 campign over levels of personal taxation, for example, suggested that Labour still clung to the ethos of redistributing wealth despite the trenchant opposition of the Conservatives. Moreover, Labour's promise that future economic growth would finance an expansion of the social services conflicted with the Conservative argument that it should be used for further tax cuts. It may also be contested that although both parties protested a commitment to the welfare state, these protestations were based on radically different analyses. Whereas the Conservatives still saw welfare provision in a short-term manner, providing a service for individuals and thus enhancing respect for (and satisfaction with) the *status quo*, there was still evidence that Labour views state welfare in the 'Croslandite' fashion – as a mechanism for creating greater equality and reducing divisions in society. All this suggests, of course, that an important philosophical difference still cuts through mainstream party politics, namely, one concerning the role and desirability of government activity.

It should also be remembered that the 1992 manifestos revealed an almost unprecedented division between Government and Opposition over constitutional matters (an extraordinary contrast with the situation prevailing in the 1950s). Labour advocated devolved parliaments for Scotland and Wales, a new second chamber to replace the Lords, proportional representation for the election of these new assemblies and a further push towards European union – all of which represented a sharp departure from the stance of the Major–Thatcher Governments. This disagreement over the very framework within which British government should be conducted made talk of a new consensus appear highly questionable; it also provided for some of the most strident exchanges during the 1992 campaign.

Important differences between the main parties therefore persisted in the early 1990s. It remains to be seen whether the 1992 election result will prompt a further convergence or divergence of party beliefs. However, Britain's ever closer involvement with the EC, and the left's loss of faith in Bennite socialism, make it unlikely that the enormous differences evident in 1983 will be replicated in the forseeable future.

## Notes

1 R. Miliband, *The State in Capitalist Society*, London, 1969.
2 R. Rose, *Do Parties Make a Difference?*, London, 1980.
3 P. Jenkins, *Mrs Thatcher's Revolution*, London, 1987.
4 J. Cole, *The Thatcher Years: A Decade of Revolution in British Politics*, London, 1987.
5 D. Kavanagh, *Thatcherism and British Politics*, Oxford, 1987.
6 Kavanagh, *Thatcherism*, chapter two.
7 R. T. McKenzie, *Political Parties*, London, 1955.
8 D. Howell, *British Social Democracy*, Beckenham, 1980.
9 D. Marquand, *The Unprincipled Society*, London, 1988.
10 R. A. Butler, *The Art of the Possible*, London, 1971, p. 160.
11 E. Butler, *Milton Friedman: A Guide to His Economic Thought*, London, 1985.
12 G. Foote, *The Labour Party's Political Thought*, London, 1985, pp. 61–4.
13 A. Horne, *Macmillan 1957–1986*, London, 1989, pp. 75–7.
14 Butler, *The Art of the Possible*, pp. 127–53.
15 Lord Carver, 'The apostles of mobility: the theory and practice of armed warfare', *Lees Knowles Lectures*, London, 1979.
16 R. Skidelsky, *Guardian*, 21 September 1987.

17 Butler, *The Art of the Possible*, pp. 133–4.
18 Butler, *The Art of the Possible*, p. 134.
19 A. Howard, *RAB: The Life of R. A. Butler*, London, 1987, chapter eleven.
20 Quoted by J. Critchley, *Observer*, 16 February 1980.
21 See D. Fraser, *The Evolution of the British Welfare State*, London, 1973, chapter seven.
22 A. Sked & C. Cook, *Post-War Britain*, London, 1984, p. 19.
23 Profile of D. Kavanagh, *Talking Politics*, autumn 1988.
24 *Guardian*, 16 July 1980.
25 Quoted by S. Foster & R. Kelly, 'Keynesians or monetarists?', *Talking Politics*, summer 1989.
26 See W. Kennett (ed.), *The Rebirth of Britain*, London, 1982.
27 P. Cosgrave, *Margaret Thatcher*, London, 1978, pp. 158–66.
28 Cosgrave, *Thatcher*, p. 45.
29 Kavanagh, *Thatcherism*, pp. 78–80.
30 See, for example, R. Hattersley, *Choose Freedom: The Future of Democratic Socialism*, London, 1987.
31 Profile of F. J. Hayek, *Guardian*, 20 April 1982.
32 See J. Critchley, *Westminster Blues*, London, 1985.
33 See R. Scruton, *The Meaning of Conservatism*, London, 1980.
34 M. Cowling (ed.), *Conservative Essays*, London, 1978.
35 See A. Gamble, *The Free Economy and the Strong State*, London, 1988.
36 P. Cosgrave, *The Lives of Enoch Powell*, London, 1989, chapters four & five.
37 Gamble, *The Free Economy*.
38 N. Kinnock, *Making our Way*, Oxford, 1987; Hattersley, *Choose Freedom*.
39 I. Crewe, 'The policy agenda', *Contemporary Record*, February 1990.
40 *Guardian*, 12 March 1992.
41 *Sunday Telegraph*, 28 August 1988.
42 *Marxism Today*, February 1991.
43 *Marxism Today*, February 1991.
44 *Guardian*, 25 March 1991.
45 *Guardian*, 26 March 1991.
46 *Times*, 17 February 1992.
47 R. Worcester & E. Jacobs, *We British*, London, 1990, p. 25.
48 Rose, *Do Parties Make a Difference?*.
49 A. Massie, *Daily Telegraph*, 14 March 1992.
50 D. Butler, 'General elections since 1945', *Contemporary Record*, autumn 1989.
51 G. Lawler, *Daily Telegraph*, 10 March 1992.
52 P. Worsthorne, *Sunday Telegraph*, 15 March 1992.

# 4

## THE CONSERVATIVE PARTY:
## THEORY AND PRACTICE

For much of the twentieth century, the term 'Conservative ideology' was considered something of a misnomer. Ideas, doctrine and theory were thought to be the preserves of the left, of parties like Labour and the Liberals. As recently as 1977, a journalist observed 'if an undergraduate returns from university on vacation and tells his parents that he has become hooked on doctrine, it is certain that he has not joined the Federation of Conservative Students'.[1] The Conservative Party, it seemed, was firmly rooted in a non-ideological approach to politics, and their well known hostility to philosophy and abstract notions was reflected in Lloyd George's famous taunt that they were the 'stupid party'. This was echoed in the more serious analyses of what Conservatism was about; White described it as 'less a doctrine than a frame of mind', while Gilmour claimed that Conservatives had 'emotions but no doctrine'.[2] Far from being offended by such descriptions, many leading Tories accepted them gladly, asserting that, unlike other parties, the Conservatives were unencumbered by grand empirical theories and could therefore act flexibly and pragmatically in response to changing circumstances. Stanley Baldwin (party leader 1923–37) dismissed the intelligentsia as 'an ugly name for an ugly thing' and this contemptuous view of the 'chattering classes' was an important part of the party's attempt to make a direct appeal to the working-class voters they needed to survive as a party of government.

## 'A determination to govern'

The party's survival as a party of government is, in fact, one of the most remarkable features of twentieth-century British politics. Indeed, not only has the party survived, it has prospered, and is by far the most successful party in twentieth-century British electoral history. By the time of the 1992 election, the Conservatives had been in government (either alone or as part of a coalition) for over two-thirds of the century. To illustrate the point in another way, the party was re-elected to government in 1900 after an emphatic election victory under the leadership of Lord Salisbury. Ninety-two years later, the party was re-elected in an equally emphatic way under the leadership of John Major. When one considers the enormous social, economic and cultural changes that had occurred in the interim one has some idea of the scale of the party's achievement. Such an achievement is rendered more extraordinary when one considers that the party has been historically associated with property and privilege and that British politics, for most of this century, has been dominated by working-class, propertyless electors.

In seeking to explain the Conservatives' durability, their hostility to doctrine provides a tempting, ready-made answer: the party has endured because it has been able to 'move with the times' and continously offer a set of policies relevant to contemporary society, and it has been able to do so largely because it has not been 'weighed down' by 'ideological baggage', a problem often linked to Labour's electoral difficulties since 1951. A former Liberal Party leader stated that the Conservatives 'do not conserve any set of principles, merely the state of affairs they happen to inherit'.[3]

Such observations clearly expose the party to the criticism that it is a slave to opportunism and expediency and bereft of any eternal principles and deeply-held ideals. Conservatism, perforce, is merely a series of ephemeral policies springing from the shifting political calculations of Conservative Party leaders; not so much an ideology as a stratagem for attaining and retaining power. Such an approach to politics is by no means indefensible.[4] It can be argued that ideas and theories are tenable only when examined from the perspective of social and economic realities, which are themselves transient. Serious political objectives and ideas must take into account practical as well as ethical requirements, and it might be the case that those who argue for 'fixed principles' in politics underestimate the changing character of society. As Michael Oakeshott (the most distinguished apologist for Conservatism's traditional, protean nature) maintained, politicians 'are adrift in a boat without harbour or destination'.[5]

## The Legacy of Burke

Not all descriptions of traditional Conservatism, however, agree that it is impossible to place Conservatism within a distinct philosophical framework and deny that the Conservative party simply does whatever is expedient without reference to certain basic principles.[6] They contend that attempts to dub Conservatism as non-ideological (and even amoral) arise from a view of ideology which is shaped, or distorted, by liberal, humanist assumptions – in other words, a view of humanity and society which is by no means unchallengeable. In their efforts to put Conservatism into an alternative philosophical context, such authors often invoke the writings of Edmund Burke, and in particular his seminal thesis *Reflections on the Revolution in France* (1790). It is ironic that Burke did not himself belong to the then Tory Party, understandably seen as the progenitor of the modern Conservative Party which emerged in the mid-nineteenth century, but was a practising Whig politician with a fairly radical pedigree on account of views expressed, for example, during the American War of Independence. Yet the outbreak of the French Revolution in 1789, and the optimistic ideals which underpinned it, were seen by Burke as profoundly dangerous and a threat to the survival of human civilisation – a view not immediately shared by most of his contemporary parliamentarians in England. Burke's *Reflections* was prompted by a belief that the French Revolution made it necessary to clarify and justify the rationale of England's existing hierarchical society. Burke's achievement was 'to make mundane virtues sound dramatic and exciting', and in so doing he provided later Conservative thinkers with an intellectual basis for their instincts and preferences.[7]

The starting point for Burke's diatribe, and of later attempts to examine British Conservatism, was a pessimistic view of human nature and human capability and a stress upon the tragic discrepancy existing between human aspiration and achievement. He therefore denounced the ideals of human perfectibility, utopianism and infinite improvement which seemed inherent to the Revolution. The doctrines of 'reason' and abstract theorising by which indefinite progress would be achieved were rejected vehemently for ignoring the realities of human potential and thereby courting disaster (the genocide and 'Terror' into which the Revolution later descended is seen naturally as a vindication of Burke's argument). Burke evidently sought to defend the imperfect society from a behaviouralist standpoint, namely, that the imperfections of society merely reflected the innate imperfections of those human beings who comprised it.

Burke was no reactionary and did not deny the need for change – 'A state without means of change is without its means of conservation' – and suggested that the French Revolution had occurred largely because orderly change had been resisted for so long (although this is disputed by many historians). Yet change had to be cautious, gradual and piecemeal, stemming from a recognition that society was not a mechanism but an organism, having evolved over a long period in a subtle, complex and mysterious way – and which would continue to evolve irrespective of actions instituted by governments. Radical change was to be avoided for the simple reason that its effects could not be fully foreseen. Existing institutions and political processes should be respected precisely because they still exist, which is in itself a measure of their practicality.

Many assessments of Burke's views, however, dispute that he (and Conservatives who later invoked him) were arguing from a detached, philosophical premise.[8] They contend that 'Burkism' merely provides a pseudo-rational gloss for an unequal, élitist society in which Burke and his later Conservative devotees had a vested interest. Burke was quite clear that the best and most 'natural' type of society was hierarchical, where 'the wiser, the more expert and the more opulent conduct . . . the weaker, the less knowing and the less provided'.[9] The small, aristocratic ruling class Burke commended was to have duties and obligations and should take a benevolent, paternalistic attitude towards the less fortunate. Yet one may infer that Burke preferred the rule of an aristocracy that was not so dutiful to the rule of what he termed 'the swinish multitude' being extolled in France. Burke's belief that the overthrow of the French aristocracy could be attributed to their 'neglect' of the lower classes strengthens the idea that the 'Tory paternalism' of later years was only the function of preserving the exalted material position of its exponents. To summarise, Burke's views upon politics and society were founded upon the notion of choosing the lesser evil, of making the best of an unpromising situation. Pessimism, cynicism and a fear of the mob – underlined by an implicit determination to maintain the vestiges of privilege and property – seemed to characterise his outlook.

The extent to which that outlook influenced and coloured later writers whose attachment to Conservatism is explicit seems considerable. In his classic work Conservatism (1912), Lord Hugh Cecil claimed that: 'Progress depends upon conservatism to make it intelligent, efficient and appropriate to circumstances . . . it is only when a man is controlling his wish to go forward with a strong sense of entering the unknown that he is likely to make effectual progress.'[10] Cecil went on to say that the attraction of Conservatism lay in that it appealed to a basic human instinct, namely, 'a distrust of the unknown and a love of the familiar'.[11] A sympathetic biographer of Disraeli observed that 'Change is irresistible; all a Conservative can do is to moderate and delay what of it he finds repugnant'.[12] Quinton Hogg's celebrated study of Conservatism in 1948 argued that 'Conservatism's indispensable role is to criticise and mould the latest heresy in the name of tradition'.[13] From such opinions it is possible to discern that, until recently, Conservatism was an essentially defensive creed, negative and reactive rather than positive and creative. Quinton claimed that Conservative opinion became clear only 'in reaction to a positive, innovative attack on the traditional scheme of things', a view echoed in a recent study by Ingle who stated that Conservatism could only be 'fully understood . . . by reference to the policies of its traditional opponents'.[14]

The negative and reactive character of the Conservative Party during the past 150 years or so probably has less to do with any applied interpretation of Burkean doctrine than a sober assessment of social, economic and political realities. The Conservative party was plainly identified with the landed, established interests in an age when the extension of the franchise (in 1832, 1867, 1884 and 1918) meant an increasing influence – at elections at least – for those with little to conserve in the material sense and no overwhelmingly obvious interest in the preservation of the existing order. Pessimistic and cautious many Conservatives may have been, yet their pessimism and caution had more to do with the apparent trends in contemporary society than any genuine sympathy towards the Burkean view of humanity's eternal shortcomings. In short, traditional Conservatism's guarded character arguably arose from a sense that 'history' was not on its side and that it was fighting a rearguard action against the apparently inexorable forces of egalitarianism. In this respect, it is easy to understand Jay's assertion (quoted earlier) that Conservatism was really about a 'determination to govern at all costs'. Unfavourable trends, inimical to property and privilege, may be irreversible, but Conservative Governments could at least endeavour (in Hogg's words) to 'criticise and mould' them in order to preserve as far as posssible the status quo in which large sections of the party had an interest. According to R. A. Butler in the 1950s, only Conservative Governments could 'maintain the old order by appeasing and accommodating the forces which threaten it'.[15]

## From Toryism to Conservatism

In seeking to ensure the election and re-election of Conservative Governments charged with this task, the party has adopted an assortment of 'libertarian–individualist' and 'authoritarian–

72

collectivist' measures which at once illustrate and explain the party's versatile character described earlier. At this point, it is germane to describe when 'Conservative Governments' and, for that matter, the 'Conservative Party' first appeared. Although certain analyses of Conservative practice unsurprisingly try to discern a thread running from those politicians known as 'Tories' in the seventeenth and eighteenth centuries through to modern Conservative politicians, the more distinguished Conservative historians (chiefly Robert Blake and John Ramsden) believe there is 'little profit' in seeking such a sequence of ideas, as political and economic circumstances during the reign of George III (1760–1829) alone had changed so much.[16]

It is instructive that Blake's authoritative history of the party begins at the end of 1834 with the premiership of Robert Peel, usually seen as the first 'Conservative' Prime Minister. Peel's accession to the premiership did not, however, mark any significant caesura in terms of his party's character. As Blake notes: 'There was no fundamental break with the past ... no drastic change occurred in Conservative as compared with Tory political ideas and attitudes', adding that Peel's view of politics had been shaped largely by the Tory administrations of Wellington and Liverpool earlier in the century.[17] The logic behind tracing the Conservative Party's official history back to Peel seems to be based largely upon nomenclature. The term 'Conservative' was first used in its modern political sense by a group of parliamentarians writing in *Quarterly Review* in 1830 who proclaimed: 'We now are, as we always have been, attached to what is called the Tory, and which might with more propriety be called the Conservative Party.'[18] Blake recalls that by the end of 1831, certain newspapers were referring to the 'Conservative party' as if it were 'a well established expression and ... it soon became the normal word for the party of the Right'.[19] There is also an organisational factor which underwrites Peel's premiership as the starting post for any examination of the Conservative Party as such: the Conservative and Constitutional Associations, the forerunners of the modern extra-Parliamentary organisation founded in 1867, were all assembled between 1834 and 1835.

Peel's leadership of the party cannot be extolled as exemplary as it led to a calamitous split in 1846 and the party's subsequent failure to secure a normal period in government for nearly thirty years. Nevertheless, Peel's strategy is useful to any assessment of Conservatism as it exhibits the influence of Burkean philosophy and some of the political calculations which were to guide later Conservative Governments. By the beginning of the nineteenth century, a new middle class consisting of merchants, traders, businessmen and *nouveaux riches* was challenging the traditional, aristocratic, landed agrarian interests associated with Peel's party. The challenge was a powerful one as it had already succeeded in changing the culture or 'prevailing morality' of society.[20] The bourgeois ideals of thrift, individualism, self-reliance and commercial *laissez-faire* were becoming increasingly widespread and seemed ill at ease with traditional Tory attitudes. Peel's resulting dilemma was compounded not just by the 1832 Reform Act, which enhanced the new middle classes' influence upon Parliamentary elections, but by the concurrent emergence of an identifiable and homogenous working class – the inevitable long-term result of urbanisation and the factory system. Both these classes had been outraged by the effects of the Corn Law of 1815, passed by a Parliament of landowners with the intention of protecting landed interests against the effects of untrammelled commerce. Peel perceived a dangerous alliance between the two classes which represented a grave threat to the existing order, and his response came from a calculation of how that order could preserve itself by harnessing these forces for change – a calculation made by countless Conservative leaders who followed him. He realised that the landed aristocracy upon which the party had traditionally depended constituted an insufficiently broad base for survival in the new political climate; he therefore sought to broaden that base by championing the interests of the new middle class by embracing *laissez-faire* ideas and by seeking to unite the two wealth-owning classes in society. In a manner that echoed Burke's prescriptions for a stable and efficient society, Peel aimed to 'compromise with the forces of change and adapt traditional institutions to new social demands', thereby preserving and

74

strengthening 'the traditional constitution of Church and state and land'.[21] Although Peel's decision to repeal the Corn Laws seemed to contradict aristocratic interests, and thereby Burke's belief in the virtues of aristocratic government, Peel claimed he was merely acting to defend and enhance it by widening the sphere of recognised privilege and status, thus making the aristocracy more accessible and thus more acceptable.

Although Peelism had disastrous consequences for the party, it nevertheless deserves attention in any essay seeking to illustrate the meaning of Conservatism and to explain the later success of the party. This is on account of Peel's leadership establishing three precedents which were to be invoked at later stages in the party's history. First of all, that the party should aim to champion the interests of all the 'haves' in society, new money as well as old, middle as well as upper classes, and should aim to be seen as the natural political advocate for those who wished to conserve their wealth. Secondly, it incorporated into Conservatism's pantheon of ideas libertarian, individualistic, *laissez-faire* notions which would later supplement the party's traditional association with collectivist themes (expressed through such concepts as the nation, the Church, the estate etc.). Finally, its direct assault upon the usual Tory icons highlighted a certain utilitarian streak which became a recurrent feature in later Conservatism – a willingness to instigate remarkable changes in policy in order to make existing society (thus Conservative prospects) more favourable.

## The legacy of Disraeli

It was not until the mid-1860s that the Conservative Party, under the guidance of Disraeli, recovered its footing as a party of government. Although Disraeli had been a vehement critic of Peel, and although he continued to denounce Peel's ministry after he had steered the party back to power, in terms of raw political calculations, the two statesmen had much in common. Disraeli's support for the Liberal-instigated franchise reform (passed in 1867) owed much to a similar desire to reflect the mood of the time, which was overwhelmingly in favour of reform, and demonstrate to the new middle-class electorate that the party was attuned to current thinking and therefore fit to govern after over twenty years in the wilderness. Likewise, the initiatives taken by Disraeli's Government of 1874–80 in the field of social reform were not, as is often supposed, expressions of Tory paternalism, a reaffirmation of the ancient bonds between aristocratic and commonality foolishly severed by Peel, but a response to new political circumstances which made the interests of the working class much more urgent. Such measures as the Factory Act (1874), the Public Health and Artisan Dwellings Acts (1875) and Disraeli's exhortations to 'trust the people' may at first seem in conflict with Burke's profound distrust of 'the people', yet they should be seen more properly as another attempt to shore up existing society in the face of new threats and pressures upon it. Disraeli also echoed the Burkean concept of respect for traditional institutions and at his famous Crystal Palace speech in 1872 (which Gilmour believes laid the foundations of twentieth-century Conservative thought),[22] Disraeli enunciated the party's 'three great objects', namely, 'to maintain the institutions of the country, to uphold the empire of England and to elevate the condition of the people'.[23]

The second of these three objects indicates what is seen by many as Disraeli's most important legacy to Conservatism. By elucidating the concept of the nation and empire, and by identifying the Conservatives with it, he bequeathed a theme that generations of Conservatives have used to unite middle-class and working-class voters. More important, by emphasising the party's 'impeccable' patriotic credentials, the party has often placed the onus on other parties to defend themselves against the charge that they are putting 'party' or 'sectarian' interests against the interests of the country. McKenzie and Silver's celebrated study of working-class Conservatism emphasises that by encouraging the powerful nationalistic and xenophobic sentiments of the working class, the party made other parties' policies seem 'utterly to be distrusted where the fate of the nation's institutions and imperial interests are concerned'.[24] McKibbin has also argued that working-class militancy in the late nineteenth and early twentieth centuries was significantly attenuated by the injection of 'jingoistic' ideas into political debate.[25] The strengths of the 'patriotic factor' for the Tory Party, and the damage it has inflicted upon its opponents, have been demonstrated on several occasions since. It was seen in *Gladstone's Irish Home Rule* policy in 1886, which split the Liberals and allowed an almost unbroken period of Tory rule for the next twenty years, in the *Boer War*, which played a central role in the re-election of Lord Salisbury's Government at the 'Khaki election' of 1900, in the *Zinoviev Letter*, which undermined the credibility of the first Labour Government and paved the way for the election of Baldwin's Conservative Government in 1924, and, more recently, in the *Falklands conflict* which had a critical effect upon the national 'mood' in the run-up to the 1983 election, along with Labour's *unilateralist* approach to nuclear disarmament which cast doubts upon Labour's patriotism at both the 1983 and 1987 elections. All these incidents suggest that the other parties face an obligation to prove they are as patriotic as the Conservatives if they are to stand any chance of defeating them at a general election.

## The legacy of liberalism

Any examination of how and why the Conservatives managed to endure as a party of government throughout the turbulence of the present century must certainly accord a major role to the weaknesses of opposing parties, in particular their failure at key moments to react to changing circumstances in a united and cohesive manner. It is easy to forget, of course, that the Tories themselves provided a spectacular example of what happens when a party becomes divided over fundamental issues of policy – in 1905, when Balfour's Government fell apart over the issue of free trade or protection, with the resulting Liberal landslide victory at the 1906 election. Yet this *débâcle* seemingly taught the party a lesson; that debate over policy should never be allowed to eclipse electoral calculations, and that differences over such calculations should be moderated, compromised and amicable. This is, in effect, one of the great prerogatives of any conservative party, a party which seeks to preserve and administer the existing order, what a later Conservative described as 'the politics of here and now',[26] with no grand designs for improving the human condition. Such a party can by its very nature afford to be more pragmatic, flexible and managerial in its view of politics than parties like the Liberals and Labour, which contain elements which take an altogether more crusading approach to government – regarding ofice as an opportunity to create a 'new' society according to some lofty vision of humanity. Problems arise, of course, when such visions are not easily reconciled with existing circumstances and current public opinion, and are compounded when members of that party cannot even agree on what the vision should be.

The disintegration of the Liberal party after 1918 – itself largely self-induced – was immensely helpful to the Conservatives, as it allowed them to project their party as the only viable opponent of socialism, and it became increasingly difficult in the inter-war years for middle-class Liberals to resist the lure of Conservatism. This development was to complete the political fusion of upper and middle class, which both Peel and Disraeli recognised as essential to the party's survival. Furthermore, the infusion of former Liberal supporters (such as Mrs Thatcher's father) enlarged the breadth of Tory values. In addition to patriotism, paternalism and a basic love of the familiar, the party was now able to project the traditionally liberal ideals of self-reliance, probity, thrift and frugality which struck a chord with many of the less class-conscious blue collar voters the party now had to attract. Such ideals were not entirely alien to the Tory tradition, as Peel's leadership demonstrates. Nevertheless, the absorption of 'Gladstonian' principles following the shambolic decline of the Liberal Party underlined and cemented the synthesis of collectivist and libertarian ideas which enhanced the party's appeal as the century wore on.

## One Nation Conservatism (1923–65)

Yet in the forty or so years leading up to Edward Heath's leadership, the relationship between collectivism and libertarianism within Conservative thought was not equally balanced. While the influence of liberal–individualism certainly embellished the party's rhetoric (exemplified by Churchill's rallying-cry of 'Set the People Free' in 1951), the behaviour of Tory Governments had inclined towards Disraelian collectivism and the maintenance of social cohesion. Stanley Baldwin, party leader from 1923 to 1937, devoted his limited energies to the cause of 'the nation' and 'unity' rather than individualism and self-help.

Such collectivist language was given a practical dimension by Baldwin's Minister of Health, Neville Chamberlain, who aimed to translate into national government many of the 'municipal socialist' ideas associated with the administration of Birmingham, his native city. At the beginning of the 1924 Parliament, Chamberlain presented the Cabinet with a list of twenty-five bills pertaining to social policy, an impressive twenty-one of which were enacted. The Tory dominated-coalition Government of the 1930s is likewise a challenge to all those who argue that the social democratic consensus emerged only after 1945. In addition to Housing, Public Health and Factory Acts (1935–37), the Government also ventured tentatively into the realms of economic planning with a series of Special Areas, as well as encouraging a measure of industrial reorganisation.

It should be emphasised that the bias of Tory leaders towards collectivist rhetoric and 'One Nation' policy during the inter-war era arose not from any conscious ideological preference but mainly from a dispassionate analysis of what was needed to secure national unity and consent and therefore the preservation of existing society – the underlying theme of Conservatism. The nature of society for much of this century (urbanised, predominantly working class and therefore relatively homogeneous) both allowed and demanded a statist approach to social and economic policy. It was not merely ethically tenable but apparently pragmatic to extend state provision in a way that would affect and benefit the mass of electors who might now be categorised as 'have-nots'. The Tories could be, and have been, accused of simply adopting other parties' collectivist ideas; yet for most of the century those ideas did seem to have, given the nature of society, a certain logic and practical urgency.

This argument was given added strength by the Labour Party's landslide victory in the election of 1945, widely seen as a popular vindication of the principles of state planning and state provision. It should be noted that the 1945 Conservative manifesto was by no means opposed to these principles, yet the party's failure to capture even 40 per cent of the vote suggested that the public had the *impression* that the party did not wholeheartedly endorse the *Beveridge Report* (on which the new system of welfare benefits was to be based) and were somehow out of tune with the general mood in favour of radical, state-inspired reform. In the three years that followed, the party, under the guidance of R. A. Butler at the Conservative Research Department, sought to correct that impression. A series of policy charters was commissioned (notably the *Industrial Charter* of 1947) which accepted the Attlee Government's commitment to a mixed economy with a much greater level of state involvement in both economic and social policy. Although the Charters did not represent any significant break with trends in Tory policy before the War, the whole point of the exercise was to suggest to a sceptical electorate that they did – to make the rejection of *laissez faire* and the recognition of state planning more explicit. To guard against the charge of flagrant opportunism and apostasy, a series of Conservative writers during the 1945–50 period went back to Disraeli to justify their enthusiasm for state intervention. L. S. Amery claimed in 1946 that: 'Conservatism has none of the old Liberal objection to the direction and control of industry or even a theoretical objection to nationalisation. Conservatism has always recognised that *laissez-faire*, unchecked, can destroy freedom and individuality.'[27] Yet as was explained earlier, Disraeli's 'Tory paternalism' owed more to shrewd political deductions rather than to any deeply held philosophy and it was this *strategy*, rather than any historic Tory doctrine, which the post-1945 party was determined to reflect. Indeed, Iain Macleod later admitted this by arguing that his party's adaptation after 1945 'demonstrated the peculiar genius of the party, a readiness to admit that it was wrong and move to where the public wanted it to be, rather than sticking to a narrow orthodoxy'.[28]

However, an often overlooked feature of British politics during that period was that by 1949 there had been a definite change in the mood of the time. After four years of rationing and general austerity, the focus of public opinion shifted from 'fairness' and sacrifice to 'freedom' and selfishness, manifested in housewives' campaigns for better rations, and a general public demand for more houses and lower taxes. Although the Labour Govenment tried to respond to this trend (for example, with its 'bonfire of controls'), the Conservatives were able to identify with it more easily, thanks to their inheritance of liberal ideas from Peel onwards. It was a useful illustration of the political benefits accruing from a party philosophy which can, according to circumstances, call upon either libertarian or collectivist ideals.

Despite the Conservatives being elected in 1951 on a libertarian slogan ('Set the People Free'), and despite the relaxation of controls instigated by Butler's term at the Treasury (1951–55), the Conservative Governments of 1951–64 broadly respected the interventionist, social democratic climate fostered by the Attlee Governments. The bulk of industries nationalised by Labour were not returned to private ownership and economic policy continued to respect Keynesian diagnoses. Harold Macmillan (Conservative leader and Prime Minister 1957–63) was determined to pursue a policy of expansion and high public expenditure and sacrificed three Chancellors in order to do so. Towards the end of Macmillan's premiership, there was a related interest in economic planning – evidenced by the creation of the National Economic Development Council – and state control of prices and incomes. Macmillan's supporters have disputed that this involved appeasing other parties' ideas, pointing to their relationship with Macmillan's book The *Middle Way*, one of the earliest pro-Keynesian statements published in 1938.[29] They would, however, accept the charge that Macmillan, like most of his predecessors as Tory leader, was appeasing public opinion, which appeared to demand short-term consumer benefits after a prolonged period of austerity. As Butler, Macmillan's deputy, is alleged to have remarked, 'if they [the people] want that sort of life, they can have it, but under our auspices'[30] – a remark which perhaps neatly summarises the whole ethos of Conservatism. It also fits in with Churchill's comment to Lord Moran after the election victory of 1951: 'I have come to know the nation and what must be done to retain power',[31] an approach which most conspicuously involved appeasing the trade unions, thought necessary partly on account of the supposed power of organised labour at that time, and partly because the party's claim to stand for 'one nation' had been damaged by its 'anti-union' reputation created in the 1920s.

The 1951–64 Conservative Governments also brought into question the relationship between the party and the concept of the nation, which, as explained earlier, plays a key role in understanding the Conservatives' electoral success from Disraeli onwards. The Suez fiasco of 1956, which brought to an end Eden's brief premiership, exposed Britain's limitations as a world power and destroyed the nostalgic, self-satisfied illusions which had flourished in the early 1950s. Coupled with Britain's slow rate of economic growth compared with other advanced nations, it provoked serious interest in the European Community. Macmillan's enthusiasm for EC membership and Gaitskell's staunch opposition on the grounds that it endangered 'a thousand years' of proud self-government (a view which echoed the reservations of many Tory activists) temporarily threatened the Conservatives' claim to be the 'party of the nation' – although there is no evidence suggesting this was in any way responsible for the party's narrow defeat at the 1964 election, and the nature of the debate was largely changed following the new Labour Government's decision to seek entry themselves.

### Towards a new Conservatism? (1965–90)

A commitment to Europe was one of the themes in the new package of Tory policies assembled by Edward Heath following his accession to the leadership in 1965. Heath epitomised a new breed of senior Tory – grammar school educated, lower middle class, meritocratic and with much less time for the patriarchal notions personified by traditional Tory leaders. Heath's election as leader, which in itself was a mark of individual merit and achievement rather than 'background' and 'tradition', was matched by a switch back to liberal, individualistic ideas which, as has been shown, have always been latent in Toryism but which were submerged by a succession of paternalist leaders who deferred to the social democratic consensus. An extract from Heath's address to the 1970 party conference illustrates this development: 'Our purpose is to make our fellow citizens realise that they must be responsible for the consequences of their own actions and nobody will stand between them and the results of their own free choice.'[32]

Although this appears to represent a break with the Conservatism of Heath's predecessors, it should be remembered that Heath (unlike Disraeli in relation to Peel) had been a loyal supporter of those Governments and never gave any public indication that he was unhappy with their statist tendencies. Heath's biographers have shown that his arguments for a more *laissez-faire* approach to society and the economy, and his belief in the virtues of limited government, were not based upon some lifelong libertarian 'world view' derived from reading the works of Hayek and Popper but derived from a sober, practical assessment of Britain's problems by the middle of the 1960s.[33] Heath had convinced himself that Britain's slow rate of economic growth, lack of investment, poor industrial relations and so on were the result of excessive government and shortage of encouragement for entrepreneurs and free market capitalism. Underlying Heath's belief in the need for a 'quiet revolution', which would relegate the role of the state and exalt private enterprise, was not a grand philosophical commitment to individual liberty but a straightforward desire to 'modernise' Britain's economy and make it more efficient. It should also be noted that Heath's initial hostility to government intervention in the economy did not extend to a full-blown scepticism towards government itself. Indeed, Heath attached enormous importance to the reform, or 'rationalisation', of a wide range of institutions (Britain's incorporation into the European bureaucracy and the reorganisation of central government being the obvious examples), stemming from a belief that institutional reform could achieve far-reaching results. It therefore appears that far from breaking the continuity of Conservative practice, Heath was maintaining it by responding in a fresh way to changing circumstances and contemporary problems while upholding the traditional Tory belief in the utility of state institutions. This thesis is corroborated by the Heath Government's spectacular 'U-Turn' in 1971.

In the eighteen months following Heath's remarkable election victory in 1970, the Government sought to apply the 'neo-liberal' flavour of its manifesto by ending prices and incomes policies, abolishing such interventionist bodies as the Wilson Government's Industrial Development Corporation and gradually adopting a deflationary, 'hands off' approach to the economy and industry. Heath's rejection of the conventional Keynesian, statist assumptions, however, was short-lived. The Government's policies helped to produce a growing number of commercial closures and bankruptcies and unemployment figures totalling one million; this in particular was a blow to the Government's self-confidence as support for the Keynesian principle of full employment was still deeply rooted in political culture and public opinion. In what amounted to a classic example of the party's versatility in response to circumstances, Heath undertook a series of policy changes from late 1971 onwards which became known as Heath's U-Turn. These new policies (all of which contradicted the spirit of the 1970 manifesto) included a highly reflationary budget in 1972, a Statutory Prices and Pay Standstill later that year, spectacular government-funded rescue schemes for 'lame duck' industries like Rolls Royce and Upper Clyde Shipbuilders and an Industry Act of 1973 which set up an Industrial Development Executive enjoying wide powers to interfere in industry.

The Heath Government's decision to abandon the cautious, deflationary tone of the 1970 manifesto and 'go for growth' was successful enough in itself. The Gross Domestic Product grew by about 6 per cent against an annual average of less than 3 per cent in the ten years before. Yet there was a high price to be paid for such expansion. Imports soared by 41 per cent, resulting in a balance of payments deficit of £1.12 billion by the end of 1973. The retail price index rose by 12 per cent between 1973 and 1974,

with interest rates rising to 13 per cent. These difficulties exacerbated the problems of operating a strict incomes policy, which
was challenged by a series of crippling strikes by unions in the
energy industries, resulting in a three-day week for industry.
Eventually, Heath thought it necessary to strengthen the mandate
to pursue his stringent policies by calling an election in February
1974, since known as the 'Who Governs?' election. The
electorate's response was scarcely the one Heath could have
expected. Although the Conservatives achieved a plurality of the
vote, they failed to retain office having won their then lowest share
of the vote (37.9 per cent) this century.

The ignominious demise of the Heath Government is also
thought to represent the end of 'traditional' Conservatism
spanning a period of roughly 140 years. The party, under a
succession of leaders from Peel to Heath, had shown a hostility to
abstract ideas and rigid doctrine and had endeavoured to react in a
variety of ways to the vicissitudes of political life, the ultimate
objective being to make existing society more stable and efficient
and thereby guarantee the inequalities and privileges many Conservatives enjoyed. Heath's reign as party leader exemplified not
only Conservatism's lack of consistency with regard to specific
policies but also its capacity to expound both neo-liberalism, with
a stress upon individualism, and collectivism/statism, with an
emphasis upon national unity. Heath's U-Turn, however, also
showed that it was the latter ideal which usually prevailed in
Conservative policy, arguably because the dominance of 'heavy'
industry in the economy, and the dominance of collectivist ideas in
British political culture, required such an approach in order to
maintain society's existing structure.

Although it was Heath's leadership which marked a change
from the traditional social background of Tory leaders, Mrs
Thatcher, elected leader in 1975, was thought to show none of
Heath's traditional Tory pragmatism and flexibility (indeed,
Heath was one of the foremost critics of Thatcherism). Her
determination to break the continuity of policy practised by previous governments differs from that of 'Heath Mark I' (1965–71)
in that it was apparently more resistant to severe difficulties and

vehement criticism. 'The Resolute Approach' and 'There is no Alternative' were in fact central to Thatcherite rhetoric and have played no small part in her electoral appeal. What Macleod saw as 'the party's peculiar genius' – 'a readiness to admit that it was wrong ... rather than sticking to a narrow orthodoxy', was scorned by Thatcher and her followers; she stated early in her premiership that she preferred 'conviction' to consensus, ascribing to the latter term inconsistency of policy and therefore much of the blame for Britain's decline.[34] The second major difference between Thatcherism and 'Heath Mark I' is that Thatcherism was not founded simply upon a desire to make Britain more 'modern' and efficient but also upon firm ideological principles (such as those enunciated in Hayek's *Road to Serfdom*) which stressed the primacy of individual liberty and the threat posed to it by statism and collectivism. Furthermore, the economic ideas embraced by the party, following Sir Keith Joseph's seminal Preston speech in September 1974, were thought to owe much to the heady theories of monetarism propounded by Professor Milton Friedman in Chicago rather than any 'practical' examination of the 'British disease'. Similarly, from 1975 onwards, the growing influence of external think tanks upon the development of Tory policy was thought to be symptomatic of a change in the party's attitude; organisations like the Institute of Economic Affairs and the Adam Smith Institute made no secret of their interest in linking policy proposals to philosophical notions of freedom and individualism and would not have been offended by the accusation that they were 'ideological' in nature.[35]

Thatcherism's belief in the need for radical as opposed to piecemeal change, its contempt for traditional practice in British government (especially in respect of economic policy) and its interest in the opinions of ideologues like Hayek all left it open to the charge that it was an affront to the cautious empiricism of Burke and therefore the conventional nostrums of Conservatism. This may not be surprising in view of the fact that Mrs Thatcher's view of human potential seemed at odds with Burke's fearful observations. Writing in 1978, Alan Watkins described her view of humanity in these terms: 'It is roughly that everyone is endowed with an equal quantity of will-power which he (or she) can then use for purposes of self-advancement . . . Her universe is not determinist but frighteningly mechanistic . . . people do not have good or bad fortune.'[36] Watkins went on to draw what could have been seen as the natural conclusion, namely that Mrs Thatcher was not a Tory at all but a liberal, and that under her leadership the Conservative Party's pragmatic, malleable, hierarchical and sceptical ethos had been sidelined by the more idealistic, abstract and anti-hierarchical notions of classical liberalism – a view reinforced by Mrs Thatcher's enthusiasm for the *laissez-faire* economic theories historically associated with the Liberal party. Further credence was given to this view by John Nott, a senior Minister in Mrs Thatcher's first Government, who claimed 'I am a nineteenth century Liberal. So is Mrs Thatcher. That is what this government is all about.'[37]

Many authors, many of whom are Conservatives, believe that the 'Thatcherite Conservatism is an aberration' school of opinion is vindicated by the record of the Thatcher Governments. 'Wet' government Ministers like Norman St John Stevas and James Prior (who claimed to represent traditional Tory principles) later expressed dismay at the way in which Thatcher and her key economic Ministers in the first Government had supposedly pursued monetarist theory with gusto by imposing drastic programmes of deflation in 1980 and 1981. The equally drastic consequences – chiefly a doubling of unemployment and the loss of a fifth of Britain's manufacuring industry – accompanied by such bracing rhetoric as 'a leaner but fitter society' and 'the lady's not for turning', were thought to exhibit a ruthlessness and dogmatism contrary to the old Tory values of pragmatism and patriarchal compassion. A more cynical interpretation was that the 'wets" dissent, based upon rapidly rising levels of unemployment, sprang from a much older Burkean trait, that is, a fear of the 'swinish multitude' and the dangers posed to the preservation of order and privilege.

Alongside the Government's 'vigorously doctrinaire' approach to inflation and unemployment went a much more strident attitude towards the reform of trade unions. The Burkean gradualism

87

of James Prior, Mrs Thatcher's first Employment Secretary, gave way in 1982 to the more 'hawkish' strategy of Norman Tebbit, a strategy reflected in the controversial legislation of 1982, 1984 and 1988.[38] Likewise, the Government's steadfastness in the face of the bitter and prolonged miners' strike of 1984–85 was criticised by the patriarchal Lord Stockton (the former Harold Macmillan) as dangerously divisive and sectarian. It was also poignant that during the strike, another old-fashioned Tory – Francis Pym – brought out a book entitled *The Politics of Consent*, which purported to be a restatement of 'true' Tory ideals, evidently championing the virtues of compromise and co-operation in place of the confrontational brand of politics personified by the Thatcher Government (from which Pym had been dismissed in 1983).

The Thatcher Governments also instigated a privatisation programme, a spirited attempt to alter radically the balance of the mixed economy respected by successive post-war Tory Governments, clearly inspired by their firm belief in the efficacy of market forces and private enterprise. This 'crusade for capitalism', as the Prime Minister called it, was again sneered at by old Toryism in the shape of Lord Stockton, who likened it to 'selling off the family silver', a reference to the widely held view that privatisation was nothing less cynical than a means of facilitating tax-cuts for society's 'haves'.[39] Another Tory dissident, Julian Critchley, claimed that the dismantling of nationalised industries was symbolic of Mrs Thatcher's deeply un-Tory distaste for established institutions, a view underlined by her hostility towards the Church, the BBC, the universities and the higher civil service.[40] After 1987, it was generally felt outside the Government that the extension of privatisation to water and electricity owed more to an 'ideological obsession' than to any practical conclusion about how to make those services more efficient.

The Government's lack of public support for the later stages of its privatisation project was emblematic of the relationship between public opinion and most of the specific policies pursued by the Thatcher administration. Traditional Conservatism was supposed to be about moving with the currents of public opinion in order to ensure electoral success, of 'giving the people what they want' (to paraphrase R. A. Butler). This, of course, was a key element of the party's 'non-ideological' attitude to political life. If the litmus-test of an ideological party is therefore a preparedness to shape, rather than reflect, common opinion and defy current preferences as a result, then it could be argued that the Thatcher Governments were the most 'ideological' in modern British history. Many of those on the left are certainly prepared to acknowledge the Thatcher regime thus; Martin Jacques described the modern Tory Party as the 'major purveyor of ideological politics in Britain', while Ken Livingstone admits that 'Thatcher has set the ideological agenda' which, he laments, the Labour Party subsequently accepted.[41] Psephologists like Ivor Crewe pointed out that the unpopularity of the third Thatcher Government's social security and National Health Service reforms highlights the extent to which the Government was out of tune with the public's still largely social democratic attitudes in these areas.[42] Indeed, Crewe argued that the public's continuing desire for expensive and extensive collective provisions in preference to a more self-reliant, individualistic society, represents 'A Crusade That Failed' on the part of the Government.[43] Yet the interesting point is that the 'warning signals' contained in the 1987 election surveys were not obviously heeded in the years that followed. The introduction of the Community Charge in the Local Government Finance Act of 1988 is perhaps the most blatant example of all of the Government ignoring overwhelming opposition from the public. It should also be noted that the Government's assault on local government, especially the abolition of the Metropolitan County Councils in 1985, is yet another example of its 'anti-Burkean' hostility to existing institutions.

To summarise, it became fashionable to argue that the behaviour of the Thatcher Governments was in stark contrast to previous, non-doctrinaire interpretations of Conservatism. This view was particularly well expressed by Critchley in 1985:

Traditional Tories are alarmed by her passion and simplistic world view. They see her as a Lincolnshire edition of Reagan, a radical populist whose objectives fall way outside those of conventional conservatives . . .

who dislike her implacable zeal, a quality which remains profoundly untypical and antipathetic to mainstream Conservatism . . . Her attempt to tie the Conservative Party rigidly to the success of the free market, rather than being pragmatic and flexible, threatens to cut the party off from its past. Her thirst for conflict is socially divisive and politically unwise. The Tories are not the natural champions of the minimalist state and fulsome support for a market economy has never been, until recently, a dominant feature of Conservative politics.[44]

## Thatcherism in perspective

Mrs Thatcher's three successive election victories, the changes seen in British politics and society during her premiership and her dynamic style of leadership certainly make the Thatcher era unique in the annals of Conservatism. Yet to argue that Thatcherism marks a complete break with previous Conservative practice is an exaggeration. To begin with, Thatcherism was not simply a regurgitation of classical liberalism, for the stress upon economic *laissez faire* was accompanied by a much older Tory emphasis upon order, authority and national self-respect. To suppose that Mrs Thatcher spent the whole of her time as Opposition leader extolling the theories of Milton Friedman and Friedrich Hayek would be false. She was also eager to show that a future Tory Government would strengthen the powers of the police, impose stiffer penalties upon offenders and reverse the 'permissive funk' generated by the liberalistic 1960s. She also adopted a much more belligerent attitude towards defence policy and Britain's relationship with the Soviet Union (earning her the sobriquet of 'Iron Lady' from *Pravda*) and sympathised with those who felt the 'traditional British character' was being 'swamped' as a result of coloured immigration. Trade union reform was advocated not just on the grounds of individual freedom but also with a view to preventing disorder caused by trade union militancy. Likewise, her belief in 'rolling back the frontiers of the state' in the economic sphere was designed not to weaken but strengthen the authority of government, which she believed had been enfeebled by governments overstretching themselves in areas where they had no legitimate business (the title of Gamble's study of

Thatcherism – *The Free Economy and the Strong State* – is itself instructive). In short, Thatcherism in no way denied the traditional Burkean stress upon authority and firm government and asserted that a more *laissez-faire* approach to the economy, far from being inimical to 'One Nation' and the maintenance of order, was actually a *precondition* given the 'crisis of ungovernability' Britain had faced in the increasingly statist 1960s and 1970s.

The authoritarian and nationalist dimensions of Thatcherism, the dimensions which recalled the character of earlier Conservatism, were exemplified clearly by the Thatcher Governments. Trade unions were curbed, police powers enhanced and (according to opposition pressure groups like Charter 88 and Samizdat) civil liberties circumscribed. The idea that Thatcherism clashed with traditional Toryism because of its rampant individualism would be considered supremely ironic by many of her opponents, while Mrs Thatcher's fervent prosecution of the Falklands conflict was hardly in the spirit of nineteenth-century liberalism; indeed, it surely stands as the most recent example of a Conservative leader playing what Disraeli termed the 'patriotic card' with devastatingly successful political results.

It is indisputable that the Thatcher Government's *official* rejection of Keynesianism and the utility of economic state planning distinguishes it from previous Conservative ministries in the post-war epoch. But the claim that this deviation amounts to a 'new' Conservatism needs qualification. First of all, there has been a gap between the rhetoric of economic policy and the practice. The money supply (the ark of the covenant for monetarists) and general government expenditure as a percentage of the Gross Domestic Product have remained at roughly pre-1979 levels.[45] Part of the reason for this lay in the Government's reluctance to curb in any dramatic way the enormous amount of public money directed towards the electorally sensitive areas of health, education and welfare. In both the 1983 and 1987 elections, the Government actually boasted about increased spending in these areas, emphasising that the NHS in particular was 'safe with us' – a strange posture for an administration supposedly devoted to reversing the social democratic consensus and 're-educating' the public in the process. The reaction to the growing trade deficit after 1987 was essentially fiscal rather than monetarist, emphasising interest and borrowing rather than the money supply, prompting Alfred Sherman (supposedly one of the Government's ideological gurus) to lament 'We are back on the Keynesian treadmill of stop-go, albeit with Friedmanite rhetoric.'[46] Thatcher's administrations, in other words, have been more willing to allow circumstances to temper their doctrinaire zeal than many of their critics allow.

Secondly, even if we assume that the Thatcher Governments were faithful to the tenets of economic liberalism, it should be remembered that this does not make them unique in Conservative terms. It might be recalled that the two major splits in Conservative history, in the 1840s over the Corn Laws and in 1905 over protectionism, were caused by the existence of a sizeable body of Conservatives favouring a more *laissez-faire* approach to economic policy. As explained earlier, the statist–collectivist tendencies in Conservatism have prevailed for most of the last hundred years, but largely because the nature of the economy and the character of the electorate demanded it if the present structure of society (and therefore inequality) were to be sustained.

This leads to the final crucial qualification. Economic liberalism returned to the fore of Conservatism after 1974 mainly in response to economic and political requirements. The problems encountered by social democratic governments (including Heath's after 1972), and their dismal falure to attain re-election, suggested quite clearly that the Keynesian assumptions underlying post-war politics might be redundant. The Conservative Party's interest in the ideas of Friedman and the IEA was therefore not the outcome of idle theorising but a practical response to the crises which seemed to threaten the existing order of the 1960s and 1970s. Conservatism, once again, was reacting to circumstances. Furthermore, this reaction was not confined to the Conservatives; by 1976 the Labour Government was denying that Britain could spend its way out of recession and had introduced a series of monetary targets and cuts in public expenditure, all of which strengthened the Conservatives' claim that their policies were pragmatic rather than ideological in origin.

Conservatism's tendency to react to social and economic circumstances has been complemented by its tendency to react to related shifts in public opinion, and there is much evidence to show that the evolution of policy after 1974 owed more to psephology than philosophy. Sarlvik and Crewe confirmed that, by the mid-1970s, there was a move rightwards in such issues as law and order, personal morality, traditional educational standards and discipline in general.[47] The party's identification with tax cuts (as opposed to further public spending) and council house sales was expressed only after a series of investigative opinion polls commissioned by the Conservative Research Department under the direction of Chris Patten. The CRD later agreed that most of the 'radical' policies enshrined in the 1979 manifesto had been 'tested' in such a way beforehand.[48]

Crewe's later studies did indicate an unusual discrepancy between the policies of the Thatcher Governments and public opinion.[49] Yet the explanation for this phenomenon, rather than being blind ideological fervour, seems to lie in the peculiar character of the economy and contemporary society. Until recently, Conservatives were inclined to think that social trends were not on their side; the inherent caution of Conservatism and its tendency to sail with the tide was very much a function of a society which was predominantly working class and a political climate governed by centre-left, statist ideals. As mentioned above, the record of social democratic governments served to weaken those ideals. Yet more important was the fact that this was paralleled by 'post-Fordist' developments in society: the fragmentation of the working class, the decline of labour-intensive heavy industry, the growth of white collar occupations, the spread of consumer affluence and home ownership, the growth of suburbia – the general *embourgeoisement* of society. For the Conservatives, whose historic role had been to mitigate working-class consciousness and protect the interests of society's 'haves', these were obviously welcome developments which made the party much less pessimistic about the extent to which they themselves could now set the political agenda. The 'crusading zeal' of the Thatcher Governments, and their willingness to risk unpopularity in the short term, stemmed largely from a conviction that 'history' was now moving in their direction and that public opinion could be moulded to their advantage. Between 1983 and 1990, this seemed to alter the function of Conservative Party leadership. The manner in which the party reacted to change (the conventional concern of Tory leaders) became allied to considerations about how change could be initiated. 'Float an idea five years ahead of its time', Mrs Thatcher is reported to have remarked, 'and it will sink; launch it two years ahead and it can lead to success.'[50]

Whereas reaction to social and economic realities once justified caution and accommodation of other parties' ideals, for Mrs Thatcher, at least, those same 'realities' justified a more adventurous and talismanic approach to politics – one which made her Governments among the most remarkable in modern British history.

## Post-Thatcher Conservatism

For many of those who had claimed that Thatcherism was an aberration (Heath, Gilmour, Critchley *et al.*), the advent of John Major's premiership was thought to signal a return to a more traditional brand of Conservative politics. This belief would have been supported by Major's transparent dislike for confrontation, his preference for consensus and compromise and his distaste for free-market dominance in the field of social and welfare policy. Major's background, of course, was starkly different from that of previous Tory leaders (even Heath and Thatcher were Oxbridge graduates). Yet for many observers, his comments about creating a nation 'at ease with itself', his undogmatic personality, his fondness for cricket and so on, recalled the style and language of Baldwin, Macmillan and Douglas Home. As explained in Chapter 3, this idea was reinforced by several policy developments between November 1990 and the 1992 election, which served as a

94

reminder that, despite the legacy of Mrs Thatcher, the grammar of Conservatism can be reconciled quite easily with support for public services and collective provision.

The appointment of Chris Patten as Party Chairman underlined the shift away from the rigorous, individualistic version of Conservatism expounded by Mrs Thatcher. In a series of interviews with various 'highbrow' journals, Patten sought to restate the Party's historic links with state intervention and its traditionally qualified view of *laissez-faire* individualism. As Patten explained (in terms that would alarm many Thatcherites), 'people express their individuality best in groups larger than themselves . . . the collective and the social are important to the working out of individualism'.[51] When tracing the roots of his 'personal philosophy', Major himself gave the clear impression that he was leap-frogging the Thatcher years by extolling Iain Macleod as the key influence upon his 'economic conservatism and social liberalism'.[52]

It would be a mistake, however, to see 'Majorism' as a serious attempt by the Conservative Party to redefine or clarify its intellectual traditions. The changes which engulfed the party after Novemeber 1990 owed more to electoral calculations than to any cerebral craving for Disraelian Toryism. In essence, the history of the Conservative Party between 1990 and 1992 demonstrates one of the oldest Tory traits of all – namely, an unqualified desire to attain and retain power. The way in which one of the most charismatic Prime Ministers this century was ditched by her own party, despite an unmatched record of electoral success, exposed once again the ruthless flexibility of a party determined to govern.

Nevertheless, the issue which precipitated Mrs Thatcher's downfall – Europe – should also be kept in mind when assessing the party's future. The divisions it has already produced – between Tory nationalists (such as Tebbit, Ridley and those belonging to the Bruges Group) and Euro-modernisers (such as Howe and Brittan) who believe that European integration is the logical sequel to the achievements made under the earlier Thatcher Governments – have already rent asunder former 'dry' allies and pose arguably the biggest threat to the party since the

1840s. It will be interesting to see whether the party's historic determination to govern can withstand and accommodate this division in the closing years of the twentieth century.

### Notes

1   J. Ibziki, *Daily Telegraph*, 16 February 1977.
2   R. J. White, 'The Conservative tradition', in P. Buck (ed.), *How Conservatives Think*, London, 1975, p. 174; I. Gilmour, *Inside Right*, London, 1977, p. 109.
3   D. Jay, quoted in J. Grimond, *The Liberal Challenge*, London, 1963, pp. 304–7.
4   See M. Cowling, *The Nature and Limits of Political Science*, Cambridge, 1963.
5   M. Oakeshott, *Rationalism in Politics and Other Essays*, London, 1962, p. 173.
6   Introduction to Buck, *How Conservatives*.
7   T. E. Lindsay & M. Harrington, *The Conservative Party 1918–1979*, London, 1980, p. 7.
8   See T. Honderich, *Conservatism*, London, 1990, pp. 5–9.
9   Buck, *How Conservatives*, p. 52.
10  Buck, *How Conservatives*, p. 130.
11  Buck, *How Conservatives*, p. 131.
12  P. Smith, *Disraelian Conservatism and Social Reform*, London, 1967, p. 106.
13  Buck, *How Conservatives*, p. 163.
14  A. Quinton, *The Politics of Imperfection*, London, 1978, p. 24; S. Ingle, *The British Party System*, Oxford, 1987, p. 28.
15  'The ideologist of inequality', *New Statesman Profiles*, London, 1958, p. 66.
16  R. Blake, *The Conservative Party From Peel to Thatcher*, London, 1985, p. 9.
17  Blake, *Peel to Thatcher*, p. 7.
18  Blake, *Peel to Thatcher*, p. 7.
19  Blake, *Peel to Thatcher*, p. 6.
20  H. Perkins, *The Origins of Modern English Society*, London, 1969, p. 273.
21  Blake, *Peel to Thatcher*, p. 25.
22  Gilmour, *Inside Right*, p. 83.
23  Buck, *How Conservatives*, p. 70.
24  R. T. McKenzie & A. Silver, *Angels in Marble*, London, 1968, p. 48.
25  R. McKibbin, 'Deference and democracy', *Times Higher Education Supplement*, 15 February 1985.

26  K. Joseph, *Freedon Under the Law*, Conservative Political Centre, London, 1975, p. 14.
27  Buck, *How Conservatives*, p. 142.
28  Quoted by J. Ramsden, 'Adapting to the post-war consensus', *Contemporary Record*, November 1989.
29  A. Horne, *Macmillan*, Vol. 1, London, 1988, pp. 106–9.
30  Quoted in Kavanagh, *Thatcherism*, p. 191.
31  Lord Moran, *Winston Churchill: Struggle for Survival*, London, 1966, p. 191.
32  *The Conservative Party Conference 1970: Report of Proceedings*, CCO Publications, London, 1970, pp. 131–2.
33  See M. Laing, *Edward Heath*, London, 1972.
34  B. Jones (ed.), *Political Issues in Britain Today*, Manchester, 1987, p. 2.
35  'Of policy and pedigree', *The Economist*, 6 June 1989.
36  A. Watkins, 'Is Mrs T a Tory?', *Observer*, 23 July 1978.
37  A. Sked & B. Cook, *Post-War Britain*, London, 1984, p. 329.
38  For details see J. McIlroy, *Trade Unions in Britain Today*, Manchester, 1988.
39  Jones, *Political Issues*, p. 115.
40  Quoted by P. Pulzer, 'From old Adam to new Eve', *London Review of Books*, 6 June 1985.
41  S. Hall & M. Jaques (eds.), *The Politics of Thatcherism*, London, 1983, p. 6; Quoted in T. Coleman, *Thatcher's Britain*, London, 1988, p. 107.
42  Crewe, 'The policy agenda', *Contemporary Record*, February, 1990.
43  I. Crewe, 'Values: a crusade that failed' in D. Kavanagh & A. Seldon (eds.), *The Thatcher Effect*, London, 1989, pp. 239–50.
44  Critchley, *Westminster Blues*, London, 1985, pp. 125–6.
45  Foster & Kelly, 'Keynesians or monetarists', *Talking Politics*, Vol. 1, 3.
46  A. Sherman, 'Time to bring back Sir Keith Joseph', *Sunday Telegraph*, 28 August 1988.
47  I. Crewe & B. Sarlvik, *Decade of Dealignment*, Cambridge, 1983, chapter eight.
48  R. N. Kelly's conversation with Peter Cropper, former Director of Conservative Research Department, 22 February 1983.
49  Crewe, 'The policy agenda'.
50  G. Brock, 'Mrs Thatcher's arithmetic', *Spectator*, 15 June 1985.
51  *Marxism Today*, February 1991.
52  *Daily Telegraph*, 16 December 1991.

# 5

# THE CONSERVATIVE PARTY: ORGANISATION, MEMBERSHIP AND AUTHORITY

A study of the Conservative Party at the beginning of the 1980s noted that, for the uninitiated, the Conservative organisation was not readily understandable.[1] Whereas the Labour Party organisation – in theory if not in practice – was relatively straightforward, appreciating the way in which the Tories conducted their internal affairs required an eye for the oblique. This may explain one of the most curious features concerning the study of modern British politics, namely, the lack of detailed attention devoted to the structure of Britain's most successful political party. Although Labour's organisation has been comprehensively assessed in a number of distinguished studies during the last twenty years – notably those of Minkin and Shaw[2] – the Conservative organisation has not recived any exhaustive treatment since McKenzie's study of *British Political Parties* in 1955.[3] As a result, the internal mechanisms of the party, in the words of its own members no less, 'remain governed by secrecy'.[4]

The arcane nature of Conservative organisation has much to do with the fact that the party has no official constitution from which scholars can compare theory with reality, appearing to function, instead, mainly on the basis of convention and *ad hoc* arrangements. Indeed, no such body as 'The Conservative Party' formally exists. Literature available from Conservative Central Office points out that 'The Conservative party' actually consists of 'three *separate* components' (authors' emphasis), leaving the outsider only to infer what organisational relationships, if any, exist between them. As the party's former Director of Organisation pointed out: 'There are virtually no absolute rules, that's why – unlike Labour – we tend not to get bogged down in procedural wrangles. We have family squabbles instead.'[5] The 1993 reorganisation carried out by Sir Norman Fowler was designed partly to overcome this somewhat anomolous situation by giving the party a governing 'Board of Directors' incorporating all three components. The effectiveness of this new body, of course, remains to be seen – especially in a party which is, in many ways, surprisingly diverse and decentralised.

The 'three separate components' cited by party literature are:

(i) *The Parliamentary party* (Conservative MPs, peers and MEPs).

(ii) *The voluntary extra-Parliamentary party* (the National Union of Conservative and Unionist Associations).

(iii) *The professional extra-Parliamentary party* (Conservative Central Office and its Area headquarters).

In common with most previous textbooks, this chapter will begin by examining the Parliamentary party, the 'component' generally considered the most important; furthermore, examination of the other two 'components' will show that the influence of the Parliamentary party pervades beyond Westminster.

## The Parliamentary party

As explained in the previous chapter, the first Conservative Government is normally assumed to be that of Sir Robert Peel (1841–46). Yet, as described presently, no formal Conservative organisation existed outside Parliament until after 1867. This point is critical to any analysis of power inside the party as it shows that Conservative MPs and ministries predate official Conservative activists outside Parliament (a situation in marked contrast to the Labour Party). In brief, the extra-Parliamentary Conservative Party was created by Conservative Parliamentarians and was intended to serve their interests.

The superiority and autonomy of the Parliamentary party has allegedly remained intact throughout the party's history; having secured nomination as candidates, and having secured election, Conservative MPs are assumed to expect loyalty and support from their extra-Parliamentary colleagues rather than instruction and dissent.

## The Conservative leader

Much of the autonomy and authority supposedly resting with the Parliamentary party is, in turn, supposedly invested in the Conservative Party leader (The term 'Conservative Party leader' is being used here colloquially, as the leader has no formal power over the party outside Parliament, indeed has little formal power at all, the authority of the office again deriving largely from convention).

The Conservatives are widely seen as as a leader-dominated party. McKenzie claimed that 'the most striking feature of Conservative party organisation' was 'the enormous power which appears to be concentrated in the hands of the leader'.[6] Rose likened the leader to a pre-constitutional monarch, surrounded by a personal court of advisers but ultimately pursuing the policy he or she prefers.[7] Even some of the more outspoken elements of the extra-Parliamentary party accept this version of affairs:

Power in the Conservative party is still excessively centralised and dominated by one person . . . We place enormous trust in that one person. We place huge responsibilities on that person – to run the government when we are in power, to choose the members of the government, to be the sole author of party policy and to be in ultimate control of the party's central organisation and its resources. Hardly surprising that we tend to glorify that person . . . it [the party organisation] is not only undemocratic, it is feudal.[8]

It was argued by Laski that the 'autocratic' character of the party merely reflected its political philosophy, one emphasising strong leadership, a clear source of power and responsibility and a society somewhat akin to the military, with unity, discipline, loyalty and respect for authority considered paramount.[9] This analogy was supported in an essay concerning the party's preparations for the 1987 election, with the author comparing the party to 'one of those armies that rely overmuch on its dashing and daring commanders.'[10]

In comparison with Labour leaders, Tory leaders certainly enjoy a large amount of freedom from institutional constraint. He or she has the exclusive right to appoint either the Cabinet or shadow Cabinet without regard to any ballot of MPs and does not have to work with an independently elected deputy leader. As Fowler's recent report on Tory organisation confirmed, he or she is granted the freedom to decide policy without being encumbered by a party conference (or any other party organ) with formal policy-making powers; the party's numerous committees and assemblies (both inside and outside Parliament) are purely advisory. Tyler's study of the party's 1987 election campaign observed that the manifesto was entirely the creation of Mrs Thatcher and a handful of senior ministerial colleagues, the so-called 'A-Team', with its details a closely guarded secret until the election was announced.[11] It should also be recalled that the leader has a crucial influence over the extra-Paliamentary party, through both the appointment of the Chairman of the Party Organisation and membership of the National Union Executive Committee (see below).

The pre-eminence of the Tory leader was arguably illustrated spectacularly by Mrs Thatcher's premiership. Her 'domineering' style, her stress upon 'conviction politics' and the 'resolute approach' and so on established her as something substantially more than *primus inter pares*, a view corroborated by a string of ex-Ministers (Gilmour, Pym, Prior, Nott, Biffen, Heseltine Lawson and Howe) who complained about the lack of collegiate decision-making and a concentration of power in the Prime Minister's office. In order to strengthen her personal control over policy-making, she gave considerable importance to various 'New Right' think tanks such as the Centre for Policy Studies, the Institute of Economic Affairs, the Adam Smith Institute and the Social Affairs Unit – bodies which 'tended to by-pass the rest of Cabinet and provide Mrs Thatcher's small coterie with detailed ideas which pre-empt suggestions from elsewhere in the party, or even Whitehall'.[12]

It could be argued that the 'feudal' power a Tory leader apparently enjoys stems from the party's lack of a constitution or grand 'Statement of Values', something which might compel the leader at least to give the impression that the party at large was helping to determine its direction. Yet this absence is probably a symptom, rather than a cause, of the 'problem'. A more tenable explanation may be found in the attitude of most Conservative party members. As the previous chapter emphasised, the Conservatives have always attached prime importance to the election of Conservative Governments; as such, there has been a general belief that the best way to secure this goal – rather like an army winning a war – is to allow the leadership discretion and flexibility and to lend wholehearted support to whichever course of action is decided upon. Yet such an attitude is itself symptomatic, in this case of a certain non-ideological approach to politics. Apart from a few general themes like the defence of private property and the constitution, the ordinary activist was unconcerned with policy details and generally happy to support whatever ideas the leadership thought conducive to electoral success. In this respect Laski was correct in surmising that a party's organisation reflected its philosophy. Constitutions prescribing a party's procedures in precise form are, perhaps, necessary only when the members of that party are keen to play an active part in determining its precise objectives and policies, which in turn, perhaps, springs from a precise view of how the party should exercise the power it may obtain.

The 'secrecy' enfolding much of the Tory organisation was, until 1965, exemplified by the manner in which Tory leaders were chosen (see table 5.1). When the leadership fell vacant (as in 1955 and 1957) it was customary for a new leader to 'emerge' after a series of clandestine discussions involving the Parliamentary Whips, senior backbenchers and peers and influential figures within the National Union. This process had the merits of attenuating public divisions inside the party and concealing the extent to which the eventual leader did not have unanimous support. It relied for its utility, however, upon the new leader immediately commanding the support of other Tory MPs and then vindicating the system further by leading the party to electoral success (as proved to be the case with Eden in 1955 and Macmillan in 1959). It foundered upon the resignation of Macmillan in 1963, as there was no clear and widely supported successor. The consequence was that the Tory conference of that year, which coincided with Macmillan's resignation, was turned into an American-style party convention where the various 'front-runners' (notably Butler, Hogg and Maudling) sought to impress both the conference and the television audience, thus eliminating the advantages of the old system outlined above. The party's dilemma was compounded by the eventual accession of Lord Home, a rather unlikely figure from whom two former frontbenchers, Macleod and Powell, withheld support when he came to form a government. In a *Spectator* article a few months later, Macleod derided the old selection system for the power it gave to what he termed 'The Magic Circle', a collection of Tory 'grandees' whose common link was an Etonian or Harrovian education.[13] The fact that the patrician Home seemed ill at ease when faced with the 'abrasive' and 'dynamic' Harold Wilson confirmed Macleod's view that the existing system of leadership selection was inappropriate if the party wished to be taken seriously in the new 'classless' Britain.

*Table 5.1* Tory leaders 1945–65

| 1945–55 | Winston Churchill | (PM 1951–55) |
| 1955–57 | Anthony Eden | (PM 1955–57) |
| 1957–63 | Harold Macmillan | (PM 1957–63) |
| 1963–65 | Alec Douglas Home | (PM 1963–64) |

The party's defeat in the 1964 general election accelerated the demise of the 'emerging' process. Sir Alec Douglas Home (as he had then become) later presided over an inquiry which duly recommended a new system whereby new leaders would hence-forth be elected in a ballot of Conservative MPs. A candidate would require the support of a nominator and seconder, and to be elected in the first ballot would need an overall majority plus a 15 per cent lead over the nearest rival (calculated on the basis of the

number who voted – later changed to the number entitled to vote).
If a second ballot were needed, a straightforward overall majority
was sufficient for victory. In the event of a third ballot being
required, the contest would involve the three most popular candidates from the second round, with an 'Alternative Vote' system of
election being employed.

Sir Alec's resignation in July 1965 provided the first opportunity for the new system to be used, with the first ballot attracting
three candidates, Edward Heath, Reginald Maudling and Enoch
Powell. Although Heath built up an impressive lead (with 150
votes to Maudling's 133 and Powell's fifteen), it did not meet the
criteria needed to secure outright victory, although a second ballot
proved unnecessary following Maudling's withdrawal from the
contest (see table 5.2).

One of the main themes of Norton and Aughey's study of the
party was that changes in both policy and organisation are usually
a response to unforeseen circumstances rather than abstract principles.[14] This has certainly been the case regarding the selection
of Tory leaders. Just as the 1965 reform was a response to the
inadequacies of the 'Magic Circle', so a further reform was considered necessary as a result of Heath's failure to secure victory
for the party in both the 1974 general elections. The 1965 reform
assumed that an unsuccessful or unpopular leader could be persuaded to resign, and made no provision for an incumbent leader
to be challenged. Heath's intransigence after the October 1974
defeat exposed the weakness of this arrangement, and the rules
governing leadership contests were altered accordingly by the
Executive of the 1922 Committee (see below). It became possible
for a Tory leader, in or out of government, to be challenged,
providing the challenger has the support of two MPs and that the
challenge is mounted within twenty-eight days of each new Parliamentary session. Provision was also made for the opinions of Tory
peers and constituency activists to be conveyed (in informal
fashion) to MPs about to vote and for candidates to enter the
contest after the first ballot (see table 5.3).

Heath became the first Tory leader to be challenged in a formal
ballot held in January 1975. In a 'three-horse' race involving only

*Table 5.2*    Tory leadership contests

---

1965
First ballot
Heath 150, Maudling 133, Powell 15, abstentions 6.
(Heath lacked victory requirements, but was elected after rivals withdrew.)

1975
First ballot
Thatcher 130, Heath 119, Fraser 16, abstentions 11
Second ballot
Thatcher 146, Whitelaw 79, Howe 19, Prior 19, Peyton 11, abstentions 2.
(Thatcher duly elected.)

1989
First ballot
Thatcher 314, Meyer 33, abstentions 27
(Thatcher duly re-elected).

1990
First ballot
Thatcher 204, Heseltine 152, abstentions 16
Second ballot
Major 185, Heseltine 131, Hurd 56
(Major lacked victory requirements but opponents declared support for him in final ballot. The 1992 Executive then declared another ballot unnecessary and so Major was elected.

---

Source R. Shepherd, *The Power Brokers*, London, 1991.

*Table 5.3*    Challenging a Tory leader
Revised rules: July 1991[a]

---

Challenge to be announced within fourteen days of a new Commons session or three months of a new Parliament. Challenger requires backing from (unnamed) 10 per cent of Tory MPs.[b]

MPs consult constituency associations

First ballot of Tory MPs. Victory involves one candidate achieving an overall majority plus a 15 per cent lead over nearest rival.[c] Otherwise . . .

Second ballot of Tory MPs. Those not initially candidates may now enter the contest. Victory involves one candidate achieving an overall majority of votes cast. Otherwise . . .

Third ballot of Tory MPs. This involves two or three leading candidates from the second ballot.[d] If three candidates are involved, the result is determined by the Alternative Vote system.

The winner (after whichever ballot) is confirmed at a Party meeting comprising MPs, Peers, MEPs, Parliamentary candidates and members of the National Union Executive.

---

*Notes*

[a] Although provision for Tory leadership contests had existed since 1965, it was not until 1974 that leaders could be challenged in an annual ballot. Neither was it possible, until 1974, for challengers to enter on the second ballot, nor were MPs obliged to consult their constituency associations.

[b] The names of backers had to be disclosed only after Meyer's 'frivolous' challenge in 1989. This was revoked following the challenge of 1990.

[c] Since 1974, this has been based upon those *entitled* to vote.

[d] Until 1991, there was no formal provision for the contest to end as a result of the leading candidate's rivals withdrawing after he or she had achieved a plurality (but not a majority) of support. Neither was a third ballot envisaged involving less than three candidates.

Source 1922 Executive Committee, *Standing Orders*, 1991.

one other shadow Cabinet Minister, Heath was surprisingly defeated; the fact that he had the overall support of the constituency parties is a further illustration of the Parliamentary party's autonomy.[15] Although Mrs Thatcher achieved only a plurality of the votes, the ignominy of being defeated by a relatively unknown colleague prompted Heath's resignation. In the second ballot, more distinguished figures like Whitelaw and Howe joined in, having been reluctant (unlike Mrs Thatcher) to embarrass their present leader. By this stage, Mrs Thatcher was no longer attracting support simply because she was not Edward Heath (as she had generally done in the first ballot), and thereby scored an emphatic victory to become the first female leader of a British political party.

The major implication of the 1965 and 1974 reforms seems to be that they have paved the way for a more meritocratic leadership – Heath, Thatcher and Major were all grammar school educated – in contrast to the traditional, aristocratic–upper-middle-class style of leader personified by Churchill, Eden, Macmillan and Home. This, in turn, may have encouraged a new style of Conservatism wherein the old paternalistic, 'One Nation' ideals give way to a greater emphasis upon individualism and self-reliance. The 1974 reform, however, along with Heath's spectacular demise, highlights what has probably always been true of Conservative leaders, namely, that their power and autonomy rest entirely upon a record or assumption of electoral success. Indeed, it could be argued that Tory leaders, for all their freedom from the sort of institutional restraints attendant upon a Labour leader, have less security of tenure. As Ingle remarked, 'only Churchill among post-war Conservative leaders retired at the time of his choosing and even he had been under great pressure to do so earlier'.[16] It seems, as Shepherd's recent study reminded us, that although Tory leaders exercise almost exclusive power inside the party, they also shoulder almost exclusive responsibility for electoral failure.[17] The fall of Mrs Thatcher demonstrates vividly the precarious nature of a Tory leader's power – even when that leader turns out to be one of the most forceful and domineering leaders this century, with a rock-solid overall majority in peacetime and with a unique record of electoral success. Indeed, it is supremely ironic that the supposedly 'autocratic' Tories should have been the first party to subject a Prime Minister to the indignity of a formal leadership challenge (from Meyer in 1989) and then the first to prompt the removal of a Prime Minister as a result of an internal party ballot. Moreover the Tories' overthrow of Mrs Thatcher in November 1990 served as a reminder that although Labour's organisation is normally considered more democratic, it is actually much harder to depose a Labour prime minister (see Chapter 7 and table 5.3).[18]

### *The 1922 Committee*

The main channel through which a Tory leader's power is circumscribed by Tory MPs is the 1922 Committee, consisting of all backbench MPs when the party is in government, and all MPs except the leader when in opposition. The Committee takes its name from a meeting of Tory MPs at the Carlton Club in 1922, following the failure of the leader, Austen Chamberlain, to take note of backbench dissatisfaction with the Lloyd George coalition (in which the party had been involved since 1918). The fact that the meeting precipitated the end of both the coalition and Chamberlain's leadership is a stark illustration of how reliant Tory leaders are upon the trust and goodwill of their fellow Tory MPs.

The 1922 meets weekly and considers all matters affecting the fortunes of the party. It has an executive consisting of eighteen MPs, and its Chairman (in 1993 Sir Marcus Fox) is widely considered 'one of the most powerful unknowns in British politics'.[19] Through regular contact with the Tory chief whip, the Chairman can be relied upon to transmit backbench mood to the leadership. Should there be a matter of particular urgency, he has the right of direct access to the leader, a right that would be exercised were the backbenchers to favour overwhelmingly a change of leadership. Since 1965, one of the Executive's most important tasks has been arranging the ballot in any leadership contest, and since 1974, facilitating any formal challenge to the incumbent leader.

The 1922 is served by a range of specialist committees (like Defence and Foreign Affairs), which are attended by a party whip who then reports their findings to the leadership. During opposition, these meetings are chaired by the appropriate shadow minister; when in government, the chairmanships are elective and eagerly contested at the start of each Parliamentary session.[20] As with the main 1922 meeting, no vote is ever taken at the end of proceedings; it is the duty of the Chairman to discern and summarise the 'mood'. This disregard for the formalities of intra-party democracy apparently makes the meetings no less potent and is, indeed, a feature of Conservative organisation generally (see below).

The extent to which these committees put a brake on the freedom of Ministers (and by implication the party leader) has been demonstrated on a number of occasions during the 1980s. Critchley maintains that Lord Carrington's decision to quit as Foreign Secretary shortly after the start of the Falklands crisis in 1982 was expedited by a 'grilling' before the Foreign Affairs committee: 'The bulk of the backbenchers turned up to see the Foreign Secretary worked over and his career destroyed by the pack . . . the most able and attractive Tory of his generation was blown out of the water.'[21] Similarly, Sir Keith Joseph's desire to increase parental contributions to the cost of higher education was scuppered in late 1984 in what was described as 'one of the most concerted onslaughts ever experienced by a Tory Cabinet Minister from his own side' and 'one of the swiftest and most effective assertions of backbench power over the executive'.[22] Leon Brittan's resignation as Trade and Industry Secretary in early 1986 was also accelerated by a meeting of the relevant specialist committee which left him in no doubt that he had lost the confidence of most Tory MPs.[23] In view of these examples, Mrs Thatcher's overthrow – far from being an explosive aberration in the behaviour of Tory MPs – may instead be seen as only the most dramatic illustration of a trend evident within their ranks throughout the 1980s, one suggesting that they would no longer dissent only when they wanted to exchange one 'all powerful' leader for another.

The increasing tendency of backbench Tories to question the leader's judgement on a policy-specific basis is considered by Burch and Moran to be partly the result of their changing background, which in turn is partly the result of the changed social background of the leadership since 1965.[24] In 1945, 83 per cent of Tory MPs were public school educated, with over 25 per cent having been to Eton. By 1983, this figure had fallen to 64 per cent, yet even more startling was the background of the 1983 intake; a majority of the 'new boys' had been educated at state secondary schools, with only 6 per cent being Old Etonians. Burch and Moran argue that the Tory MPs elected in 1979 and 1983 were 'among the most rebellious in the modern history of the Conservative party', claiming that such MPs were more likely to be rebellious on account of arriving in Parliament on the basis of their own efforts and abilities rather than through any 'old boy network'. They may find loyalty and discipline less instinctive than the old 'knights of the shire' whose background often lay in the army and whose upbringing emphasised 'service' and 'duty' rather than individualism, competition and achievement. Another striking feature of the 1983 intake was that a majority had some experience in local government, a factor which Burch and Moran believe may have a profound impact upon the power of the leader in relation to the rest of the Parliamentary party: 'They would have been among the ablest councillors. As chairmen of committees they would influence budgets worth millions of pounds. Articulate, experienced and opinionated councillors do not make good lobby fodder at Westminster.' This trend seems to have been underlined by the behaviour since the 1992 election of Tory MPs, ninety of whom signed (in June 1992) an 'early day' motion criticising the Government's approach to Europe. Of even greater interest was that these dissidents contained almost a third of those new MPs elected less than two months earlier.

## The voluntary extra-Parliamentary party

The body embracing all voluntary Conservative activity outside Parliament, that is the area and constituency parties, the Young

Conservatives, the Conservative Women's and students' organisations and so on, is the National Union of Conservative and Unionist Associations. Originally known as the National Union of Conservative and Constitutional Associations, it was set up by Disraeli and Henry Raikes in 1867 as a response to the second Reform Act. In contrast to the arrangements prescribed in Labour's Constitution, the extra-Parliamentary Tory party was established not as an exercise in grass-roots power or mass party democracy but as an election-winning machine designed to secure office for Conservative Parliamentarians in the new electoral climate. As Norton and Aughey stated, 'It was created to support, not question or control, the party in Parliament'.[25]

This situation broadly obtains today. It is significant that whereas a Labour Party membership card reprints the party's constitutional commitment to common ownership, a Conservative membership card points out that members are obliged to offer whatever help they can in 'Parliamentary, local and European elections'. The structure of the National Union also remains largely unchanged, with the *Maxwell-Fyfe Report* of 1949 being the only significant re-examination. The National Union's current rule book gives it five principal functions:[26]

(i) To support and encourage the development of the principles and aims of the party.

(ii) To secure the election of Conservative candidates.

(iii) To form and develop Conservative associations in every constituency.

(iv) To form a centre of united action and to act as a link between the leader of the party and all sections of the party.

(v) To work closely with Conservative Central Office.

The governing body of the National Union is the Central Council, a yearly gathering of about a thousand senior Conservatives, including the leader, MPs, peers, candidates and senior officials from the constituencies and various party sections. Its functions include the election of the NU Chairman and three Vice-Chairmen, although this usually means simply ratifying the recommendations of its Executive Committee (see below). It discusses and votes upon any changes to the NU organisation, although its main function these days is to act as a mini-conference in which policy matters are reviewed.[27] Just as the official powers of the Labour Party conference are, by necessity, delegated to a smaller and more frequently assembled body (the NEC), so the responsibilities of the Central Council are delegated to the National Union Executive Committee, a body consisting of about two hundred people which meets five times a year. Its chairman, in 1993 Sir Basil Feldman, is normally a businessman who serves for several years after being elected in a postal ballot giving each constituency party three votes. He has been described as 'one of the most powerful and influential men within the party machine', his principal duty being to convey the views of the voluntary party to the leadership and vice-versa.[28]

It must be restated that the NUEC, like the National Union overall, has no formal input into party policy and has only an advisory role. Furthermore, the composition of the NUEC betrays the pervasive influence of the Parliamentary leadership. Almost half of its members are *ex officio*, comprising not only the leader but about a dozen MPs and eighty party bureaucrats whose positions depend upon the leader's support. Additional doubts about the ability of the NU hierarchy to reflect the wishes of its rank and file arise from the fact that much of the NUEC's routine business is conducted by its General Purposes Committee. This has sixty-five members, of whom only eleven are elected to their positions by the membership. According to one activist broadsheet, the key figures on this committee are the Chief Whip, the Party Chairman and his Vice and Deputy Chairmen, all of whom are appointed by the leader.[29] It remains to be seen whether the committee's importance will be undermined by Fowler's new 'Board of Directors', of which NUEC officials will be *ex-officio* members.

The NUEC embraces and works closely with the various National Union Advisory Committees which represent the various sections of voluntary Tory activity. These include the Young Conservatives, the Conservative Women's Organisation, Conservative Trade Unionists, the Conservative Local Government Department and the Conservative Collegiate Forum (which replaced the controversial Federation of Conservative Students in 1986). A study carried out by one of the present authors found that these NACs are responsible for a surprising degree of diversity and semi-autonomous activity within the voluntary party, contribute a good deal of specialist advice to the Parliamentary leadership and undermine any attempt to portray a 'typical' Tory activist.[30]

### Conservative conferences

One of the most exacting tasks falling upon the NU leadership is organising the annual party conference – officially known as 'The Conference of the National Union and Conservative Associations'. Responsibility for this four-day event rests largely with a sub-committee of the General Purposes Committee, which invites policy motions and then decides upon the agenda. The potential size of the conference is between eight and nine thousand, making it in theory one of the largest political gatherings in any western democracy. Those who attend are known as representatives and, although they are supposed to communicate the views of their various constituencies and sections, are not mandated to vote in any particular way. Voting, in any case, does not appear to be a very important feature at Conservative conferences. Most of the rather bland and uncritical motions are passed by an overwhelming majority with a show of hands, and formal ballots are rare.

This peculiar feature helps to explain why the Tory conference has been sneered at in most studies of British party politics. Ostrogorski dismissed it as 'a show body', Lowell as 'a transparent sham', while McKenzie saw it as 'primarily a demonstration of support for its own leaders'.[31] This contempt was apparently shared by the Parliamentary leadership who, until 1965, rarely attended until the final afternoon. The conference is of course purely advisory, yet Balfour (leader 1902–11) remarked that he would sooner take the advice of his valet (although it may be revealing that Balfour was one of the party's least successful leaders). Only in a handful of areas, like law and order, defence and immigration, could Tory conference-goers be expected to exhibit any independent fervour, while the only clear-cut example of the conference influencing policy was generally taken to be the 1950 housing debate, when the leadership accepted a target of 300,000 new homes after a series of impassioned speeches from the floor.

This traditionally negative view has been challenged in a detailed study of Tory conferences by one of the present authors.[32] It asserts that the main October conference cannot be properly understood in isolation from the sixty or so sectional and regional conferences which precede it each year. Debates at these conferences tend to be much more frank and critical and there is considerable evidence to show that the rapturous ovations Ministers receive at the main conference spring not from deference but from a recognition that their speeches have acknowledged and articulated much of what they heard from the floor at earlier Tory conferences held that year. As one con-stituency vice-chairman explained at the 1986 conference: 'The practicality and implications of a particular policy as seen within a local situation will be made known to the central policy makers, thereby allowing policy to be moulded in the light of experience . . . this follows in a system where grass roots opinion is taken into consideration.'[33] Such remarks scarcely accord with either the conventional view of Tory conferences or the stereotype version of Tory activists.

The 'specialist' advice offered by Tory activists at their numerous 'secondary' conferences had a particular impact upon policy during the 1980s. The 1980, 1982 and 1984 trade union reforms echoed much of the advice rendered by the conferences of Conservative Trade Unionists; the reform of married women's taxation in the 1988 budget echoed the results of questionnaires circulated at a series of special conferences arranged by the Conservative Women's organisation; the abolition of domestic rates proceeded only after Kenneth Baker's Green Paper had been critically discussed at the party's 1986 Local Government conference – indeed, the decision to re-examine alternatives to rates was taken only after the Scottish Conservative conference of 1985 expressed outrage at the effects of rate revaluation and warned of dire electoral consequences. There have also been signs recently that activists are prepared to embarrass Ministers at the main conference. The decision not to 'phase in' the Community Charge was forced upon Nicholas Ridley at the 1987 conference, while two years later it was pressure from the floor which persuaded a reluctant platform to sanction Conservative Party candidates in Northern Ireland.

The *embourgeoisement* of society gives Tory leaders an added incentive to heed the advice of Tory conferences. With the spread of white collar employment and home and share ownership, the vested interests of Tory activists are rapidly becoming those of an electoral majority. This trend largely accounts for the increasingly bullish tone of modern Tory conferences; as representatives realise that they may embody the new average voter, they are increasingly reluctant to accept meekly the leadership's initiatives and are increasingly impatient with those leaders who do not give serious thought to their own ideas. Such developments have far-reaching implications not just for the reputation of the Tory conference but for any analysis of power and authority inside the modern Conservative Party.

### Sub-national organisation

At 'local' level, the National Union was until recently divided into twelve 'areas', including Scotland which has a greater degree of autonomy from the NUEC than the eleven areas in England and Wales. In 1989, the figure became thirteen with the creation of a new Northern Ireland Area Council, after pressure from the party's supporters in Ulster (notably Dr Lawrence Kennedy) who wished to create constituency organisations and contest Parliamentary elections. As a result, the first official Conservative candidate in Northern Ireland for over seventy years contested the Upper Bann by-election in May 1990 – and lost her deposit.

Acting through the Area Councils, the Area parties' main function is to supervise and co-ordinate the work of the constituency parties ('associations') and their various sections (YCs, CTU, CWO etc.). According to a report in 1985, membership of the constituency associations stood at 1.3 million, a marked fall from the peak of 3 million reached in the 1950s.[34] One of the present authors later made the arresting discovery that over a million of these were women – a discovery endorsed a few years later in a separate study by Morris.[35]

The traditional view of Tory constituency activity tends to stress its largely 'apolitical' nature. Gamble claimed, for instance, that in respect of policy, the party had a 'sleeping membership'.[36] This view was reinforced by a (female) official of the Brentwood association who remarked that a 'typical year's activity' consisted of 'cheese and wine parties, sherry parties, garden parties, coffee mornings, quiz evenings, carol evenings and family days at the houses of members with swimming pools'.[37] There is, however, evidence to suggest that this situation is not universal. Tappin's study of Tory activists in Scotland found that prime emphasis was given to policy-making and that 'ideology' was the main motivation for membership.[38] The aforementioned study of Conservative conferences also discovered that at least twenty thousand Tory activists were attending at least one Tory conference each year with a view to having some input into party policy.[39]

One of the most important functions of the constituency parties lies in the selection of Parliamentary candidates (see table 5.4). The independence that local Tories enjoy in this sphere prompted a Deputy Chairman of the party to make the interesting claim that 'the nature of the party is determined by its grass roots . . . the Parliamentarians may have the final word over policy, but then how does one become a Parliamentarian to begin with?'[40] The Chelmer Committee, set up by the NUEC in 1968 to 'investigate ways in which the party outside Parliament might be made more democratic' (its recomendations were shelved), stated that the right of the associations to choose their own candidates without outside interference was 'paramount', while Rose has argued that local Tories have more autonomy in this area, and exhibit greater party democracy, than constituency Labour parties – a view likely to have been reinforced by the recent interventionist tendencies of the NEC under Kinnock (see Chapter 7).

Since 1988, most aspiring Conservative candidates must first

*Table 5.4*   The selection of Tory Parliamentary candidates

**National level**
NATIONAL UNION STANDING ADVISORY COMMITTEE
Recommends most applicants to

↓

NATIONAL UNION PARLIAMENTARY SELECTION BOARD
Recommends about 60 per cent of applicants to

↓

NATIONAL UNION APPROVED LIST
Interested candidates apply to

**Association (constituency) level**

'unapproved' candidates[a]

EXECUTIVE SUB-COMMITTEE (about 20)
Interviews about 20 candidates and reduces short-list to
between 3 and 6

↓

EXECUTIVE COUNCIL (about 60)
Interviews remaining candidates and recommends one or more to the
whole association[b]

↓

GENERAL MEETING
*Either* makes final selection (if more than one remaining candidate) *or*
formally adopts candidate recommended by the Executive.

*Notes*

<sup>a</sup> Dudley Fisher, successful candidate at the Kensington by-election in 1988, is a rare example of a would-be MP sidestepping the Approved List. Such applicants must be endorsed by the Standing Advisory Committee before any final decision is made. The Committee's endorsement applies only to the Association concerned

<sup>b</sup> If only one candidate is recommended to the whole Association, he or she must have received an overall majority of votes cast by the Executive Council. Opponents of John Taylor in Cheltenham claimed this criterion was not met and anyhow rejected the principle of *fait accompli*.

Source *Rules and Standing Orders of the National Union*, revised 1990.

secure a place on the National Union's approved list of candidates, attained (since 1979) through a gruelling series of tests arranged at weekend retreats by the National Advisory Committee on Candidates (chaired by a backbench MP). Those on the list may then apply for any vacancy that occurs, with the NAC making appropriate recommendations to the association concerned. Two things need to be emphasised here which relate to the distribution of influence inside the party. The first is that, unlike in the Labour party, would-be candidates do not *have* to be approved beforehand by the Conservatives' national organisers; the candidate chosen by the Tyne Bridge association in 1991, for example, had been rejected by the National Advisory Committee only a few weeks beforehand. Secondly, although the national organisers undoubtedly have 'favourites' on the approved list, whom they try to push into winnable seats, there is no guarantee that they will be successful. This was illustrated by the Ribble Valley association in 1990, which caused much chagrin at Central Office by rejecting three of its 'strongly recommended' candidates – including ex-Labour minister John Horam – in favour of Nigel Evans, a Welshman who had just fought a notably unsuccessful campaign at the Pontypridd by-election

The task of sifting through the applications is usually done by the Association Chairman and Agent, who then draw up a short list (of twenty-one in the case of Kensington, 1988).[41] These candidates are then interviewed by a sub-committee of the association governing body, the Executive Council (in the case of Kensington, the sub-committee consisted of twelve members).

Having reduced the short list to between three and six, it is then customary for the remaining candidates to appear before the full Executive Council (sixty-five people in Kensington), which includes the representatives of the association's various sections. A ballot is normally taken, after which the successful candidate appears before an association general meeting for formal adoption. A growing number of associations are now following the idea pioneered by Reigate in 1968, whereby the Executive Council is bypassed and those on the final shortlist appear before the general meeting which itself holds a ballot on the final choice.

Mandatory reselection is not a feature of Conservative organisation and the vast majority of Conservative MPs are re-adopted unopposed. Those MPs who fail to secure re-adoption are usually guilty of 'personal' rather than 'political' shortcomings – such as John Browne (Winchester 1990, following an acrimonious divorce case and dubious financial dealings), Sir John Stradling-Thomas (Monmouth 1990, following a dismal record of attendance in the Commons), and Harvey Proctor (Billericay, 1987, after newspaper stories concerning his unusual sexual proclivities). Sir Anthony Meyer's deselection by Clwyd North West, following his challenge to Mrs Thatcher's leadership in late 1989, was the first clear example of 'political' or 'ideological' deselection inside the party for over thirty years. However, the growing self-confidence and assertiveness of Tory activists may encourage them in future to be less tolerant of an MP whose version of Conservatism does not correspond to their own. This was borne out by the dozen or so Tory MPs (such as Michael Mates and Cyril Townsend) who were threatened with deselection after their outspoken support for Heseltine's leadership challenge. The notion that an MP is owed the loyalty of her or his constituency party was obviously weakened (in the eyes of many Tory activists) by the lack of loyalty shown by their MP towards the leader – a leader who retained the overwhelming support of grass roots Conservatives. The friction generated within the Cheltenham association in 1990, amid claims that the black candidate John Taylor had been 'imposed' by Central Office, offered further evidence that the compliance of local Tories in relation to the

119

national party establishment can no longer be taken for granted. Fowler's review of party organisation in 1992 looked closely at ways of eroding the associations' independence in the area of candidate selection – especially for by-elections, which, as Labour has already realised (see Chapter 7), have implications going beyond a particular constituency.

The process of selection is normally overseen by the constituency agent, a full-time official trained by Central Office to ensure that associations function efficiently and with a reasonable measure of uniformity. The party's relative wealth enables it to afford more full-time agents than other parties; in 1986 there were 350 constituencies with full-time agents compared to only sixty in the Labour Party.[42] Craig argued that the Tories' superiority in this respect was worth between six and twelve seats in a general election.[43] Although there is some potential for conflict between a professional 'outsider' and local volunteers jealous of their autonomy, such conflict is rare and most association chairmen value their organisational expertise.[44]

Whatever independence the associations may have could be a consequence of the enormous contribution they make to party funds. In 1983–84, the party's overall income was £12 million of which £7.8 million came from constituency rather than company donations.[45] As Pinto-Duschinsky reported:

Company contributions have normally supplied . . . approximately 30 per cent of overall income. The fact that individual Conservative membership has been far larger than Labour's has given the party a vital additional source of money. The large number of small contributions raised by members of Conservative associations, mainly through coffee mornings, jumble sales or wine and quiche receptions have produced in total more than the money given by companies.[46]

The generosity of the constituencies' donations also has much to do with the generous subscriptions paid to their individual associations by the party's many wealthy individual members (such as Stanley Kalms, chairman of Dixon's). Many of these members pay an additional £100 a year to join the Businessmen's Section now found in most associations.[47] The fact that such individuals make it their business to keep abreast of popular tastes and spending power may give the Parliamentary party an extra incentive to listen carefully to the advice tendered by party activists.

## Conservative factions

It should be stated immediately that the term 'Conservative factions' is considered a misnomer by many authors. Both Rose and Norton prefer the term 'tendencies' given that: 'tendencies lack the organisational coherence associated with factions . . . the Conservative structure limits group roles to those of publicists for particular policies, whereas in the Labour party the formal participation of ordinary members in policy and leadership choices enables greater lassitude to active factions.'[48] Within a section of the chapter dealing with the extra-Parliamentary party, it is also prudent to note that many of the party's 'tendencies' are dominated by MPs.[49]

One of the most enduring and popular of these groups is the *Bow Group*, formed in 1951 and with a membership of around a thousand.[50] Until the 1980s, it had a reputation for 'progressive', 'social democratic' Conservatism, supporting an interventionist state out of the belief that it could enhance individual freedom and create a more cohesive society. Recently, however, its policy ideas have become more eclectic and have given qualified support to the economic liberalism of the Thatcher Governments. Its journal, *Crossbow*, has recently carried articles from such party luminaries as Sir Geoffrey Howe and Chris Patten.

The *Monday Club* represents what could be termed the 'old right', stressing the primacy of authority, order, discipline and national sovereignty while attacking immigration, the EEC and, before its demise, the dangers of Soviet communism. It was formed in 1961 to combat the Macmillan Government's 'softness' on race and claimed to have two thousand members in 1984.[51] Although principally concerned with 'authoritarian' ideas, it has given broad support to the libertarian drift of government economic policy since 1979, despite expressing grave concern about the implications of European integration. Enoch Powell was its 'guest of honour' at a fringe meeting arranged at the 1989 conference.

The *Tory Reform Group* was formed in 1975 and claims to propound the 'One Nation' Conservatism epitomised by most of the party's leaders prior to Thatcher. It therefore has reservations about free market economics, fearing they could imperil national unity and stability, and takes a much more sympathetic view of government interference in the economy. Many of its criticisms are aimed at what it calls the 'hanging and flogging' element inside the party, and it is the 'enemy within' of the Monday Club. During the final years of his life, the TRG provided a platform for Lord Stockton's sardonic attacks on government economic policy and has recently lent support for the neo-corporatist ideas of Michael Heseltine. A statement issued by the TRG at the 1991 Conservative conference expressed 'confidence that John Major's leadership would revitalise our influence inside the government'.[52]

The *Libertarian Alliance* was set up in 1984. Although it is considered to represent right–wing thinking, its priorities are the antithesis of the Monday Club's. Its unqualified support for *laissez-faire* economics extends to an almost anarchic emphasis upon individual liberty. Hostile to any state interference which curtails an individual's freedom of choice (provided it does not encroach upon the freedom of others), it supports free abortion, a reduction of censorship and has even called for the legalisation of heroin and incest. Its influence was particularly strong inside the Federation of Conservative Students (leading to the latter's closure in 1986), and claims to have the sympathy of MPs like Theresa Gorman and Michael Forsyth. Given that Thatcherism is a mixture of libertarian *and* authoritarian ideals, however, its influence in the 1980s should not be overstated.

Since the resignation of Mrs Thatcher, a number of other groups have come to attract the interest of Conservative MPs and activists. Perhaps the most colourful of these is the *No Turning Back Group*, founded in 1983 by some of Mrs Thatcher's most ardent backbench supporters; its frontbench members have since included Peter Lilley, Michael Fallon and Michael Forsyth. Its pamphlets have called for extensive privatisation and the virtual dismantling of the present welfare bureaucracy. As Prime Minister, Mrs Thatcher was a regular guest at its monthly dinners and, as the group's name implies, it is committed to preserving and building upon Thatcherite free market principles. Although John Major promoted some of its members to ministerial posts, its collective influence is thought to have been much diminished since 1990.

A group with similar objectives to the No Turning Back Group is *Conservative Way Forward*, launched in March 1991 'as a vehicle for those who support what Margaret Thatcher stood for'.[53] Chaired by Cecil Parkinson and endorsed by a gallery of ex-ministers like Norman Tebbit, Lord Joseph and John Moore, it has been unkindly described as a 'sunset home for superannuated Thatcherites'.[54] Although it was thought to have a ready audience among the many grass roots Tories aggrieved by Mrs Thatcher's departure, there was – after a year of its existence – little evidence that it achieved anything save undermining further the Party's reputation for unity and cohesion.

Although not an exclusively Tory group, the *Bruges Group* deserves to be noted because it has since 1990 provided a focus for those senior and aspiring Tories worried about European integration. Its president is Mrs Thatcher and it has received vigorous support from Nicholas Ridley, Teddy Taylor and Nicholas Budgen. Having criticised Britain's ERM membership, and issued dire, anti-federalist messages prior to and since the Maastricht Treaty of 1991, it has enabled Conservatives to express doubts about official Conservative policy in a conveniently semi-detached fashion.

From the angle of party organisation, the most interesting Tory group is the *Charter Movement*, set up by activists in Kent in 1981 to campaign for greater formal party democracy. The aims enshrined in its constitution, 'The Charter', include: a new Policy Committee accountable to Central Council, which would give members a clearer role in policy-making; ending the formal separation of the National Union and Central Office by giving activists the right to elect the Party Chairman in a postal ballot; an end to automatic re-adoption of most MPs; the reorganisation of the National Union's ruling bodies to ensure that a majority of its members are elected directly by party activists, and control of the party conference to be transferred to a new committee elected by Central Council. Until the 1992 election, at least, there was little support for Charter's aims among the bulk of representatives, who seemed to feel that the sort of institutionalised democracy demanded by Charter was unnecessary given that members' wishes were already noted in a more informal and unofficial way. It is possible, however, that Charter's prescriptions may attract more support in the event of electoral defeat – especially if members believe that defeat has been caused by the leadership giving insufficient weight to their advice

## The professional extra-Parliamentary party

Conservative Central Office (CCO), set up in 1870, represents the headquarters of the party's professional 'civil service'. It employs about 250 full-time staff, and is supported away from London by eleven Area Offices, plus a Scottish Central Office which has slightly more autonomy.

CCO's official function is to service Tory MPs and the various organs of the National Union with information, literature and organisational support. It also houses the Conservative Political Centre, set up in 1949 to stimulate discussion of Conservative principles among activists, and the 'permanent officials' of the various National Advisory Committees. It is under the indirect control of the party leader, who appoints as its overall controller the Chairman of the Party Organisation. It would be wrong, however, to see the position in purely organisational terms. At least since the early 1960s it has involved extensive campaigning and the 'marketing' of party policy. This has been underlined in recent years by the appointment of seasoned politicians like Norman Tebbit and Kenneth Baker. Indeed, the current appointment of a new 'chief executive' or 'director general' to run the party's new Board of Directors may release the Chairman from much of his organisational responsibilities, leaving him free to concentrate on the propagandist elements of the job.

Pinto-Duschinsky has described CCO as 'the leader's personal machine', as through the Party Chairman the leader can insist that CCO is run in the way that, and pursues the priorities that, the leader considers appropriate.[55] After the 1987 election, for example, when Mrs Thatcher was apparently reduced to tears of rage by CCO's inadequacies, she appointed Peter Brooke as Chairman with a brief to 'streamline' party headquarters. The result of Brooke's labours were announced in August 1988. The seven directorates which formally existed with equal standing in relation to the Chairman were reduced to three: Campaigning and Organisation, Research and Communications, with a General Director of Campaigning (in 1992 John Lacy) acting as *primus inter pares*.

This reorganisation did little to allay widespread disquiet among Conservative activists at the performance of CCO. The publications of the Charter Movement routinely lambast CCO for its 'arrogance', 'inefficiency' and 'secrecy', claiming it aspires to master rather than servant status.[56] That the National Union's ruling bodies have such a strong CCO *ex-officio* presence naturally fuels this anxiety. Complaints about CCO's efficiency were again heard after the 1992 election when it became fashionable inside the party to assert that it had won despite, rather than because of, the efforts of its bureaucracy at Smith Square. This prompted Major to appoint to the position of Party Chairman Sir Norman Fowler, whose wholesale examination of party structure (involving an ambitious level of consultation across the party) was initiated just before the 1992 Tory conference. As expected, Fowler's report emphasised the need to streamline CCO, whose labyrinthine structure had largely survived Brooke's inquiry five years earlier. Yet Fowler also unveiled (as already indicated in this chapter) a new Board of Directors intended to supervise all aspects of Conservative activity outside Parliament, while ensuring that the activities of both CCO and the National Union were complementary and co-ordinated. Very few grass roots Tories believe that Fowler's 'commitment to efficiency at all costs' will be achieved by extending intra-party democracy (*vide* the influence of the National Union's mass membership); most believe that it will simply enhance the power of the party's apparatchiks over its ordinary members – a view reinforced by the fact that the Board's 'Director General', like the Party Chairman, will not be directly accountable to constituency activists.

Much of the concern about CCO, and much of the Fowler inquiry's attention, were related to CCO's precarious finances for which its Treasury Department has responsibility. It was estimated that CCO was overdrawn by £10 million in 1992, a situation which Charter claims can only be rectified by giving the National Union's membership more control over CCO by allowing it to elect the Party Chairman.[57]

At a time of soaring election expenditure, the party Treasurers (in 1993, Lord Laing and Tim Smith MP) have one of the most important jobs within the party organisation, namely, raising campaign donations in the run-up to an election. The available figures suggest a fair measure of success. Between 1990 and 1991 alone, company donations rose by over £3 million and by the time the 1992 election was called, CCO had raised almost £20 million for expenditure on the campaign – more than the other parties combined.[58] Although some details of party accounts have been published since 1984, the source of company donations has remained much of a mystery, many companies making their contributions through such 'filter' organisations as British United Industrialists. However, journalistic investigation reveals that the biggest donors in 1991 included Allied Lyons (£110,000), Tarmac Construction (£55,000) and Scottish and Newcastle Breweries.[59] The contributions made by the various brewers' organisations appeared to have a controversial influence upon Government policy in 1989, when a proposal to limit the number of public houses owned by a single brewery was amended after a series of deputations to Lord Young and CCO. There was also disquiet when it was revealed in 1992 that CCO had received large donations from the defunct Polly Peck which had been in violation of the Companies Act.

Yet it is wise to recall that the bulk of party funds in non-election years comes from the membership. The importance this can have upon party policy was demonstrated during the poll tax controversy of 1989–90 when a number of local parties (notably Morecambe) threatened to withold their regular contributions to CCO funds in protest. It was interesting that at the Central Council of 1990, the Local Government Minister (David Hunt) announced major concessions regarding eligibility for poll tax rebates, admitting to representatives 'You were right. The policy was a mistake. We will go on listening to you.'[60]

## Conclusion

This chapter has aimed to show that the Conservative Party is easily, and usually, seen as an oligarchic, 'top-down' party with activists playing a generally subservient role. Yet the changing character of society, with the growth of the middle-class electorate and the increased scope for the 'upwardly mobile', have produced changes in the nature of both Tory MPs and activists which threaten the hegemony of the Parliamentary leadership. Back-benchers and extra-Parliamentary activists are now less satisfied with merely supporting the leadership until they want to change it and are much more inclined to tell the leadership what it should be doing in the first place – albeit without the paraphernalia of ballots, resolutions and formalised party democracy. The indivi-dualistic ethos expounded by Mrs Thatcher is both a cause and effect of these developments, a connection highlighted in a letter writen by the Chairman of the Hornchurch association to Kenneth Baker shortly after his appointment as Party Chairman:

Statements from Central Office appear to ignore totally one particular facet of the many changes the last ten years have seen; namely that as people respond to the constant urging to be more self-reliant, so they also become more independent and will resist any attempt to impose authority on them. We have been told, rightly, that the man in Whitehall no longer knows best. Why, then, should we still assume that the man in Central Office (or even Downing Street) knows best when it comes to the ordering of this party's affairs?[61]

This new, questioning mood among activists was aggravated by events in November 1990. Charter's demands for greater formal party democracy have so far gained little support from activists who, by and large, trusted their MPs to sense and respond to their informally expressed opinions. That trust was severely shaken by the deposition of a leader who retained their overwhelming support, and by the apparent 'dilution' of the Thatcherite agenda in the year that followed.

Following the Party's re-election in 1992, it was possible to argue that the ousting of Mrs Thatcher had been vindicated – along with the traditional, tacit assumption inside the Party that its MPs 'know best'. It would be a mistake, however, to suppose that this epoch-making triumph will automatically stifle demands for greater rank and file influence inside the party. Indeed, the belief (encouraged by the 1992 victory) that the Conservatives were now 'unbeatable' may only encourage further the self-confidence of a rank and file whose concerns are no longer alien to most 'ordinary' voters. It is not immediately certain whether the Government's diminished majority will increase or constrain the dissenting tendencies evident among Tory MPs in the 1980s, although their response to the Maastricht Treaty, the ERM and the proposed redundancies in the coal industry all point to the former. It also seems probable that dissent at grass roots level will manifest itself more forcefully as the 1990s progress.

### Notes

1 P. Norton & A. Aughey, *Conservatives and Conservatism*, London, 1981, p. 231

2 L. Minkin, *The Labour Party Conference*, Manchester, 1978; E. Shaw, *Discipline and Discord in the Labour Party*, Manchester, 1988.

3 R. T. McKenzie, *Political Parties*, London, 1955.

4 Charter Movement, *A Charter To Set The Party Free*, Beckenham, 1988.

5 Conservative Political Centre, *Conservative Central Office*, London, 1987; R. Morris, *Tories*, Edinburgh, 1991, p. 60.

6 McKenzie, *Political Parties*, p. 21.

7 R. Rose, *The Problem of Party Government*, London, 1976, p. 154.

8 *Charter News*, Beckenham, September 1989.

9 H. J. Laski, *Parliamentary Government in England*, London, 1938, p. 71.

10   M. Trend, 'The Tories' battle plans', *The Spectator*, 28 February 1987.
11   R. Tyler, *Campaign!*, London, 1987, chapter three.
12   'Of policy and pedigree', *The Economist*, 6 May 1989.
13   See R. Churchill, *The Fight For The Tory Leadership*, London, 1964.
14   Norton and Aughey, *Conservatism*, chapter five.
15   Norton and Aughey, *Conservatism*, p. 197.
16   S. Ingle, *British Party System*, Oxford, 1987, p. 47.
17   R. Shepherd, *The Power Brokers*, London, 1991.
18   See R. Kelly & S. Foster, 'Power in the Labour party', *Politics Review*, September 1991.
19   'Senior Tory backbencher', quoted in *Daily Telegraph*, 11 December 1989.
20   P. Goodhart, *The 1922*, London, 1973, p. 209.
21   'A party rages in room 14', *Guardian*, 22 January 1986.
22   Ingle, *British Party System*, p. 56.
23   *Guardian*, 22 January 1986.
24   M. Burch & M. Moran, 'Who are the new Tories?', *New Society*, 11 October 1984.
25   Norton & Aughey, *Conservatism*, p. 203.
26   'Rules and Standing Orders of the National Union and Conservative Associations', London, 1988.
27   Kelly, *Conservative Conferences*, chapter five, Manchester, 1989.
28   *Daily Telegraph*, 2 July 1986.
29   *Charter News*, winter, 1988–9.
30   Kelly, *Conservative Conferences*, chapter five.
31   Kelly, *Conservative Conferences*, chapter one.
32   Kelly, *Conservative Conferences*, chapter five.
33   Kelly, *Conservative Conferences*, p. 157.
34   *Times*, 7 October 1985.
35   Kelly, *Conservative Conferences*, p. 119; Morris, *Tories*, pp. 33–5, Edinburgh, 1991.
36   A. Gamble, 'The Conservative party', in H. Drucker, *Multi-Party Britain*, p. 40.
37   Quoted by S. Benton, 'The mass sherry party', *New Statesman and Society*, 7 October 1988.
38   Quoted in Norton and Aughey, *Conservatism*, p. 217.
39   Kelly, *Conservative Conferences*, p. 179.
40   Peter Morrison, speech at Manchester Grammar School, 25 March 1988.
41   *Sunday Telegraph*, 2 July 1988.
42   Information obtained by R. N. Kelly from Conservative and Labour Headquarters, February 1986.
43   F. W. S. Craig, *British Parliamentary Election Statistics 1918–70*,

London, 1981, pp. 65–6.

**44** R. D. Bayman, Conservative party Eastern Area Agent, conversation with R. N. Kelly, 15 September 1987.

**45** *Times*, 7 October 1985.

**46** M. Pinto-Duschinsky, 'The funding of political parties since 1945', in A. Seldon (ed.), *UK Political Parties Since 1945*, Hemel Hempstead, 1990, p. 95.

**47** S. Benton, 'The mass sherry party'.

**48** V. McKee, 'Conservative party factions', *Contemporary Record*, Autumn 1989.

**49** V. McKee, 'Conservative party factions'.

**50** From W. Coxall and L. Robins, *Contemporary British Politics*, London, 1989, p. 239.

**51** Coxall and Robins, *British Politics*, p. 239.

**52** *The Reformer*, Tory Reform Group Journal, October 1991.

**53** *Sunday Telegraph*, 17 March 1991.

**54** E. Pearce, *Guardian*, 18 March 1991.

**55** M. Pinto-Duschinsky, 'Central Office and "power" in the Conservative party', *Political Studies*, March 1972.

**56** *Charter News*, 1987–89.

**57** S. Heffer, 'A very expensive party', *Spectator*, 15 June 1991.

**58** *Guardian*, 4 March 1992.

**59** *Guardian*, 4 March 1992.

**60** *Daily Telegraph*, 31 March 1990.

**61** *Charter News*, Party Conference Issue, October 1989.

# 6

# THE LABOUR PARTY:
# THEORY AND PRACTICE

Labour has often been described as a 'broad church' in the sense
that its ideological boundaries are wide. Bealey's 'peasant's
stockpot' metaphor for the ideas of a political party, then, is
certainly applicable to Labour.[1] Indeed, this is hardly surprising
given that, since the decline of the Liberals in the 1920s, Labour
has been the major party on the centre-left of British politics and a
number of impressive volumes have sought to document the
variety of ideas that have been put forward within the confines of
the party.[2] Our purpose, however, is more limited. In a book of
this size it is necessary to focus on the ideas that have had the
biggest impact in the party's development. By so doing, it is
possible to identify what may be described as a mainstream
ideology which has remained dominant as a guide to the actions of
the Labour leadership since 1918.

## Labour Party socialism

Before considering its origins and the challenges it has faced
during the party's history, it is worthwhile sketching out the major
characteristics of Labour's dominant ideology, which we will refer
to as Labour party socialism. It might be argued that a more
appropriate term for this ideology is social democracy. The problem here, though, is that in the early part of the present century,
the label social democracy had Marxist connotations. Thus, the
Social Democratic Federation in Britain – which for a short time

was affiliated to the infant Labour Party – was a Marxist group and the very fact that it felt unable to remain within the party illustrated its ideological incompatibility.[3] It was only in the post-war period that the label social democrat began to be regularly applied to certain (moderate) individuals and factions within the Labour Party to denote their acceptance of the mixed economy created by the 1945 Labour Government and to distinguish them from those who sought a further socialist transformation. In practice, it has been the social democrats, apart from a brief period in the 1970s and early 1980s, who have dominated the party. It is doubtful, though – for reasons that will be explored below – whether such a distinction can be profitably applied in the inter-war years. Furthermore, many of those in the post-1945 Labour Party who would not have described themselves as social democrats would accept at least some of the characteristic features of what we have described as Labour Party socialism.

So, what are these characteristics? In the first place, Labour's theory and practice have been fashioned around a *belief in the primacy of parliamentary action*. Mainstream Labour socialism regards legislative enactments as the only means of achieving its aims. Extra-parliamentary action is considered to be both illegitimate and unnecessary. A corollary of this is a belief in the *neutrality of the state*. The state is not, as for Marxists, the vehicle of an economically dominant class but is infinitely malleable, to be used effectively by any government with a majority of MPs in the Commons.

Secondly, Labour socialism is a *classless doctrine*. The existence of classes is recognised as is the point that the working class stands to gain most from socialism. Socialism, however, is not a doctrine aimed at one particular class or section of society and does not, as Marxists would claim, involve a class war the result of which would be the victory of the working class. Rather, changes in a socialist direction will come about when people from *all* sections of society come to see the validity of the arguments put forward.

Thirdly, Labour socialists have regarded *public ownership and state action* in general as the main means to achieve their ends. The ends themselves have changed significantly over time. The early

*Labour: theory and practice*

Labour socialists, exemplified by Ramsay MacDonald – the first Labour Prime Minister, assuming office in 1924 – consistently stated that their long-term objective was the creation, albeit gradual, of a socialist society in the sense of the emasculation of private ownership of the economy. Post-1945 Labour socialists, on the other hand, as we shall see, have had the less visionary aim of the effective and just management of the mixed economy which has within it a substantial private sector. This can, as we indicated, be more profitably described as a social democratic approach. In practice, however, the distinction between the two really became apparent only after the achievements of the 1945 Labour Government.

These are the major characteristics of the doctrine that we have described as Labour socialism. Obviously, as we shall see, the bare bones of the principles elaborated above have been fleshed out in different ways over the years and the basic principles have been challenged, from within the party, with varying degrees of success. Nevertheless, the continuity of the dominant set of ideas has been striking.

## The impact of the trade unions

Before we consider the ideological development of the party in different historical periods, it is essential to discuss in general terms the role of the trade unions. No adequate account of Labour's ideology can ignore the impact of the trade unions. It was the desire for independent labour representation in the latter part of the nineteenth century that led to the creation, in 1900, of the Labour Representation Committee which was renamed the Labour Party after the 1906 general election. Admittedly, a number of socialist societies – the Fabians, the Independent Labour Party (ILP) and the Social Democratic Federation – were also involved. It was the finance and numerical strength of the trade unions, however, which was vital in the party's development. As the next chapter will show in detail, Labour has continued to rely on the trade unions to an enormous degree.

Given the dominance of the trade unions it is important that we tackle immediately their impact on Labour's ideological development. The established orthodoxy amongst commentators seems to be that the trade unions had, and continue to have, a moderating influence on the Labour Party. Bealey, for instance, concludes that for the most part the purpose of the trade unions has been 'highly practical and immediate'. Similarly, Foote regards the aim of desiring a better reward for workers within a capitalist society as the 'Labourist' boundaries of the party's political thought. For any ideological faction to have any success within the party, he argues, it must 'adapt itself to the Labourism of the trade unions'. Ingle is equally adamant that the trade unions moved 'Labour decisively away from socialism, making it very much a trade union party'. Finally, McKibbin, in his study of Labour's development up to 1924, suggests that the party's adoption in 1918 of a socialist commitment was unimportant because the trade union organisational dominance ensured it would never be put into effect.[4]

It can be seen that these authors ascribe to the unions a particular ideological contribution. For want of a better word this may be defined as *labourism*. Labourism refers to the theory, in so far as it exists, and practice of the protection and elevation of working-class living standards. Thus, it is concerned with the sectional interests of the working class within the existing framework of society rather than with attempts to change that society fundamentally. Thus, as Peter Gay has written:

A trade union leader, if he wishes to stay in power, must produce immediate and tangible results; higher wages, shorter hours, better working conditions. He knows that man cannot live on hope alone nor can present hunger be satisfied by thoughts of the happiness of future generations. He knows too that short run gains are best achieved by working within the existing social framework.[5]

Before 1918, certainly, the party was little more than a pressure group for the trade union movement. Thus, the main purpose of the Parliamentary Labour Party (PLP) was not to aim at forming a government but to put pressure on the government of the day to adopt legislation in the interests of organised labour. After 1918, however, Labour was transformed – partly, at least, because of the impact of the Representation of the People Act which massively increased the number of working-class voters – into a national party of government with a constitution emphasising socialism as its objective.

Clearly, there is a conflict between the labourism of the trade unions and the Labour socialism we identified above. In the first place, labourism lacked the vision of early Labour socialism. The former seeks only the improvement of working-class living standards. The latter, at least in its early days, advocated the creation of nothing less than a new kind of society. R. H. Tawney, a leading Labour socialist thinker in the inter-war years, put the difference nicely when he pointed out that the ultimate aim of socialists was not simply a society 'in which money and economic power will be somewhat differently distributed' but one 'in which money and economic power will no longer be the criterion of achievement'.[6] Secondly, and more importantly in practice, labourism asserts the interests of one section or class of society. This is clearly at odds with the Labour socialist denial of the value of a class-specific doctrine and the desire of all Labour Governments to govern in the 'national' interest.

The conflict between labourism and Labour socialism has manifested itself on numerous occasions in the party's history. In the 1920s, for instance, the first Labour Government's defence of the 'national' interest when refusing to support the striking transport workers in 1924, and the leadership's lukewarm support for the general strike in 1926, were both illustrations of the conflict.[7] In the modern period, the Labour Government's unsuccessful attempt to reform the trade unions in 1969 and the imposition of pay norms in the late 1970s were both sources of conflict as was the Kinnock leadership's lukewarm response to the miners' strike in 1984, the latter providing a classic case study of the traditional Labour socialist view that the party should not condone industrial action conducted by one section of society to the detriment of society as a whole. That is not to say, of course, that the justice of the particular group of workers taking industrial action cannot be proclaimed; only that the methods utilised to correct this injustice are unfortunate, a last resort requiring speedy resolution.

The response of Labour Governments to the activities of trade unions, of course, has been inspired as much by electoral considerations as by a principled stance. This is not, on the other hand, to say that Labour leaders have not had a choice. They have, and on most occasions they have chosen to sacrifice the interests of particular sets of workers, or even the trade union movement as a whole, in order to uphold what they have seen as the national interest. As a consequence, there have often been bitter recriminations within the party, usually fought out at the Labour conference and, in the case of *In Place of Strife* in 1969, the Labour Government was forced – owing to pressure from within the Parliamentary party and even in the Cabinet as well as the bulk of the extra-Parliamentary party – to back down.

Clearly, then, we cannot ignore labourism as an ideological force within the Labour Party. Its importance, however, should not be exaggerated.[8] In the first place, labourism does not provide a programme for government. Before 1918, the PLP could simply act as a mouthpiece for the trade union movement because it was not in a position to take on the reins of government. After 1918, when Labour was seeking to replace the Liberals as one of the two main parties, the party needed a programme dealing with a wide variety of issue areas and appealing to a wider audience than the organised working class. This was recognised by Arthur Henderson, the party's secretary and a key figure in the reorganisation after 1918, when he wrote that Labour's appeal up to 1918 was limited because:

it was regarded as the party of the manual wage-earners. Its programme was assumed . . . to reflect the views of trade unionists not as citizens with a common interest in good government, but as workers seeking remedies for a series of material grievances touching hours of labour, rates of wages, conditions of employment.[9]

Thus, after 1918, the trade unions were forced to rely on the Labour socialists to formulate a general programme which would attract wide enough support for the party to win elections. The demands of trade unionists constituted a part, but only a part, of that programme.

Secondly, at certain times of the party's history, the trade unions have been forced to depend on the political leadership of the Labour socialists since their bargaining power in the industrial sphere, through recession and/or legislation, has been severely limited. This happened in the 1920s after the exhausting failure of the general strike in 1926 and the Conservative Government's draconian trade union legislation enacted in the following year (see Chapter 7). It has also occured in the period of Conservative Governments since 1979 for the same reasons. Then, as now, the union movement has needed above all a friendly government to legislate in its interests.

The final point to make here is that although we have identified one facet of the ideological make-up of the trade unions, it would be too simplistic to ascribe to them an homogenous labourism which has been universally hostile to Labour's socialism. This would be to underestimate the difficulty of locating the unions within Labour's overall theory and practice.[10] Some trade unionists have regarded themselves as socialists with a vision or a goal of what society should look like which goes way beyond the limited aims of labourism and indeed the social democracy of Labour's post-war Parliamentary leadership as well. For example, as we shall see in Chapter 7, Labour's move to the left in the 1970s and early 1980s came about at least partly because the major unions had elected a more left-wing leadership who had become hostile to the moderation of the party's Parliamentary leadership in the 1960s and 1970s. Before then in the 1950s, on the other hand, the key union leaders, far from representing an ideological and political threat, were fully behind Hugh Gaitskell's social democratic leadership of the party.

## The inter-war years

Labour socialism was established as the party's mainstream ideology in the 1920s. Labour's 1918 Constitution had two vital provisions. First, there was the opening up of the party to individual members in local constituencies to supplement the existing affiliated membership. This had the effect of reducing the dominance of the trade unions thus making Labour look more like a national political party capable of governing rather than merely a pressure group. Secondly, there was the adoption of a socialist objective (Clause IV, Part V of the party's Constitution). This committed the party for the first time to:

secure for the producers by hand and by brain the full fruits of their industry, and the most equitable distribution thereof that may be possible, upon the basis of the common ownership of the means of production and the best obtainable system of popular administration and control of each industry and service.

Two statements of aims were also published in the 1920s, *Labour and the New Social Order* in 1918 and *Labour and the Nation* in 1927. Both remain classic examples of Labour socialism, committing the party to the eventual creation of a socialist society through nationalisation in addition to various reforms to improve the lot of the working class until that change could be effected. Both programmes were to be carried into completion: 'by peaceful means, without disorder or confusion, with the consent of the majority of the electors and by the use of the ordinary machinery of democratic government'.[11]

Central to the adoption by Labour of these aims were the activities of three individuals. First, Sidney Webb, the leading Fabian thinker, was instrumental in drawing up *Labour and the New Social Order*. Indeed, much of what we have described as Labour socialism derives from the gradual, evolutionary socialism advocated by the Fabian Society. Secondly, Arthur Henderson, as previously mentioned, played a key role in Labour's reorganisation after 1918. He saw that it was vital that Labour should become a national party capable of legislating in the interests of all classes. Finally, and most importantly, there was Ramsay MacDonald. Dominating the party as Labour leader from 1922 until 1931, he did most to popularise Labour socialism both by his actions and in a series of books written immediately before and after the First World War.[12]

Labour socialism was also seen in action during the 1920s. We have observed it in the leadership's response towards the trade unions. It was also evident in the party's continual refusal to allow the Communist Party of Great Britain to affiliate and the expulsion of known communists within the Labour party. The ideological incompatibility between communism and Labour socialism was noted in a letter sent out by Labour's National Executive Committee (NEC) to all affiliated societies in 1924:

The Labour Party seeks to achieve the Socialist Commonwealth by means of Parliamentary democracy. The Communist Party seeks to achieve the 'Dictatorship of the Proletariat' by armed revolution. The Labour Party realises that ... this country possesses almost a wholly enfranchised adult population, and a Parliament and system of government that will respond to the direction of the working people, so soon as they express intelligent desire for change through the ballot box.[13]

It is an established fact that the two Labour Governments in the 1920s achieved very little in the way of carrying out their programme. In 1924, MacDonald was clearly concerned above all to show how moderate and respectable Labour was in order not to frighten off the voters. Nevertheless, there were other excuses. Both Labour Governments were minorities so they did not have a mandate to carry out their full programme. In addition, the second Labour Government between 1929 and 1931 was overwhelmed by an economic crisis with which it had little idea how to deal. Arguably, this failure was rooted in the party's ideology. Labour socialism in the inter-war years – before the party absorbed Keynesian economics – consisted largely of an ethical vision of a new social order. Consequently, it had litle idea how the transition was to be achieved in practice and even less how to handle a capitalist economy in crisis.[14]

Of course, the Labour socialism of MacDonald and others did face opposition within the party. We have already seen the challenge presented by the industrial militancy of the trade unions. Another came from the left of the party centring on the ILP. The ILP, originally dominated by MacDonald loyalists, came to be the focus of opposition to Labour's gradualist socialism. Led by the fiery Clydesider James Maxton, the ILP mounted a campaign for *Socialism in our Time* which sought a Parliamentary road to socialism but one which would be achieved rapidly. It had little impact on Labour's development, however, and after the *débâcle* of 1931, the ILP disaffiliated from the party.[15]

A more serious challenge to Labour socialism came after the events of 1931. With the Government's collapse and MacDonald's decision to stay on as Prime Minister of a National Government, a number of key thinkers began to question the validity of a cautious Parliamentary approach. One kind of analysis, represented by Stafford Cripps and Tawney, concentrated on the need for a future Labour Government to act quickly to control the power of capital. They remained committed, however, to a parliamentary approach.[16] The second kind, represented by Cole and Laski, adopted an uncompromising Marxist analysis which involved the – for them – pessimistic conclusion that socialism was not obtainable by constitutional means.[17]

Despite the increased influence of Marxism amongst British socialists in the 1930s, the decade was marked by the refinement of Labour socialism rather than its abandonment. Crucial here was the absorption of Keynesian economic management techniques and the general idea of planning into mainstream Labour socialism.[18] The party also settled upon the public corporation model of nationalisation, popularised by Herbert Morrison. Thus, industries were to be run by a board of experts replacing the earlier participatory ideals of public ownership in British socialist thought exemplified by Cole's Guild Socialism.[19] These refinements were included within the two Labour programmes published in the period, *For Socialism and Peace* in 1934 and *Labour's Immediate Programme* in 1937.

## Revisionism versus fundamentalism

The Labour Government elected in 1945 carried out much of the programme adopted in 1918 and refined in the 1930s. With the consent of the people, manifested in a huge Parliamentary majority, Labour nationalised a whole range of industries, from coal to road haulage, and took it upon themselves to provide and maintain full employment through the use of demand management techniques derived from Keynes. In addition, through the creation of the welfare state, a safety net was provided below which no one was to fall. As explained in Chapter 3, this was to provide the basis for the social democratic consensus which dominated British politics for the next twenty-five years. After the fall of the Labour Government in 1951, however, an ideological battle broke out within the party. Put very simply, on the one side were the *Revisionists*, led by Hugh Gaitskell and Tony Crosland and on the other were the *Fundamentalists*, whose main champion, at least for the first part of the 1950s, was Aneurin Bevan.

The ideological divisions were provoked by the need for Labour to come off the fence. Prior to the Second World War, Labour socialism was sufficiently vague to keep the party relatively united ideologically. More specifically, the gradualist socialism, propagated most of all by MacDonald, had the effect of keeping those who regarded Labour's true purpose to be the creation of a socialist society active within the party whilst not frightening off those with less ambitious aims. Thus, for the latter group, socialism was so far off as not to be worth worrying about, whilst for the former socialism was still very much on the agenda.

This ideological glue was not available for Labour after 1951. MacDonald, Snowden and other Labour leaders in the 1920s could be described as social democrats in the sense that they would probably have accepted the mixed economy and the welfare state as Labour's ultimate goal. Certainly, their actions, as opposed to their writings, suggest this. Because, however, they were not put to the test of implementing their preferred programme in the inter-war years they avoided the inevitable debate about Labour's future direction. After 1951, however, such a debate was unavoidable. It was after then that the labels socialism and social democracy began to have great importance within the Labour Party.

The main theoretical exponent of Revisionism was Tony Crosland.[20] Crosland argued that capitalism had been 'reformed and modified almost out of existence'.[21] State management ensured that the economy worked effectively, guaranteeing a high level of economic growth and employment, thereby proving Marxist predictions of the collapse of capitalism unfounded. In addition, the Marxist model of two classes – the bourgeoisie and

141

the proletariat – with diametrically opposed interests and in constant conflict, failed to take into account the fact that financial ownership of the private sector was now increasingly separate from its day-to-day control which tended to be in the hands of a class of salaried managers with their own set of goals and motives. Crucially, too, the welfare state was in position to provide free health care and education as well as various social benefits for those in need of help. Yes, Crosland argued, the main mechanism of the economy was still the profit motive but this was a necessary device in any society. The key difference since the War was that part of this profit was taken and used by the state in the interests of all.[22]

For Crosland, then, further public ownership of the economy was irrelevant to the achievement of the basic socialist goal of equality. Instead, Crosland suggested, Labour's goal of further nationalisation should be abandoned and the mixed economy/ welfare state accepted as the permanent social arrangement within which the party should work. Labour should then turn its attention to removing the remaining inequalities in society through a programme of social reforms including the introduction of comprehensive education and reform of the tax system.

Crosland had powerful support for his views within the party's leadership. Above all, it was Gaitskell – Labour leader after Attlee's retirement in 1955 – who fought for Revisionism. Thus, he sought (unsuccessfully) to remove Clause IV (which, it will be remembered, indicated that Labour's main means to the socialist end was to be public ownership) from the party's Constitution at the 1959 conference.[23] Despite this failure, the party's policy documents at this time (including the 1959 manifesto) were fully in line with the Revisionist prognosis and Labour Governments in the 1960s, with Crosland as a member, were essentially committed to the Revisionist analysis in that they aimed to institute greater planning of the mixed economy rather than any significant change in the mixture (the nationalisation, or renationalisation, of iron and steel being the only such measure carried out between 1964 and 1970).

Crosland's analysis, and its attractiveness to most of Labour's

Parliamentary leadership, were very much a product of the political and economic environment of the 1950s. During this decade, the British economy was booming and in these circumstances it was easy to see how it could be thought that the depression and mass unemployment of the 1930s were a thing of the past. In addition, the three consecutive Conservative election victories in the 1950s led to claims that, because of the growing prosperity of the working class, Labour would never win an election again unless it significantly modified its approach and image.[24]

This Revisionist approach was challenged from the left of the party. During the 1945–51 Labour Governments, the left's voice was muted. There was some disquiet at the Government's moderation – the generous compensation given to the former owners of nationalised industries, for instance, and the failure to take into public ownership more of the profitable parts of the private sector – and the *Keep Left* group of Labour MPs was formed in 1947 to urge the Government to take bolder measures. Divisions were concerned mainly, though, with foreign and defence policy with dissent provoked by the strong anti-Soviet line of the Foreign Office under Ernest Bevin's ministerial leadership.[25] The largest conflict, linking together external and domestic policy, occurred in 1951 when financing the Korean War necessitated the introduction of charges in the NHS. The subsequent resignation of three Ministers – Bevan (who, as Minister of Health, had been responsible for piloting the National Health Service Bill through Parliament), Harold Wilson and John Freeman – was to provide the impetus for left-wing opposition to Labour's leadership when the party lost the 1951 election.

During the 1950s, internal wrangling became a feature of Labour Party politics. Defence again, and particularly the Labour leadership's support for an independent British nuclear weapons system, was a key source of division.[26] In 1955, Bevan was expelled from the PLP for mounting a Commons attack on Attlee's pro-nuclear sympathies and, with the growing support for CND (itself formed in 1958) within the party, the 1960 conference voted for a unilateralist resolution, thereby inflicting a rare defeat on the Parliamentary leadership (see Chapter 7). By this time, though, Bevan himself had patched up his differences with the leadership and, as Shadow Foreign Secretary, he instituted a remarkable about-turn by imploring delegates at the 1957 conference to accept multilateral nuclear disarmament as Labour's goal.[27]

In domestic policy, the left, with very little success, opposed the Revisionists' claim that nationalisation was no longer relevant. Bevan's *In Place of Fear*, published in 1952, became the main text of this Fundamentalism. In it, he argued that Labour had not transformed capitalism. Indeed, the basic class and power structure in Britain had hardly been touched. Consequently, further nationalisation was necessary in order to change the balance between the public and private sectors. Bevan's analysis was also significant in the sense that its class-based approach differed from the mainstream Labour socialism we have described. The aim of Labour should be – as, for Bevan, it always had been – the transformation of society in the interests of the working class. This could be achieved only by an attack on the class who owned private property.[28] Bevan, though, shied away from criticising the neutrality of the state. Universal suffrage had provided the potential for the conflict between classes to be fought out in Parliament. It was Labour's job to make sure that Parliament performed this function.[29]

By the early 1960s, however, the debate between the Revisionists and the Fundamentalists was overtaken by events. Of crucial importance was Harold Wilson's arrival as leader after the shock of Gaitskell's early death in 1963. Wilson was able to unite the party for three main reasons. First, by the early 1960s, the Conservative Government was running into difficulties, not least because of the state of the economy, and Labour began to pull ahead in the opinion polls. The prospect of winning after so long in the wilderness had a disciplining effect and all sections of the party rallied around the new leader. Secondly, Wilson was in a good position to secure unity. He was respected by all sections of the party. His gritty no-nonsense northern image was attractive to a working-class party and, in addition, he was regarded as 'one of us' by the left who had not forgotten his resignation, with Bevan, in 1951. Finally, Wilson was able to transcend the ideological dispute in the party by emphasising the need for Labour to modernise the economy. Not only was this a skilful way of bypassing the divisions within the party – modernisation was a neutral term which did not involve coming down on the side of the Fundamentalists or the Revisionists – it was also an ideal weapon with which to attack the Conservatives. Thus, the old aristocratic Tories were to be swept away as Labour portrayed itself as the only party able to capitalise on, in Wilson's words, the 'white hot heat of the technological revolution', thereby promising significant economic growth with all the benefits that would derive from that.

## The Labour Governments 1964–70

For much of the period between 1964 and 1970, the left – with what seems in retrospect as hopelessly misplaced optimism – was willing to give Wilson the benefit of the doubt until it became clear that his pragmatism was not furthering the socialist cause, as they saw it, one bit. The Labour Governments of the 1960s were clearly social democratic in tone. As we indicated above, they concerned themselves with the management of the mixed economy created by preceding post-war governments rather than with any attempts to transform that system. For the Fundamentalists, of course, this was a betrayal of the party's true purpose. For the Revisionists, many of whom were actually in the Governments, this mixed economy was no longer a capitalist one. This clash was inevitable, as we have seen, once Labour's basic programme was implemented. Whereas in the 1950s the clash was merely theoretical, from the 1960s onwards it was to go to the heart of what Labour Governments actually did. Wilson was the first Labour Prime Minister to face this problem. In reality he was no more or less moderate than, say, MacDonald had been in the 1920s. He was forced, however, to come off the fence and declare himself.

The cause of the social democrats was not helped by the fact that Wilson's Governments were in their own terms largely a failure. True, some of the Revisionist themes were heeded. Welfare benefits rose, particularly for those in the direst need, as did the number of houses built in the public and private sectors. In addition, the Government began to create a system of comprehensive education, a key Croslandite proposal.[30] Nevertheless, the attempt to carry through Britain's first National Plan, the flagship of the administration, was a flop and general economic decline undermined the Revisionist claim that socialism should now be concerned with the more effective redistribution of abundant resources.

It all started well enough. The Government created a Department of Economic Affairs – with equal status to the Treasury – to develop and co-ordinate the Plan, and a National Prices and Incomes Board. By 1966, however, following a balance of payments crisis, the Government was forced to abandon the planned growth in the economy and introduce severe cuts in public spending. Despite the confidence boost of the general election victory in 1966, things did not get any easier. The following year, the recurring problem of Britain's balance of trade forced the Government to devalue sterling and initiate another round of spending cuts. In addition, the growth of strikes (particularly unofficial ones) provoked the Government into introducing a White Paper aimed at reducing the power of the unions in order to curb wage rises. The ignominy of having to drop the proposals, owing to pressure from within the party, seemed the final nail in the coffin of an exhausted government.

## The Labour Governments 1974–79 and the challenge of the left

After the failures of the Wilson Governments in the 1960s, the left began to flex its muscles and engage in some serious thinking about Labour's objectives and the strategies which would bring them about. During the 1970s, a number of intellectuals – such as Michael Barratt Brown, Ken Coates and Stuart Holland – produced a series of articles and books seeking to articulate a new approach.[31] Central to the Fundamentalists' challenge to the social democratic leadership was their divergent economic policy which became known as the Alternative Economic Strategy.[32]

Some of the features of the left's new programme were familiar. The demand for class-based action and its willingness to support extra-Parliamentary activity were still the essential features which distinguished the left from the Labour socialist leadership. In addition, the left regarded itself as the heir of Labour's 'true' purpose, the transformation of capitalism. Thus, the goal was to create full employment and economic growth through increased state intervention and planning in the form of the creation of a National Enterprise Board (to raise the rate of investment in manufacturing industry) and the nationalisation of the clearing banks together with many of the most profitable manufacturing companies. In addition, a Keynesian reflationary policy was advocated with a permanent prices and incomes policy to combat inflationary pressures.

There were also innovations in this strategy as the old Fundamentalist left, to some extent, had been transcended. In the first place, the Fundamentalism of the 1950s had been tinged, from outside the party, with the ideas of the New Left. This New Left was created in the late 1950s by a number of intellectuals who, disillusioned by the excesses of Stalin, left the Communist Party in 1956.[33] The New Left emphasised that socialism was about power relationships in society as much as it was about economic equality. Thus, a top-heavy suffocating centralism was not conducive to the quality of life whether it occured in a socialist or a capitalist society or, more to the point, whether it occured in a Morrisonian public corporation or a multinational. As a consequence of this analysis, a decentralised, participatory socialism was advocated and long forgotten issues such as industrial democracy and workers' control rediscovered. Indeed, many of the arguments used were remarkably similar to those of the Guild Socialists who, earlier in the century, had attacked the Fabians for their vision of a socialist society run by state technocrats.[34]

Secondly, and crucially, the new strategy recognised the importance of external constraints on a Labour Government. If Labour was to be able to pursue the radical domestic policy intended – and not be directed off course by foreign capitalist interests who would seek to impose their will on a Labour Government – it would have, as far as it was possible, to cut its ties with the world economy. This would necessitate controls on imports (through quotas) and the export of capital together with Britain's withdrawal from the European Community.[35] Clearly, this strategy was based upon the experience of the Labour Governments in the 1960s who were forced to deflate the economy, and eventually devalue, because of persistent balance of payments difficulties. By the end of the 1970s, the left's analysis provoked even more discussion given the influence of the International Monetary Fund on the Labour Government's economic policy (see Chapter 3 and below).

Perhaps the most significant feature of this period was that Tony Benn (the man who was, by the end of the 1970s, to become the unchallenged leader of the left, following in the footsteps of James Maxton in the 1920s and Aneurin Bevan in the 1950s) was, in the early 1970s, beginning to emerge as the political leader of the left's attack on the social democratic leadership. Peter Shore, a leading Labour politician in the 1970s, has described Benn as probably the most important single figure in the history of the Labour Party. There is a good deal to be said for this. Not only was he, in the 1970s and early 1980s, an inspirational orator and the 'darling' of the party's rank and file, he also had the key advantage of being an initially uncritical member of the Labour Governments of Wilson and Callaghan. He could therefore speak with authority, as an 'insider', about their failings and the need for Labour, as he saw it, to adopt a more left-wing standpoint.[36] We should not, however, exaggerate Benn's role. By the end of the 1970s he had become the figurehead of the Labour left but, as Patrick Seyd rightly points out, he was not the primary 'source of Labour Left ideas and neither did he provide the organisational drive for Labour Left campaigns'. In addition, his middle-class social origins and his participation in successive social democratic Labour Governments provoked some hostility on the left.[37]

Benn, although a Fundamentalist in his support for class-based activity and his refusal to condemn extra-Parliamentary action, was also influenced by the New Left emphasis on democracy.

148

Thus, he rejected the public corporation model of social ownership in favour of industrial democracy, supporting the work-in at the Upper Clyde shipbuilders' in 1971 and encouraging the development of workers' co-operatives as Industry Secretary between 1974 and 1975. His characteristic concern, though, has been with the democratisation of the British constitution itself. Only a system which was truly open and democratic could, he argued, be fully accountable to the electors. To this end, he has proposed a whole series of measures from a Freedom of Information Act to the ending of the Royal Prerogative and the abolition of the House of Lords. His attacks on nuclear weapons, Britain's membership of the European Community and the influence of international capital are based on the same grounds. All three, for Benn, are undermining Parliamentary sovereignty and the right of British people to participate in decisions which greatly affect them.[38]

As the 1970s progressed, and Britain's economic situation worsened, the Labour Party began to move leftwards. Crucial here was the adoption at the 1973 conference of *Labour's Programme* which marked a decisive shift to the left. Amongst other things, it proposed the creation of a National Enterprise Board to purchase controlling interests in twenty-five leading firms (a proposal which was only narrowly accepted by Labour's ruling National Executive Committee), a major redistribution of wealth, the institution of planning agreements, industrial democracy and controls on the movement of capital. This programme was confirmed and built upon by other documents during the 1970s. The party's manifesto for the February 1974 general election was a watered-down version of the policy programmes approved by conference (not surprisingly, given the Parliamentary leadership's greater control over the manifesto content and Wilson's antipathy to much of the left's programme). Nevertheless – with promises to extend nationalisation in areas such as ship building and road haulage, an expansion of welfare provisions, steeply progressive income tax proposals and the introduction of a wealth tax – as David Howell points out, its 'tone and the contents were more radical than anything produced by the party since 1945'.[39]

The opportunity to implement this programme came with Labour's return to government (as a minority administration between February and October 1974 and with a small overall majority after the October general election). Initially, there was relatively little for the left to complain about. Wilson appointed Benn and Foot to two important posts – Industry and Employment – which offered some prospect of the left's programme being translated into action. In addition, there was a generous settlement with the miners, legislation was introduced improving the legal status of trade unions and the economy was expanded through deficit financing, thus enabling the Government to keep its side of the bargain in the 'social contract' with the unions. Ultimately, though, the hopes of the left, and indeed the party in general, were to be sorely disappointed.

Despite Benn's appointment, the centre-right of the party held the senior posts in the Governments and Wilson, Callaghan (who became Prime Minister in 1976) and Healey (who was to remain as Chancellor throughout the period between 1974 and 1979) regarded much of the left's programme as unacceptable. In particular, the National Enterprise Board created by the Industry Act of 1975 was a pale reflection of the socialist 'battering ram' envisaged by the left. Deprived of the necessary funds and bereft of its power to institute compulsory planning agreements, its major function was to bale out firms in financial trouble.[40] Benn fought his corner at the Department of Industry, seeking to prevent the downgrading of the National Enterprise Board and encouraging workers' co-operatives, but he was gradually isolated as his departmental officials sought to obstruct him, probably on Wilson's orders. After the defeat of the anti-marketeers in the 1975 referendum, Wilson took the opportunity to demote Benn to the Department of Energy, thus effectively ending his influence within the Government.[41]

As we explained in an earlier chapter, even the Labour Government's commitment to Keynesian social democracy was, by the end of their period in office, severely in doubt. To be fair to the Government, the long-term weaknesses of the British economy had, by the middle of the 1970s, led to the phenomenon of 'stagflation' – both rising unemployment and rising inflation – provoking an agonising choice. The massive deflation adopted, in addition, was to a large degree necessitated by the conditions of the IMF loan required as a result of a serious run on the pound in 1976. Nevertheless, there was a left group in the Cabinet – including Benn, Foot, Albert Booth and Stan Orme – who (together with the more cautious Peter Shore) unsuccessfully sought the adoption of an alternative strategy based upon reflation and import controls.[42]

As it was, monetary discipline precipitated a growth in unemployment whilst at the same time the Government reneged on its part of the 'social contract', imposing lower and lower ceilings on wage rises despite public spending cuts and still high levels of inflation. The Government stumbled on through 1977–78, deprived now of an overall majority and dependent upon the smaller parties, until the outbreak of a succession of strikes amongst low-paid workers in the 'Winter of Discontent' put paid to hopes of a recovery in its fortunes. After losing a vote of no confidence in the Commons, Labour was defeated in the May 1979 election by the Conservatives under the radical leadership of Margaret Thatcher. The time was ripe now for the left to mount its most successful challenge to the prevailing social democracy within the party.

## The left in charge 1979–83

By ignoring much of the left's programme between 1974 and 1979, the Parliamentary leadership had demonstrated clearly that the party's constitution insulated it from the decisions taken at Labour conferences. The final straw came when Callaghan supposedly used his position to determine the (moderate) nature of Labour's 1979 election manifesto. Thus, after the election defeat in 1979, the left (now firmly in control of the extra-Parliamentary party) sought to change Labour's Constitution in order to make the leadership more accountable to the party outside Parliament. The causes and nature of these changes will be considered in more detail in the next chapter. For now, it should be noted briefly that the campaign to involve all sections of the party in the election of the leader and his deputy and to give local activists greater powers to remove sitting Labour MPs succeeded because the left secured enough support from the trade unions at conference. This was partly because there were more left-wingers in key union positions. More important, perhaps, was the labourist demand from trade unions in general that any future Labour Government be under their control, thereby preventing any repeat of what they saw as the attacks on the organised labour movement between 1974 and 1979.

By the early 1980s – with the left in the ascendant – the social democrats, associated with the failed policies of the Wilson and Callaghan Governments, were on the defensive. After Callaghan had stood down, Michael Foot – the most left-wing Labour leader since the War although no friend of Benn – was elected. Foot's election and the conference's confirmation of the constitutional reforms (discussed in Chapter 7), were the final straws for a number of key social democrats who left in 1981 to set up their own party (see Chapter 8). The way was left clear for Benn to utilise the new constitutional provisions. He duly challenged Denis Healey for the deputy leadership at the 1981 conference and, in a nail-biting climax, was narrowly defeated. Despite this setback for the left, the party went into the 1983 election with a manifesto which at last reflected the left's dominance over conference policy-making. A considerable extension of state intervention in the economy was coupled with other proposals – such as withdrawal from the European Community, unilateral nuclear disarmament and abolition of the House of Lords – which had long been on the left's agenda. Labour's resounding defeat – which was at least partly to do with the tone of the manifesto – was the beginning of the end for the most successful challenge to the party's dominant ideology ever mounted by the left.

## The re-establishment of Labour socialism

After the disastrous 1983 defeat the party was at a low ebb. Foot stepped down as leader immediately after the election and was replaced by the so-called 'dream ticket' of Neil Kinnock and Roy Hattersley. From this point on, the influence of the left substantially declined. Indeed, Kinnock's re-establishment of a moderate reformist social democracy as Labour's main ideological contribution occurred with remarkably little opposition. Obviously, the left's claim that, if properly explained, its policies are electorally popular, was severely dented by the 1983 defeat. Subsequently, Kinnock made a good deal of the truism that principles are of little use without the power to put them into effect. For the trade unions in particular, as we pointed out earlier, a Labour Government legislating in its interests was, and remains, a necessity.

Changes in personnel also helped Kinnock's cause. A new generation of moderate trade union leaders such as Bill Jordan, Gavin Laird and John Edmonds and the virtual eclipse of left-wingers such as Arthur Scargill, enabled the new Labour leadership to get its own way at conference. In addition, a new breed of talented Labour socialists such as John Cunningham, Bryan Gould, Gordon Brown and Robin Cook emerged to aid Kinnock in the same way that Crosland and others aided Gaitskell and Wilson in the early 1960s. The Bennites were isolated as a realignment of the left saw the bulk of the old Tribune group of Labour MPs gravitating towards the Kinnock camp. Benn's demise was complete when, in the autumn of 1988, he polled little over 10 per cent of the vote in his attempt to unseat Kinnock as leader (see Chapter 7).

Although in his younger days Kinnock was a left-wing radical, as leader he espoused the main features of the Labour socialist position. Obviously, this is to some extent the result of electoral expediency. Like other Labour leaders before him, Kinnock was well aware of the overwhelming importance of vote-catching. Nevertheless, it would be less than generous to impute some conviction here too. His attack on the 'entryism' of the Trotskyite Militant Tendency within the Labour party and his readiness to condemn the tactics of Scargill during the 1984 miners' dispute, were, for instance, predicated on a principled belief in parliamentary democracy. Kinnock, too, rejected the class-based appeal of the left. Indeed, he denied the existence of a great

153

uniform mass of working-class voters to whom Labour could centre its appeal. For Kinnock, social change had produced a small opulent class at the top followed by the bulk of the population living in reasonable comfort and prosperity with only a small proportion of people in dire need forming an underclass at the bottom.[43] Thus, as he wrote in 1983, Labour's socialism must be 'as appealing as a source of efficiency and justice to the affluent and secure as to the impoverished and insecure if it is to succeed'.[44]

Perhaps the most significant feature of Kinnock's socialism and his period as Labour leader, was his explicit acceptance of the market. This was announced in the first official statement of socialist values since Clause IV was incorporated into Labour's Constitution in 1918. Written primarily by Kinnock and Hattersley, and approved by the 1988 conference, the document, *Aims and Values*, stresses that market forces provide a 'generally satisfactory' method for allocating most goods and services. Thus, only in a few narrow areas such as health, education and the public utilities is public ownership justified.[45] Kinnock, therefore, came down very much on the Revisionist side of the fence.

Kinnock's moderation of Labour's aims was largely accepted by the party as a whole. Gone, for instance, from the 1987 election manifesto were the left-wing demands for withdrawal from the European Community, abolition of the second chamber and a major extension of public ownership. Even the party's defence policy was weakened. Unilateral nuclear disarmament remained but Labour was committed to an increase in spending on conventional defence within NATO.

Kinnock's ideological hold on the party tightened after the 1987 election defeat when the party undertook a major examination of its policies. Seven policy groups were set up with a brief to consult widely (itself an illustration of Labour's greater willingness to compromise principles in order to win votes) before drawing up a report to be discussed by the NEC and the conference. This two-year policy review culminated in the publication, in May 1989, of a 70,000-word document, *Meet the Challenge Make the Change*.[46] This report was primarily a set of policies rather than a restatement of basic principles but, together with a revised, slimmer 'son of the policy review' called *Looking to the Future* published in May 1990, it provided the best guide available to the future course a Labour Government was likely to take and, indeed, it formed the basis of Labour's 1992 election manifesto.

The similarities between Kinnock's stated preferences and these policy documents were marked. Labour, it was said, should be a party of economic efficiency as much as social justice and the market was accepted as an essential instrument of wealth creation. Although a large role was envisaged for the state in organising investment and training, the government's role in the actual ownership of industries and services was to be minimal. Gone were the 'shopping lists' of nationalisation intentions prevalent in Labour documents during the 1970s and early 1980s. Indeed, even the public utilities privatised by the Conservatives were only to be returned to public ownership if 'circumstances' allowed.[47] On the trade unions, similarly, the emphasis in *Looking to the Future* was on the acceptance of much of the Thatcher Government's reforms – secret ballots, abandonment of the closed shop and picketing restrictions – although the restoration of a limited right to secondary picketing was proposed.[48]

The limits on trade union powers were just one illustration of the review's attempt to focus attention on the consumer in the hope that Labour would not be targeted, as it has so often been before, as the party of and for the producer. Thus, in the areas of health and education, it was argued that consumer interests demand that the state intervenes since the market 'restricts individual choice to individual resources' thereby denying these vital provisions to many.[49] This emphasis on 'real' choice was the means by which socialism was to be reconciled with individual liberty. Thus, in the *Aims and Values* document (itself echoing the major theme in Roy Hattersley's book *Choose Freedom*) it was argued that individual liberty can be maximised only through the redistribution of power and wealth since 'unless we have the power to choose, the right to choose has no value'.[50] Thatcherism was to be condemned, then, not for its espousal of individual choice but for its failure to use the state to make that choice a reality for many people.

Perhaps the most innovative policy area concerned constitutional change. Labour planned to replace the House of Lords with a new elected second chamber, introduce a Freedom of Information Act and create separate assemblies for Wales, Scotland and the English regions.[51] Finally, to rub further salt in the wounds of the left, the party's commitment to unilateral nuclear disarmament was replaced by a commitment to bilateral and multilateral initiatives, despite the opposition of the largest union, the TGWU, and its leader Ron Todd.[52]

## Conclusion: the search for a big idea

What is surprising in an examination of the theory and practice of socialism in the Labour party is not the variety but the similarity of the ideas which have informed Labour's practice. Thus, the basic programme of the party written in 1918, and developed during the 1930s and early 1940s, was largely implemented between 1945 and 1951 and remained a central plank of both major parties in the twenty or so years of consensus that followed. For the left, which has very rarely come close to challenging this mainsteam doctrine, this is an damning indictment of Labour's failure to transform fundamentally the capitalist system. For many others, it is a confirmation of Labour's central role in creating a more humane and civilised society.

In 1979, this consensus was abandoned, at least in part, by the Thatcher Government and by a Labour Party increasingly dominated by the left. Under Neil Kinnock's leadership, Labour moved firmly back to the social democratic position which has characterised much of post-war British politics. As indicated, concessions were made to the Thatcherite project but at the heart of the policy review was a collectivism which was anathema to Thatcherism, although less so to the Major brand of Conservatism (see Chapter 3). The fact that the Conservatives felt they had to dispose of the services of Mrs Thatcher, in the context of a large Labour lead in the opinion polls, suggests the enduring popularity of many themes in Labour's revised social democracy.

It remains the case, however, that the main function of the policy review was to abandon electorally negative policies rather than to articulate new themes which would positively attract voters. That search goes on under a new leadership.

That the party was decisively beaten in the 1992 election has not been the occasion for a renewed challenge from the left. Indeed, there is a widespread recognition within the party that if Labour is to challenge the Conservatives effectively, it will have to move even further away from its collectivist roots, championing the consumer as much as the producer – necessitating loosening its ties with the trade unions – and relying more on renewed economic growth, rather than an emphasis on redistributive taxation, as a means of funding improved social provision (see Chapter 9 for a further discussion of Labour's problems). Whether John Smith, who – more than anyone – was associated with the taxation policies put forward by Labour during the 1992 election, can help to fashion a relevant set of policies to attract the voters is at the time of writing an open question. One thing is for sure. The left of the party, which has been strangely irrelevant in Labour's election post-mortem, badly needs a new set of organising principles with which to make sense of a society which has changed so fundamentally since 1945.

### Notes

1   F. Bealey (ed.), *The Social and Political Thought of the British Labour Party*, London, 1970, p. 1.
2   See G. D. H. Cole, *History of Socialist Thought*, five volumes, London, 1953–60; M. Beer, *History of British Socialism*, two volumes, London, 1921; G. Foote, *Labour Party's Political Thought*.
3   H. Pelling, *A Short History of the Labour Party*, London, 1972, pp. 9–10.
4   Bealey, *Social and Political Thought*, p. 6; Foote, *Labour Party's Political Thought*, pp. 1–6; S. Ingle, *British Party System*, Oxford, 1987, pp. 136–7.
5   P. Gay, *The Dilemma of Democratic Socialism*, New York, 1962, p. 130.
6   Quoted in R. Terrill, *R. H. Tawney and his Times*, London, 1973, p. 188.
7   See H. A. Clegg, *A History of British Trade Unions Since 1899 –*

*Volume II 1911–33*, Oxford, 1985, pp. 370–3.

8  Note here too that it is incorrect to characterise labourism as having a moderating influence since it allowed for militant and bitter industrial action, if only for limited ends.

9  A. Henderson, *The Aims of Labour*, London, 1918, p. 22. Henderson was later to hold senior positions in both inter-war Labour Governments and he became leader for a brief period in 1931.

10  The ideological variety of trade unionism is admirably documented in L. Minkin, *The Contentious Alliance*, Edinburgh, 1992.

11  *Labour and the Nation*, London, 1928, p. 13.

12  See B. Barker, *Ramsay MacDonald's Political Writings*, London, 1972.

13  *NEC Minutes*, 24 September 1924.

14  See R. Skidelsky, *Politicians and the Slump*, London, 1967.

15  See R. E. Dowse, *Left in the Centre*, London, 1966.

16  S. Cripps, *Can Socialism Come by Constitutional Means?*, London, 1933; R. H. Tawney, 'The choice before the Labour party', *Political Quarterly*, July–September 1932.

17  G. D. H. Cole, *What is this Socialism?*, London, 1933; H. Laski, *The State in Theory and Practice*, London, 1935.

18  See R. Samuel, 'The cult of planning', *New Socialist*, 34, January 1986, pp. 25–9.

19  See A. W. Wright, *G. D. H. Cole and Socialist Democracy*, Oxford, 1979.

20  See C. A. R. Crosland, 'The transition from capitalism', in R. H. S. Crossman (ed.), *New Fabian Essays*, London, 1953 and C. A. R. Crosland, *The Future of Socialism*, London, 1956.

21  Quoted in A. W. Wright (ed.), *British Socialism*, London, 1983, p. 19.

22  Crosland, *Future of Socialism*, p. 35.

23  See S. Haseler, *The Gaitskellites*, London, 1969.

24  See M. Abrams, R. Rose & R. Hinden, *Must Labour Lose?*, London, 1960.

25  Ball, *British Political Parties*, London, 1987, pp. 163–4.

26  Ball, *British Political Parties*, pp. 167–8.

27  See M. Foot, *Aneurin Bevan Volume II 1945–1960*, London, 1973.

28  Foote, *Labour Party's Political Thought*, London, 1985, pp. 272–4.

29  Foote, *Labour Party's Political Thought*, pp. 274–7.

30  S. Ingle, *British Party System*, Oxford, 1987, p. 110.

31  See M. Barratt Brown, *From Labourism to Socialism*, Nottingham, 1972; K. Coates & T. Topham, *The New Unionism*, London, 1972; S. Holland, *The Socialist Challenge*, London, 1974. For an excellent summary of left ideas in this period see Foote, *Labour Party's Political Thought*, chapters thirteen & fourteen.

**32** P. Seyd, *The Rise and Fall of the Labour Left*, Basingstoke, 1987, pp. 21–9; See A. Gamble, *Britain in Decline*, London, 1990, pp. 157–79 for a summary of the alternative economic strategy. The most important statements of it are to be found in Cambridge Political Economy Group, *Britain's Economic Decline*, Nottingham, 1975.

**33** E. P. Thompson and Raymond Williams are the best-known figures. In 1960, a journal called *New Left Review* was created as an arena for new left ideas.

**34** See Wright, *G. D. H. Cole*, pp. 50–71.

**35** Gamble, *Britain in Decline*, London, 1985, pp. 157–61; 174–9.

**36** Quoted in P. Whitehead, *The Writing on the Wall*, London, 1985, p. 356.

**37** Seyd, *Rise & Fall*, pp. 95–9.

**38** See T. Benn, *Arguments for Socialism*, London, 1980, *Arguments for Democracy*, London, 1981 and *Parliament, People and Power*, London, 1982.

**39** D. Howell, *British Social Democracy*, p. 291.

**40** See J. Dearlove & P. Saunders, *Introduction to British Politics*, Oxford, 1984, pp. 276–86.

**41** Whitehead, *Writing on the Wall*, pp. 140–7.

**42** Whitehead, *Writing on the Wall*, pp. 194–201.

**43** *Guardian*, 5 October 1988.

**44** *Labour's Choices*, Fabian Society Pamphlet, July 1983, p. 10.

**45** *Labour Party News*, June 1988, p. 24–5.

**46** See R. Garner, 'Modernisation and the policy review: the Labour party since the 1987 election', *Talking Politics*, 3, 1989, pp. 101–4.

**47** *Meet the Challenge Make the Change*, Labour Party, London, 1989, p. 15.

**48** *Guardian*, 18 April 1990.

**49** *Meet the Challenge Make the Change*, p. 41.

**50** *Labour Party News*, June 1988, p. 25; R. Hattersley, *Choose Freedom*.

**51** *Meet the Challenge Make the Change*, pp. 55–65.

**52** *Meet the Challenge Make the Change*, pp. 84–8.

# 7

# THE LABOUR PARTY:
## ORGANISATION, MEMBERSHIP AND AUTHORITY

This chapter has two main functions. The first is to describe the various elements that together make up the modern Labour Party. The second is to consider the relationship between these elements in order to examine the distribution of power in the party. Both these tasks have become more difficult in recent years. Since 1979, organisational reform has been a continual theme in Labour Party politics, inextricably linked both with ideological conflict and with the party's poor electoral performance. Between 1979 and 1981, in a climate of turmoil within the party, the left won the battle for the creation of an electoral college for the election of the leader and deputy leader and the introduction of mandatory reselection of Labour MPs, thus seemingly altering the balance of power in the party towards the extra-Parliamentary elements. During Neil Kinnock's leadership between 1983 and 1992, further organisational reform was carried out but, unlike the earlier period, it was initiated from the top down by an increasingly centralised authority structure under the control of the leader. Labour's fourth consecutive electoral defeat in 1992 precipitated an extension of the reforms begun under Kinnock. Once completed, these changes – focusing, in particular, on the role of the trade union links within the party – will, almost certainly, fundamentally alter the nature of Labour's internal structure, thus effectively marking the end of an era in British party politics.

## A unique organisation

Labour is unique amongst the major British parties. It is the only one that originated outside Parliament. Both the Conservatives and the Liberals originated as groupings within Parliament grafting on extra-Parliamentary organisations when, from 1867, it was increasingly necessary to attract the votes of the newly enfranchised. The Labour Party, on the other hand, was created because of pressure from below. In particular, the party was created in order to secure representation in Parliament for the trade unions. Prior to this, trade unions had relied mainly upon the Liberal Party to put forward legislation in their interests. Indeed, trade union officials were often chosen as Parliamentary candidates by local Liberal parties who were well aware of the growing need to appeal to working-class voters. For a variety of reasons (not least the fact that the Conservatives had dominated electoral politics since the mid-1880s), as the nineteenth century drew to a close, this arrangement was no longer regarded as satisfactory by many unions.[1] In 1900, because of the growing demand for independent labour representation, a number of unions – together with a small number of socialist societies – formed the Labour Representation Committee which, after winning twenty-nine seats in the 1906 election, was renamed the Labour Party.

The role of the trade unions is the key to understanding the nature of the party. Before 1918, Labour existed as a Parliamentary mouthpiece for the unions and, since it was possible to join only through one of its affiliated unions (or socialist societies), the party was a loose confederation of autonomous organisations. The new Constitution drawn up in 1918 created a system of party branches and direct party membership under the control of the ruling NEC, but this structure did not replace, but simply co-existed with, the affiliated trade unions who remained in control of their internal affairs.[2] In reality, the massive financial contribution of the unions has always ensured that they have maintained a privileged position within the party. As we turn now to look in detail at the four main constituent elements of the party – the constituency Labour parties (CLPs), the annual conference, the NEC and the party bureaucracy, and the Parliamentary party – it will be seen how the influence of the unions permeates each of them.

## Constituency Labour parties

Most Parliamentary constituencies in Britain have a CLP. As with the Conservatives, to become an individual member of the Labour Party it is necessary to become a member of one of the local parties. Since January 1989, as part of the campaign to increase Labour's membership, it has been possible to join the party nationally. The party's headquarters (which now keeps a computer record of members) provides applicants with provisional membership which becomes permanent if the relevant local party raises no objections within eight weeks.[3] Each CLP contains a number of ward parties which elect delegates to the ruling body of the CLP – the General Committee – which, in turn, elects an executive committee to deal with the day-to-day running of the party.

In common with other parties, Labour has experienced a decline in membership during the last thirty years or so. The extent of this decline is difficult to gauge because over the years different methods have been used to calculate the numbers. Prior to the new national computerised system, the figures were based upon the affiliation fees paid by each CLP but these did not provide an accurate measure because each party had to affiliate a minimum number of members. Between 1963 and 1980 this figure was 1,000 giving a minimum number of around 600,000 members in total. Many parties, however, did not have anywhere near the minimum figure of 1,000.[4] From 1980, the minimum affiliation fell to under 200 so it was possible to provide a more realistic guide. Thus, in April 1988, the membership was calculated at 288,829, a fall of 8,500 (2.9 per cent) on the previous year and a further fall to around 265,000 was recorded between 1988 and 1989.[5] Initially, the membership drive begun in 1989 did increase the membership (to 296,000 by December 1989) but by 1992 the attempt to create a mass-membership party had flopped as a report to the NEC suggested that numbers had dropped below 270,000.[6]

In addition to individual members, each CLP replicates the party's national structure by having an additional type of membership, of those belonging to various autonomous organisations which affiliate to the local party. These could be socialist societies like the local branch of the Fabians or the co-operative society but the affilated membership at the local level is dominated by members of union branches situated within the boundaries covered by the CLP. Branches are entitled to send delegates to the General Committee and, depending upon the particular area, can dominate the proceedings, not least because union affiliation brings badly needed cash into the local party coffers.

The evidence suggests that the decline in individual membership is due, in large part, to the decline of working-class participation in Labour Party politics – itself a product of social changes which have reduced the number of manual workers and fragmented working-class communities (see Chapter 9). As a consequence, the public sector middle class – those such as teachers, lecturers, health service and local government employees (what Peter Jenkins referred to as the 'lumpenpolytechnics') – now play a much more important role in the activist strand of CLPs.[7] This was confirmed by the largest ever survey of Labour's membership, undertaken by Patrick Seyd and Paul Whiteley, which revealed that only 22 per cent of the party's individual membership is working class whilst 56 per cent of party members are in the salariat (teachers, lecturers, social workers etc.).[8] Two consequences flow from all of this. In the first place, the membership decline in the late 1960s left some inner-city constituencies (those in Liverpool being the most notable examples) moribund and ripe for takeover by committed hard-left activists associated with revolutionary organisations such as the Militant Tendency.[9] Secondly, as Eric Shaw points out, middle-class activists joining in the 1970s 'tended to be radical in outlook and imbued with a participatory ethos' and thus less likely to be deferential to the party's leadership.[10]

CLPs have a number of important functions. In the first place, they are electoral machines concerned with trying to get Labour candidates elected to local councils and the Commons. This involves making sure that potential supporters are registered to vote, canvassing support during the campaign and making sure that previously identified supporters turn out on polling day. The importance of this function is often underestimated, the accepted wisdom being that the national – media-orientated – campaign is all that matters. Research has shown, however, that in the 1992 election there was a correlation between the level of local political activity amongst Labour members and the Labour vote, with the additional votes gained by more active CLPs proving the difference between winning and losing in marginal seats.[11]

For the work that party activists put in, it is not unreasonable for them to expect some influence within the Labour Party. According to John Prescott, however, the NEC's attempts to deny this influence in recent years offers a clear reason for Labour's declining membership. Yet, despite Prescott's complaints, there have been a number of recent organisational changes designed to enhance the importance of CLP members. All party members are now balloted to decide which candidates should be supported in the electoral college for the election of the leader and deputy leader, who should be the conference delegates from each CLP (although general committees still decide the stance the delegates take at conference), and (since 1991) which candidates should be supported in the elections for the constituency section of the NEC. In addition, the proposed changes to the trade union vote at conference will provide individual party members with more influence over national policy making (see the relevant sections below for further details of these points).

Finally, the most important power in the hands of CLPs is the selection and reselection of Parliamentary candidates. This is a key function in the British political system, because, since most seats are 'safe' for one or other of the two major parties, the selection of a Parliamentary candidate is, in effect, to choose the MP. It is not surprising, then, that a great deal of the internal organisational debates within the Labour Party has focused on the role of the CLPs in candidate selection and the extent to which they should have the autonomy to determine the nature of the PLP.

When a vacancy occurs, CLPs can take advantage of the approved lists of candidates maintained nationally (list A consisting of union-sponsored candidates, list B of candidates recommended by CLPs, list C of candidates recommended by the Co-operative Society and, since 1988, list W of candidates recommended by Labour's Women's Section). It is usually the case, though, that CLPs will wait for candidates to apply for consideration. To be considered for selection, candidates must be nominated by an affiliated branch of the local party – either a union, socialist society or ward branch – each affiliated organisation being entitled to nominate one candidate. Once the nominations are in, it is up to a CLP subcommittee to draw up a shortlist. They do not have a free hand. The committee must add to the shortlist those with a quarter of the nominations and, since 1988 – if nominated – at least one woman. In addition, the shortlist must contain at least five candidates (if five or more candidates applied) and, if a reselection contest, the sitting MP must be nominated. Finally, the shortlist can be accepted, amended or rejected by the general committee of the CLP.[12] Union-sponsored candidates are obviously attractive to CLPs because of the finance attached. Usually, a trade union will provide a grant of £2,000–£3,000 towards its candidate's general election expenses in addition to £500 per annum paid directly to the candidate's CLP. After the 1992 election, a record number of 152 Labour MPs (out of 271) were sponsored by trade unions, the TGWU (sponsoring thirty-eight) and the GMB (eighteen) being the two largest union-groups in the Commons.[13]

The major changes have occurred in relation to the electorate entitled to vote in the final choice of candidate, and the decision on the exact system to be used in the next round of selections will not be taken until the 1993 conference at the earliest. Before 1989, it was the delegates on the general committee who would make the final choice. At the 1987 conference, however, it was decided to introduce – from January 1989 – an electoral college

*Table 7.1*   The selection of Labour Parliamentary candidates

| *Before 1989* | *1989–92*[a] |
|---|---|
| NEC LISTS OF 'APPROVED' CANDIDATES (List A: TU sponsored) (List B: CLP recommended) (List C: Co-op recommended) | NEC 'APPROVED' LISTS[b] |
| | As before 1989 |
| ↓ NEC recommended candidates to be considered alongside direct applications to ▼ CLP | ▼ |
| *GMC SUBCOMMITTEE | GMC SUBCOMMITTEE |
| ↓ Presents short list to | ▼ As before 1989 |
| GMC (includes senior CLP officers, and branch and TU delegates) | CLP ELECTORAL COLLEGE (votes of individual CLPs' members must comprise at least 60 per cent of votes cast) |
| ↓ Request ratification from | ↓ Request ratification from |
| NEC SUBCOMMITTEE | NEC SUBCOMMITTEE |

* GMC = CLP's General (Management) Committee

whereby at least 60 per cent of the vote was allocated to individual members of the CLP and a maximum of 40 per cent to affiliated organisations (see table 7.1). For many in the party – including Kinnock – this was to be a step towards an eventual one member, one vote (OMOV) system and the 1990 Labour conference did approve the abolition of the electoral college to take effect in the next round of selections after the 1992 election. In 1991, the NEC decided upon a replacement which was approved by that year's conference. The replacement to the electoral college introduced OMOV for individual party members but, in addition, proposed that a ballot of individual members should be held before each contest to decide if affiliated unions should continue to have a vote. If this is answered in the affirmative, each union member who pays the political levy (see below) is entitled to a vote but this

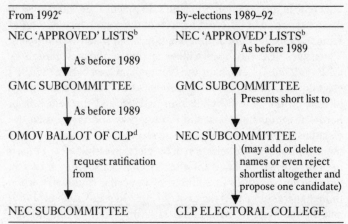

| From 1992[c] | By-elections 1989–92 |
|---|---|
| NEC 'APPROVED' LISTS[b] | NEC 'APPROVED' LISTS[b] |
| As before 1989 | As before 1989 |
| GMC SUBCOMMITTEE | GMC SUBCOMMITTEE |
| As before 1989 | Presents short list to |
| OMOV BALLOT OF CLP[d] | NEC SUBCOMMITTEE |
| request ratification from | (may add or delete names or even reject shortlist altogether and propose one candidate) |
| NEC SUBCOMMITTEE | CLP ELECTORAL COLLEGE |

*Notes*

[a] These changes were approved by the 1987 Labour conference, though not implemented until 1989.

[b] As before 1987, but with the addition (since 1988) of List W – candidates recommended by Labour's Women's Section, from which at least one candidate must be drawn.

[c] The decision to introduce OMOV was agreed by the 1990 and 1991 conferences but after the 1992 election the whole issue was referred to the committee of inquiry looking into party-union links.

[d] It was agreed at the 1991 conference that, before a selection contest is held, a ballot of individual members would decide whether to allow trade unionists residing within a particular constituency to vote. If they are permitted to participate, their votes will equal one-third of those cast by individual party members.

Source R. Kelly and S. Foster, 'Power in the Labour party: A decade of organisational change', *Politics Review*, September 1991, pp. 26–30.

vote should count for only one-third of a full party member's vote. After the 1992 election, however, the NEC – under pressure from trade unions – agreed to refer the whole issue to the review committee which was set up to consider, as a whole, Labour's links with the unions. Its proposals – on candidate selection together with other aspects of the party-union link – were to be considered by the NEC and put before the 1993 conference.[14]

In theory, the NEC, as the party's ruling body, has the power to intervene in the selection procedure. In practice, its willingness to do so has varied in different periods of the party's history. Under Kinnock's leadership, an interventionist approach was adopted. Thus, the NEC has been willing to veto candidates chosen by CLPs as it did in Lewisham and Nottingham East before the 1987 election. In addition, following Labour's heavy defeat at the hands of SNP at the Govan by-election in 1988 and the selection of hard-left candidates (as at the Bermondsey and Greenwich by-elections in 1983 and 1987 respectively) the NEC decided to take more control over the selection of by-election candidates. Thus, it became normal practice for the NEC to liaise with CLPs in drawing up shortlists in addition to imposing candidates when thought necessary, as in the case of Kate Hoey in Vauxhall (1989) and Sylvia Heal in Mid-Staffs (1990) – both of whom won impressive victories.[15]

In recent years, too, the issue of the reselection of sitting Labour MPs has been a contentious issue. In 1980, a system of 'mandatory reselection' was introduced. Here, those CLPs who had a sitting MP were obliged to initiate a reselection contest at least once during the lifetime of a Parliament and, even if no challenger to the incumbent emerged, an affirmative vote was still necessary. This came about partly as a result of the left's campaign to make getting rid of a sitting MP less cumbersome and to end the reliance on the NEC's permission which was previously required in every case. This is not to say that the deselection of Labour MPs did not take place before the 1980s. On the contrary, conflict between CLPs and right-wing Labour MPs was endemic in the 1970s with MPs such as Eddie Griffiths (in Sheffield Brightside), Frank Tomney (in Hammersmith North), Dick Taverne (in Lincoln) and Reg Prentice (in Newham North-East) all being deselected.[16]

Mandatory reselection was a key reform on the left's agenda in the 1970s and its effect, although not as dramatic as many had feared (or hoped), was significant in moving the PLP to the left (see below). It was hardly surprising, therefore, that under Kinnock's leadership the 'mandatory' principle was effectively abandoned. It was agreed at the 1990 conference that in future a reselection contest would take place only if a ballot of CLP members desired it. Ironically, it is now more difficult to remove a sitting Labour MP than it was before mandatory reselection was introduced when the power rested with CLP general committees, subject to NEC approval.[17]

## The annual conference, the block vote and the trade unions

Labour's conference normally meets annually for a period of five days in the autumn. The conference is where delegates from all sections of the party come together to discuss organisational and policy matters. The key feature is its voting system which has traditionally given the trade unions a massive predominance. In return, the unions provide the vast majority of Labour's finances. Traditionally, votes at conference have been allocated in proportion to the number of members each union affiliated to the party. Each member of a union affiliated to the Labour Party, unless he or she 'contracts out', pays a political levy and thereby becomes an affiliated member of the party. As a result, the union membership outnumbers massively the individual membership. Of course, this does not mean that these affiliated members are Labour activists or even Labour voters for that matter. In addition, unions do not have to claim their full entitlement of votes and many have failed to do so primarily in order to save money.[18]

Conservative Governments have, on two occasions, sought to weaken this link between the unions and the Labour Party. In 1927, the Trade Disputes Act replaced 'contracting out' with 'contracting in' and the dramatic fall in Labour's affiliated membership that resulted demonstrated that paying the political levy was not, for many trade union members, a sign of their political commitment to the party. In 1984, the Thatcher Government's Trade Union Act stipulated that all trade unions had to ballot their members every ten years in order to confirm a commitment to retaining a political fund. The unions mounted a hugely successful campaign for a 'yes' vote and every union voted by a large majority to retain such a fund.

The consequence of Labour's rules has been that the unions

controlled about 90 per cent of the votes at conference. In 1989, the four biggest unions (TGWU – 1.25 million; GMB – 725,000; AUEW – 700,000; NUPE – 600,000) accounted for about half of the total conference vote and each had more votes than all the CLPs put together. It is a convention that each affiliated organisation, including the CLPs, casts its vote in a block. Thus, no account is taken of minority opinions. If a union executive, for instance, decides by 51 per cent to 49 per cent to vote for a particular motion then all of the union's vote is used to back that motion at conference.

The union's role at conference is notoriously controversial and its implications for the distribution of power in the party will be discussed later. For now, it should be noted that the trade union role within the conference, and the Labour Party generally, is now under serious examination and it will certainly change, and probably change radically. One decision already taken (at the 1990 conference) is that from 1993 an electoral college system will be introduced at conference whereby the union (and socialist society) delegates have 70 per cent of the vote and the CLPs 30 per cent. In addition, for every 30,000 increase in the party's individual (or non-affiliated) membership the proportion of the vote going to the CLPs will rise by 1 per cent. Thus, the future role of the trade unions at conference would, under this plan, depend upon Labour's ability to attract new members. A doubling of individual membership would cut the block vote to 50 per cent.[19]

The shock of the 1992 election defeat, and the indisputable evidence that Labour's links with the trade unions, in their present form at least, remain an electoral liability, led to the decision to appoint a fifteen-strong committee of inquiry which, as indicated above, will make proposals to be considered at the 1993 conference. It is inconceivable that the party will untie the union knot completely. As Lewis Minkin has pointed out, such a move might have undesirable effects.[20] The trade union link is vital to Labour in a financial sense (particularly in the absence of a mass membership and state funding for parties) and enables Labour to give political expression to the demands of a large section of the workforce. According to Minkin, any denial of this function would tear away Labour's roots and deprive it of any real purpose. The fate of the SDP is an apposite reminder to those who would advocate a complete break.

This does not, however, rule out significant reforms, particularly given that moderate union leaders such as Bill Jordan also favour the ending of the block vote in its present form. The most likely outcome is the creation of a new category of 'associate party membership' consisting of those trade unionists who pay, in addition to the political levy, an extra fee direct to the Labour Party. This would remove each union's right to decide how many members it wishes to affiliate and would limit their vote at conference to the number of associate members they are able to recruit into the party. In addition, all union delegations at conference will be accountable to their associate members and will be allowed to split their vote in accordance with the wishes of their members. In this way, the block vote will disappear but the union-party link is retained.[21]

## The National Executive Committee and the party bureaucracy

The NEC is elected by and is, in theory, the servant of the annual conference, looking after the affairs of the party and reporting to conference each year. The NEC consists of twenty-nine members. The leader and deputy leader are *ex-officio* members. In addition, there are twelve members elected by trade unions, seven elected by constituency parties, and one place each for the socialist societies and, since 1973, the Young Socialists. Finally, five places are reserved for women and for the party treasurer who are elected by the whole conference. The 1990 conference approved a proposal to consider ways in which the proportion of women on the NEC could be increased (to around 40 per cent) although this had not, by 1992, been put into practice. The key fact to note is that, since the unions dominate conference votes, they can, in effect, control eighteen of the seats on the NEC.

The NEC is the major source of party policy. Trade unions and CLPs do put forward motions to the conference, but the debates have traditionally been structured around NEC proposals. Much policy has been developed in NEC committees, most importantly, the Home Policy and International committees. The NEC, in conjunction with the Parliamentary leadership, is responsible for drawing up the party's election manifestos. Largely because of the success of the policy review undertaken after the 1987 election, in which policy was discussed in specially created policy groups independent of the NEC, the party has discussed overhauling its policy-making machinery in a way which would devalue the role of both the conference and the NEC (this reform is discussed further towards the end of this chapter).

In addition to its policy making-role, the NEC has an equally important organisational role. The extent to which it has inter-vened in the affairs of local parties has, as we saw above, varied. Under Kinnock's direction after 1983, as well as vetoing candi-dates selected by local parties and imposing candidates on CLPs, the NEC mounted an ultimately effective strategy to rid Labour of the Militant Tendency who, during a more liberal NEC regime in the 1970s, had been allowed to take root in a number of CLPs.[22] The major organisational change that occurred as a direct conse-quence of the Militant 'experience' was the decision (taken in 1986) to set up a National Constitutional Committee. This body – consisting of eleven members elected by various sections of the party – was set up because Militant was able to persuade the courts that natural justice was not being observed because the NEC was both judge and jury in the moves to expel them. As a result, these two functions were separated with the new body now adjudicating on cases brought before it by the NEC.[23]

Unlike the Conservative Party – in which the professional bureaucracy is indirectly controlled by the party leader through the appointment of the party chairman (see Chapter 5) – the NEC, and not the Parliamentary leader, supervises the party outside Parliament which is run from Walworth Road (the venue for NEC meetings). As a result of Labour's poorly organised election campaign in 1983, Neil Kinnock, after becoming leader, set about persuading the NEC to reorganise the party machine. Larry Whitty replaced Jim Mortimer as General Secretary and Peter

Mandelson was appointed by the NEC as the party's first Director of Campaigns and Communications (Mandelson is in 1993 a Labour MP. His successor was John Underhill who was subsequently replaced in 1991 by David Hill, the incumbent in 1992). Since 1983, as a result, there has been a much greater emphasis on the presentation of the party. In 1986, Mandelson set up the Shadow Communications Agency – consisting of Labour-supporting advertising and marketing experts – which was to play a key role in transforming Labour's image.[24] A sign of the change was the jettisoning of the red flag (the symbol, for many, of hard-line socialism) in favour of the much more 'voter-friendly' red rose. The glossy presentation of the party in the 1987 and 1992 elections and the slick pre-election policy launches (in stark contrast to the early 1980s and indeed, arguably, any time in Labour's history) demonstrated how far Labour had accepted the requirements of the modern television age.

Predictably, some in the party (not just on the left) were critical of what they dubbed 'designer socialism', the triumph of style over substance and the tendency to follow, rather than lead, public opinion (a complaint which has some justification given Labour's failure to win either election). The resignation of John Underwood in 1991 was itself a product of this dispute since, after replacing Mandelson, he wanted to move the presentation of the party from an image-based approach towards a more content-based approach but felt unable to counter the influence of those such as Mandelson and Colin Byrne (Underwood's deputy) who still, along with the Shadow Communications Agency, had the ear of Kinnock.[25] It is worth speculating that, with the less flamboyant John Smith as leader, Labour will tone down the glitz in future and concentrate more on the message rather than the way in which the message is communicated.

## The Parliamentary Labour Party

The PLP consists of all those who accept the Labour whip in the House of Commons. When in opposition, unlike the Conservative Party, Labour MPs elect annually a Parliamentary Committee which, together with the deputy leader, the chairman of the PLP, the Chief Whip and a number of Peers, is moulded by the leader into the shadow Cabinet. Each MP is entitled to as many votes as there are places available on the committee (eighteen at present) and, as a result of a ruling in 1989, at least three of these votes must be cast for women (if three or more are standing for election). Once in government the leader, since 1980, has been obliged to appoint in his first Cabinet those who held Shadow Cabinet posts although he or she is not restricted in any later reshuffles. This is a half-way house between the leader's previous free hand as Prime Minister and the demands of those such as Tony Benn who have argued that Labour Cabinet ministers should all be elected by the PLP.

Factions have traditionally been discouraged in the Labour party but in the 1960s and 1970s they began to proliferate particularly outside Parliament. Within the Commons, the *Tribune Group* is the oldest surviving faction. Created in 1966, it was, until the early 1980s, the only home in Parliament for left-wing Labour MPs. By the end of the 1970s its membership was eighty-six, 27 per cent of the PLP. It has always been a weak group both numerically and in terms of its organisation. It does not put forward a statement of aims and its members are not instructed to vote in particular ways in the chamber.[26] Following the acrimonious deputy leadership election in 1981 (when the failure of a number of Tribunites, including Kinnock, to vote for Benn led to his narrow defeat by Denis Healey) and the decision to purge the party of Militant in 1982, the Parliamentary left split. Those supporting Benn and opposed to what they regarded as a 'witch-hunt' of 'good socialists', the so-called 'hard left', formed the *Campaign Group* in 1982 (which has a membership of about forty-five) whilst the majority, who have come to be known as the 'soft left', remained in the Tribune Group. Most of the latter group tended to support, not always wholeheartedly, the leadership of Kinnock not least to 'protect' him from the clutches of the right of the PLP.[27]

Right-wing Labour MPs have tended to be slower to organise, and they have not been helped in recent years by the fact that a number of leading members of the *Manifesto Group*, founded in 1974, defected to the SDP in the early 1980s. Mention should also be made of the *Solidarity Group* which was set up in 1981 by 150 Labour MPs who opposed the constitutional changes adopted by the party that year and subsequently backed Healey in the 1981 deputy leadership election. By the end of the 1980s, the party had (with the exception, perhaps, of the 'hard left' who by then had been marginalised in any case) come to unite behind the leader in the elusive search for electoral success, and factionalism within the PLP had become far less pronounced.

*Table 7.2*   Labour leadership contests 1922–80 (PLP ballot)

| Leader | | | | |
|---|---|---|---|---|
| 1922 | R. MacDonald | 61 | | |
| | J. R. Clynes | 56 | | |
| 1935 | C. Attlee | (58) | 88 | |
| | H. Morrison | (44) | 48 | |
| | A. Greenwood | (33) | – | |
| 1955 | H. Gaitskell | 157 | | |
| | A. Bevan | 70 | | |
| | H. Morrison | 40 | | |
| 1960* | H. Gaitskell | 166 | | |
| | H. Wilson | 88 | | |
| 1961* | H. Gaitskell | 171 | | |
| | A. Greenwood | 59 | | |
| 1963 | H. Wilson | (115) | 144 | |
| | G. Brown | (88) | 103 | |
| | J. Callaghan | (41) | – | |
| 1976 | J. Callaghan | (84) | (141) | 176 |
| | M. Foot | (90) | (133) | 137 |
| | R. Jenkins | (56) | – | – |
| | T. Benn | (37) | – | – |
| | D. Healey | (30) | (38) | – |
| | A. Crosland | (17) | | |
| 1980 | M. Foot | (83) | 139 | |
| | D. Healey | (112) | 129 | |
| | J. Silkin | (38) | – | |
| | P. Shore | (32) | – | |

| *Deputy leader* | | | |
|---|---|---|---|
| 1952* | H. Morrison | 194 | |
| | A. Bevan | 82 | |
| 1953* | H. Morrison | 181 | |
| | A. Bevan | 76 | |
| 1956 | J. Griffiths | 141 | |
| | A. Bevan | 111 | |
| 1960 | G. Brown | (118) | 146 |
| | F. Lee | (73) | 83 |
| | J. Callaghan | (55) | – |
| 1961* | G. Brown | 169 | |
| | B. Castle | 56 | |
| 1962* | G. Brown | 133 | |
| | H. Wilson | 103 | |
| 1970 | R. Jenkins | 133 | |
| | M. Foot | 67 | |
| | F. Peart | 48 | |
| 1971* | R. Jenkins | (140) | 140 |
| | M. Foot | (96) | 126 |
| | T. Benn | (46) | |
| 1972 | E. Short | (111) | 145 |
| | M. Foot | (89) | 116 |
| | A. Crosland | (61) | – |
| 1976 | M. Foot | 166 | |
| | S. Williams | 128 | |

*Notes*

\* denotes challenge to incumbent.

Figure in parentheses denote inconclusive ballot.

Prior to 1980, the Labour leader (and deputy leader), as with the Conservative leader since 1965, was elected by MPs alone although, unlike the Conservative Party, there was no formal procedure to challenge the leader when Prime Minister (see table 7.2). This was to change when the 1980 conference agreed to a widening of the franchise and to end the anomaly preventing a challenge to a Labour Prime Minister. As table 7.3 shows, the new system differs slightly depending upon whether Labour are in opposition or in government. In opposition, a challenger requires the backing of at least 20 per cent of his or her Parliamentary colleagues (increased from 5 per cent in 1988 after Benn's fruitless challenge). For a contest to take place when the party is in

*Table 7.3*   Challenging a Labour leader (since 1981)

| *In opposition*[a] | *In government* |
|---|---|
| Challenger secures 20 per cent backing from PLP[b] | Challenger secures 20 per cent backing from PLP[b] |
| ↓ | ↓ |
| Following six months: PLP, CLP, TU votes courted and block votes organised[c] | Principle of contest approved by two-thirds majority at annual conference |
| ↓ | ↓ |
| Annual conference: electoral college votes collated and result announced | Following three months: PLP, CLP, TU votes courted and block votes organised[c] |
| ↓ | ↓ |
| | Special party conference: electoral college votes collated and result announced |

*Notes*
[a] When there is a vacancy for the leadership or deputy leadership (as in 1992), the party follows the procedure used for challenges in opposition. The NEC then has the right to shorten the length of the contest and announce the result before the annual conference.
[b] Increased from 5 per cent in 1988.
[c] Since 1989, the CLPs' block votes have had to be preceded by a ballot of individual members. In 1992, this idea was embraced by some (the GMB, for example), but not all, trade unions.

government, at least one challenger must reach the 20 per cent threshold and, in addition, the contest must be approved by at least a two-thirds majority at the annual conference.[28]

Once the contest is approved, the electoral college comes into play. Under this system, affiliated societies (the vast majority being trade unions) and CLPs are entitled to participate as well as MPs with the votes weighted in a formula (determined at the special Wembley conference in 1981) of 40 per cent, 30 per cent, 30 per cent respectively. If no candidate receives 50 per cent of the vote at the first attempt, a second ballot is held in which the second preferences of the bottom placed candidate are redistributed. The procedure has been used on four occasions (see table 7.4). The elections for the deputy leadership have proved to be closer than those for the leader although, even here, only one contest (when Healey defeated Benn in 1981) proved to be close enough to require a second ballot. John Smith's election in 1992 could well be the last under the present system as, in line with the move towards OMOV in other areas of party decision-making, there is strong pressure for removing the union's present influence. As with the selection of candidates and the voting system at conference, no final decision will be made until the 1993 conference.

## The distribution of power in the Labour Party

We have now sketched out the bare bones of Labour's organisation. It seems appropriate at this juncture, particularly given the surfeit of organisational reforms in recent years, to consider the relationship between the different organs of the party. Locating where power lies in a complex, pluralistic structure like the Labour Party is no easy task. The major debate has surrounded the relationship between the PLP leadership and the extra-Parliamentary party. Clause V of Labour's 1918 Constitution (reflecting the fact that the party originated as a mass movement outside Parliament) states that 'the work of the party shall be under the direction and control of the party conference'. A contrary view was provided by Robert McKenzie's major study of political parties written in the 1950s. For McKenzie, power in the Labour Party

178

*Table 7.4*   Labour leadership contests since 1981 (electoral college) (%)

|  | *TU* | *CLP* | *PLP* | *Total* |
|---|---|---|---|---|
| *Leader* | | | | |
| 1983 | | | | |
| N. Kinnock | 29·04 | 27·45 | 14·77 | 71·27 |
| R. Hattersley | 10·87 | 0·57 | 7·83 | 19·28 |
| E. Heffer | 0·04 | 1·97 | 4·28 | 6·32 |
| P. Shore | 0·03 | 0·0 | 3·1 | 3·13 |
| 1988* | | | | |
| N. Kinnock | 38·96 | 24·36 | 24·9 | 88·64 |
| T. Benn | 1·04 | 5·64 | 5·1 | 11·76 |
| 1992 | | | | |
| J. Smith | 38·51 | 29·31 | 23·16 | 91·02 |
| B. Gould | 1·48 | 0·69 | 6·82 | 8·98 |
| *Deputy leader* | | | | |
| 1981* | | | | |
| first ballot | | | | |
| D. Healey | 24·69 | 5·36 | 15·30 | 45·36 |
| T. Benn | 6·41 | 23·48 | 6·37 | 36·64 |
| J. Silkin | 8·09 | 1·15 | 7·95 | 18·00 |
| second ballot | | | | |
| D. Healey | 24·99 | 5·67 | 19·75 | 50·43 |
| T. Benn | 15·00 | 24·32 | 10·24 | 49·57 |
| 1983 | | | | |
| R. Hattersley | 35·23 | 15·31 | 16·71 | 67·26 |
| M. Meacher | 4·73 | 14·35 | 8·80 | 27·88 |
| D. Davies | 0·0 | 0·24 | 3·28 | 3·54 |
| G. Dunwoody | 0·03 | 0·09 | 1·19 | 1·32 |
| 1988* | | | | |
| R. Hattersley | 29·2 | 13·8 | 22·8 | 66·8 |
| J. Prescott | 12·7 | 8·4 | 2·6 | 23·7 |
| E. Heffer | 0·07 | 7·2 | 2·3 | 9·5 |
| 1992 | | | | |
| M. Beckett | 25·39 | 19·04 | 12·87 | 57·30 |
| J. Prescott | 11·63 | 7·10 | 9·41 | 28·13 |
| B. Gould | 2·98 | 3·87 | 7·72 | 14·57 |

*Notes*

* denotes challenge to incumbent.
Electoral college gives trade unions 40 per cent, CLPs 30 per cent and the PLP 30 per cent.

rested with the Parliamentary leadership. 'No major Parliamentary party in the modern period', he argued, 'has allowed itself to be
relegated to the role of spokesman or servant of its mass organisation.'[29]

The validity of both of these two diametrically opposed positions can be questioned. The constitutional emphasis on the
sovereignty of the extra-Parliamentary party quite clearly over-
estimates its actual influence. The Parliamentary leadership consists of full-time, experienced politicians permanently engaged in
defining party policy on the national stage and reacting to day-to-
day events. In such circumstances, and particularly when Labour
is in government, it is impossible to refer every decision to conference or the NEC and, more often than not, these bodies can
only pass retrospective judgements on the Parliamentary leaders,
who are, of course, skilled in the art of defending the decisions
they have made through the media or to the party directly.

Labour leaders, in any case, have usually been able to 'manage'
the party in such a way that it follows their broad preferences. In
the past, the leadership has had to secure the agreement of only a
small number of unions with large block votes to ensure victory at
conference and ensure the election of a supportive NEC. This
was graphically illustrated at the 1989 conference when Kinnock
was able to muster enough support from trade union delegations
to secure the abandonment of unilateralism against the wishes of
many CLPs and the TGWU delegation led by Ron Todd. Such
'management' of conference votes is far from new. Indeed,
throughout the period 1949–60, conference voted against the
platform on only one occasion, as the triumvirate of moderate
trade union leaders, Williamson (general and municipal workers),
Lawther (mineworkers) and Deakin (transport workers) delivered
their block votes into the leader's hands time after time.[30] Finally,
it should also be remembered that, as we commented in the last
chapter, there are times when the unions desperately need a
Labour Government to legislate in their interests and this gives
the Parliamentary leadership the opportunity to demand, in
return, a large degree of independence to pursue their electoral
strategy. In these circumstances, too, loyalty and discipline can be

invoked (as it was by Kinnock) since any internal party conflict will hinder the achievement of success at the polls.

If conference or NEC decisions are made which are contrary to the wishes of the leadership there is the option of ignoring or diluting them. Labour leaders have traditionally denied they are the mere spokesmen of the party in the country. As early as 1907, for instance, Keir Hardie, Labour's first Parliamentary leader, refused to take instructions from conference over the women's suffrage question.[31] Clement Attlee, too, despite writing in 1937 that the PLP must carry out the instructions of conference, reneged on this in 1945 when he refused to accept the NEC's claim that Labour would not be bound by foreign policy commitments he had made whilst deputy leader of the wartime Coalition Government.[32] Hugh Gaitskell, similarly, reacted to the conversion of the 1960 conference to unilateral nuclear disarmament by remarking that 'What sort of people do you think we [the PLP] are? Do you think we can simply accept a decision of this kind?'[33]

It was during the period of Harold Wilson's leadership, however, that the rejection of conference decisions became a regular occurrence. As Lewis Minkin points out: 'Rarely in modern times can a parliamentary leadership have appeared so impervious to the policy preferences of its extra-parliamentary supporters.'[34] There are numerous examples. In 1968, for instance, the Government ignored a conference vote of five to one against its prices and incomes policy; in 1975, the Government supported Britain remaining in the EEC despite conference's opposition (a referendum was held on the issue because the Cabinet was split, but official Government policy was in favour of staying in); in 1978, the conference voted against the Government's economic strategy by 3.6 million to 2.8 million.[35] Wilson, of course, was not chosen by the electoral college system, the aim of which was to make a future Labour Prime Minister more accountable to the party outside Parliament. But, ironically, it can be argued that in some ways the electoral college system actually makes Labour leaders more secure. In the first place, Labour leaders now have greater authority since they are elected by all sections of the party and not just MPs. Furthermore, the process of challenging the leader is cumbersome and prevents Labour MPs from quickly deposing a leader, a possibility which exists within the Conservative Party (see Chapter 5).

Finally here, the leader has enormous influence over what goes in the party manifesto. By convention, the NEC and the Shadow Cabinet decide which parts of the party's programme approved at conference should be included. In practice, the leader holds all the aces. Callaghan illustrated this in 1979 when he apparently threatened to resign if what he regarded as unacceptable proposals – such as the abolition of the House of Lords – were included. As a result, the Prime Minister was able to veto 'the most extreme of the NEC's proposals as contained in the *Labour's Programme 1976* document' and fudge 'phraseology dealing with their more moderate proposals'.[36] Even in 1987, with a leader who had been elected by the whole party, the manifesto was a pale reflection of the policies carried by conference. On defence, for instance, although unilateralism remained there was no recognition of conference's desire to cut spending on conventional defence.

Does all of this mean, then, that the extra-Parliamentary party has little or no influence? Was, in other words, McKenzie right? The answer must be no. In the first place, no leader can ignore conference. Its proceedings are extensively publicised in the media and, if its decisions are regularly contrary to the wishes of the leadership, this can only damage the party's electoral prospects, as well as the leader's personal position. Thus, the important feature of Gaitskell's denuciation of unilateralism in 1960 was not that he threatened to ignore it but that he went back a year later and got the decision reversed.[37] Similarly, it would have been inconceivable for Kinnock to have abandoned unilateralism in 1989 without the backing of conference. To have done so would have made his position untenable.

In addition, it is worth mentioning that, unlike their Conservative counterpart's relationship with their extra-Parliamentary party, the PLP does not have a privileged position at conference or on the NEC – where, although the leader and deputy leader are automatically members, there is no PLP section as such. Conference has traditionally been marked by the lack of deference shown to the party's Parliamentarians, symbolised by the reservation of the platform for NEC, rather than PLP, members – the latter do not even have a right to vote unless they are acting as delegates of affiliated organisations. Traditionally, even a senior member of the Shadow Cabinet or – if Labour is in office – the Cabinet itself was not entitled to sit on the platform or make a keynote speech unless he or she is also a member of the NEC – although, as an example of Kinnock's dominance over the party, Shadow Cabinet members were permitted to speak from the platform during conferences in the run-up to the 1992 election. This deference is unusual in Labour Party politics. Thus, to give the classic example of the traditional lack of deference, Denis Healey, Chancellor in the Wilson and Callaghan Governments between 1974 and 1979, was given the floor for five minutes at the 1976 conference, as any other ordinary delegate would be, to explain and defend, amongst much heckling, the Government's acceptance of a loan from the International Monetary Fund.[38]

As we intimated, the conference has been effectively 'managed' by the leadership in the past. But the very fact that it requires 'managing' demonstrates that it has some importance and if the leadership loses control it can spell trouble. This became patently obvious in the period between the late 1960s and the early 1980s when the traditional consensus between the Parliamentary leadership and the major union delegations broke down. This resulted, as we saw, in a growing divergence between what conference voted for and what Labour Governments were doing. After Labour's defeat in the 1979 election, the conflict engendered by this dichotomy exploded as the conference demanded that future Labour leaders be made more accountable to the extra-Parliamentary party. The consequence was that conference accepted, in 1980, the electoral college system for choosing the leader and mandatory reselection of MPs. The third proposal on the agenda, that the NEC have the final say in the drawing-up of the manifesto, was narrowly rejected.

The adoption of the reforms was the culmination of nearly a decade of campaigning by various left-wing groups. A small group of Labour activists, provoked by Wilson's rejection of the left-wing programme approved by conference in 1973, formed the *Campaign for Labour Party Democracy* (CLPD), which, initially, worked virtually alone to promote change.[39] Its campaign was expertly organised. By circulating 'model resolutions' on mandatory reselection to CLPs and unions it was able to co-ordinate effectively the left's conference challenge. In addition, although in favour of a left-wing programme of policies, it was able to achieve a broad base of support by focusing exclusively on the case for greater intra-party democracy without reference to policies which may have alienated it from many.[40] The movement for constitutional change was strongly associated with Tony Benn. Benn, however, played little part in the early part of the campaign only joining once Labour had been defeated in 1979. By this time, the CLPD had garnered significant support from other left-wing groups, CLPs and union branches. In May 1980 it joined together with various other left-wing groups, including Militant and the *Labour Co-ordinating Committee*, to form the *Rank and File Mobilising Committee*.[41]

It was clear why the left should want to impose controls on a right-wing leadership. But they had no chance of success unless they could persuade enough unions to use their block votes to back the proposals. They managed to achieve this for a variety of reasons. First, from the late 1960s onwards, a number of major unions began to move to the left. This was obviously crucial since the leadership's success in 'managing' conference had been based upon the support of key right-wing union leaders. Increasingly bereft of this support, the Parliamentary leadership was in trouble. The move left began as early as 1956 when Frank Cousins replaced Arthur Deakin as General Secretary of the TGWU, a vital factor in the union's 'conversion' to unilateralism at the 1960 conference. The extensive drift to the left did not really begin, however, until the middle-to-late 1960s. With the election of Hugh Scanlon as President of the Engineers in 1967 and Lawrence Daly as General Secretary of the NUM in 1968, the Parliamentary leadership had lost their key conference allies. Although in the 1970s some unions remained loyal and some (such as the

Engineers who moved back to the right with the election of Terry Duffy as President in 1978) had shifting alliances, the party's leadership could no longer rely on enough solid support to get their way consistently. They were not helped by changes in employment patterns which increased the block votes of traditionally left-led unions such as NUPE and the Association of Scientific, Technical and Managerial Staffs.[42] The consequence of this was that increasingly left-wing proposals were carried by conference.

The leftward move, though, is only a partial explanation for the trade union disenchantment with the Parliamentary leadership which led to support for the constitutional changes. Even many moderate union leaders were disturbed about the way in which the Labour Governments of Wilson and Callaghan had interfered in industrial relations. They remembered the 1969 White Paper *In Place of Strife* – introduced by the Wilson Government to limit union powers – and the centrality of pay restraint to the economic strategy of Labour Governments in the 1960s and 1970s (Frank Cousins, Minister of Technology in Wilson's Government resigned in 1966 to lead the union opposition to the Government's prices and incomes policy). There was initial agreement and, for some (such as Jack Jones the leader of the TGWU), enthusiasm about the social contract, whereby unions moderated pay claims in return for the Government's maintenance of a range of social benefits.[43] By 1978, however, most unions regarded the imposition of a rigid 5 per cent ceiling on wages coupled with cuts in public spending as unacceptable.[44] Finally, it should be remembered that some unions were still willing to side with the leadership in the debates on constitutional reform fearing the increase in power for the left that was likely to accrue. Indeed, there was a good deal of good fortune associated with the campaign for party reform. At the special conference in 1981 the choice was between the eventual vote distribution of 40 per cent, 30 per cent, 30 per cent and the leadership's favoured option giving the PLP 50 per cent and the unions and CLPs 25 per cent each. This option, giving the PLP considerably more influence, failed only because the AUEW, adopting a principled position, abstained rather than vote for a proposal which failed to give the PLP a majority of the vote.[45]

Changes to the ideological balance within trade unions also inevitably affected the composition of the NEC, which moved gradually leftward during the 1970s. As a result, the social democratic leadership was isolated further. The left's control of the NEC meant that it was able to develop its policies within NEC sub-committees (Benn being chairman of the influential Home Policy Committee at this time) and put them before conference from the platform, thus giving the policies an air of authority which they had not had when tabled, often by CLPs, from the floor of the conference. The left's control of the NEC also meant that the Parliamentary leadership was no longer able to use procedural mechanisms to prevent issues being debated.

Finally, the way in which the party outside Parliament was managed by the NEC changed fundamentally in the 1970s. From the 1930s to the 1960s, in what Shaw describes as a period of 'social-democratic centralism', the party's rank and file was rigorously controlled from the centre and its authority to exercise this control was largely recognised by Labour activists.[46] In the 1970s, however, this authority structure broke down. A much more liberal regime was introduced – symbolised by the abolition, in 1973, of the Proscribed List of ideologically incompatible organisations (resulting in the Militant 'problem' in the 1980s) and the unwillingness of the NEC to intervene to 'save' right-wing Labour MPs who had been deselected by their CLPs. Furthermore, Labour activists were much less willing to accept the edicts of the centre. This was partly because the new breed of middle-class activists was not as deferential as the party's working-class membership. Equally important was that the previous loyalty of the rank and file had been based upon an acceptance of majority decisions taken at conference but when conference decisions were blatantly ignored by the Wilson and Callaghan Governments, the legitimacy of direction from the centre took a severe mauling.[47]

By the end of the 1970s, then, the 'élite consensus' amongst the PLP, NEC and major trade unions that had been a feature of

Labour Party politics in the social democrat centralist era had crumbled and the ensuing conflict centred on the attempts to restrict constitutionally the autonomy of the Parliamentary leadership. It is important to understand the significance of this for the debate about the location of power in the Labour Party. The assertion of conference authority after 1979 did not so much shift the balance of power in the party away from the PLP leadership as confirm the power that the conference or, to be more accurate, the biggest unions already possessed. It was not necessary to exercise that power previously because of the essential agreement between leading unions and the Parliamentary leadership, both of whom were committed to the social democrat consensus. But, as Minkin has pointed out, this 'bond of mutual confidence was a contingent and not an endemic feature of the pattern of power within the Party'.[48] Thus, whilst conference has never been sovereign in the sense that it can dictate to Labour Parliamentarians, its constituent elements, particularly the trade unions, have always had more power than McKenzie realised.

## Kinnock's organisational legacy

The election of Neil Kinnock as leader, after Labour's election defeat in 1983, precipitated another era of organisational change. There were two facets to the Kinnock strategy. In the first place, under his leadership, central authority was restored – seen in the Militant 'purge' and the greater interventionism in the affairs of CLPs.[49] As we pointed out above, this came about primarily because the leader was able to rely on a new generation of moderate trade union leaders. In addition, the left's aspirations were severely dented by the disastrous defeat in 1983 and the need for the party to recover its electoral standing.

Secondly, and rather paradoxically, Kinnock used the leader's greater authority within the party to initiate a series of reforms to widen the involvement of ordinary members in the party's affairs. These changes have interesting implications for the distribution of power in the Labour Party. We have suggested that, whilst it would be an exaggeration to describe Labour's extra-Parlia-

187

mentary organisation as sovereign, McKenzie's thesis under-estimates its influence. This is not to say, however, that the party's organisation is much more *democratic* than McKenzie led us to believe. Indeed, as McKenzie well understood, power in the party has traditionally rested with small élite groups in Parliament, the trade unions and the CLPs. This is far removed from the intra-party democracy envisaged in Labour's Constitution.[50]

Despite the fact that their political levy keeps the party financially afloat, the views of ordinary trade union members are not represented adequately in decisions made at Labour con-ferences or in the election of the party leader. Unions, as we saw, often fail to affiliate for their full entitlement of votes, and minority views are not represented in the block votes cast by either unions or CLPs. More seriously, unions are not obliged to consult their members anyway. A 'bewildering and generally unrepresentative range of methods' are used to decide how a delegation will cast its vote. Some are mandated by their own conferences, some by their executives, and some take decisions immediately before or during the conference itself.[51] It would be wrong to suggest, therefore, that no consultation takes place and that union delegations are immune from grass roots pressure but it is common for union leaders to play a decisive role. The TGWU delegation, for instance, supported Benn in the second ballot in the deputy leadership election in 1981 despite the fact that a survey of members' views revealed support for Healey.[52]

In the CLPs, too, small cliques on General Committees have tended to take the most important decisions – on candidate selection and reselection, NEC elections and conference votes. In the past, ordinary individual members who were not particularly active in their local parties were not consulted, and neither were affiliated members in local union branches. This enabled union activists to use the influence provided by their branches' vote on the General Committee to get their own views adopted.

Of course, this lack of democracy in the trade unions and the CLPs suited the left. As trade union leaders moved to the left in the 1960s and 1970s, the block vote was, as we have seen, increas-ingly used to back left-wing policies. Similarly, those extremely active in CLPs tend to be more left-wing than ordinary party members and the more liberal regime of the left-controlled NEC gave them much greater autonomy.

It is in this context that the left's support for the electoral college and mandatory reselection should be seen. When the former was used for the first time in 1981, no less than 83 per cent of the CLPs voted for Benn compared to 28 per cent of his Parliamentary colleagues.[53] The introduction of the latter offered the prospect of an increasingly left-wing PLP. True, between 1981 and 1983 the relatively small number of eight, mainly right-wing, Labour MPs were deselected and there were fewer in the 1983–87 Parliament but these figures do not give the full picture of the reform's impact. Many of the twenty-eight Labour MPs who defected to the SDP faced deselection as did a number who chose retirement rather than going through with the procedure. A survey at the end of 1981 of twenty-five Labour MPs who had announced their intention of standing down at the next election showed that seventeen had voted for Healey in the deputy leadership election and that all twenty-five were replaced by candidates further to the left.[54] Finally, some Labour MPs no doubt took more notice of the opinions of their local parties and modified their behaviour in order to avoid deselection.[55] It was not just the left who tended to pay lip-service to intra-party democracy. The 'Gang of Three', who left the Labour Party to set up the SDP after the Wembley conference in January 1981, were highly critical of the influence given to the unions in the electoral college but they were not quite so vocal when the votes of the leading union leaders protected the PLP against the more left-wing demands of the CLPs.

Under Kinnock's leadership, as we have seen, there were moves to eradicate some of the more undemocratic aspects of the party outside Parliament and these will continue now that Kinnock has been replaced by John Smith. Clearly, the rationale behind the changes are electoral and ideological (as are the moves to establish a greater role for women on party bodies and in Parliament since the principle of greater sexual equality coincides with the so-called 'gender gap' in voting behaviour whereby

Labour is more popular amongst men than women). Just as the left sought to promote their viewpoint through constitutional change, the aim of the reforms initiated by Kinnock has been to give more influence to the ordinary, more moderate, members of the party. In this sense, the formula (agreed at the 1990 conference) for any further reduction in the union vote is extremely astute, since it depends upon any further increase in party membership and therefore minimises the possibility of a left-wing activist element dominating conference in the future. Even this has now probably been taken over by events. Labour's electoral defeat in 1992, and the contribution made to it by the party's links with the unions and old-style collectivism, mean that the block vote may not survive in any form.

Graphic illustrations of the moderating strategy have occurred in the decisions of CLPs. In 1989, for instance, John Hughes – the left-wing Labour MP for Coventry North-East – was deselected. For the first time, under the electoral college system, individual members were entitled to a vote in a secret ballot and the sitting left-wing MP (a member of the Campaign Group) won only eighty-seven out of the 283 votes they cast. Similarly, it is significant that the CLPs' obligation to ballot individual members before casting a vote in the NEC elections coincided, in 1991, with the election of Gerald Kaufman, the first right-winger to be elected to the constituency section of the NEC for sixteen years.[56] Finally, it is also revealing that John Smith (the centre-right candidate) won as much as 90 per cent of the CLP vote in the 1992 leadership election – a figure which was surely boosted by the participation of ordinary members.

Any attempt to remove the influence of trade union delegations at conference, though, will make it more difficult for the leadership to 'manage' conference in the event of any future conflict with party members and so, to some extent, it is a risky strategy. No doubt it is for this reason that the leadership has also proposed to alter the way in which policy is made. At the 1990 conference, the idea of a National Policy Forum was approved.[57] This reform has its origins in the success of the policy review undertaken between 1987 and 1989 and the increasing dissatisfaction with conference as a policy-maker.[58] The policy review enabled NEC and Shadow Cabinet members to consider policy in detail thus providing for much needed, and previously often absent, co-operation betwen the Parliamentary and extra-Parliamentary wings of the party. In addition, the groups were able to take on board the views of affiliated organisations and CLPs *before* presenting their proposals to conference.[59]

The proposal is that the new National Policy Forum, consisting of 194 members elected from all sections of the party, would split up into seven policy commissions, based on the policy review groups, who would draw up policy on different subject areas. Motions from trade unions and CLPs would then be sent to a commission rather than to the conference. If rejected by a commission, a motion would then be voted upon at conference if the proposers so wished. The commissions would work on a two-year cycle, producing reports on half of their subject area each year. These reports would then be considered by the NEC and then put before conference which, unlike previously, would not have to attempt the impossible task of adequately dealing with every item of policy each year. Whereas before, policy required a two-thirds endorsement from conference to be included in the party's programme, the commission reports would have to win majority support from both the trade union and constituency sections.[60]

The creation of these policy commissions should benefit the leadership. As with the policy review, members of the Shadow Cabinet would be heavily involved in policy-making (they would be *ex officio* members of the Policy Forum). In addition, the new policy-making rules would prevent affiliated bodies from being able to submit resolutions on areas of policy that are being considered by a commission as part of the two-yearly policy cycle. Delegates, though, would have the advantage of being able to amend the reports of the commissions (which they are not at present able to do with NEC policy statements) and would be able to consider these reports in advance of the conference.[61]

In conclusion, it will have become apparent that Labour's organisation is extremely complex and locating where power lies in the party is no easy task, particularly given the state of flux that has existed in recent years. Arguments about intra-party democracy are inextricably interwoven with ideological positions and electoral strategies as different groups seek to impose their version of Labour's 'true purpose'. The fourth consecutive election defeat in 1992 has intensified the debate about organisational change and at the end of the process it seems likely that a very different Labour Party structure will emerge, different not just from the one that was drawn up in 1918 but also from the one presided over by Wilson and Callaghan in the 1970s.

### Notes

1   H. Pelling, *Origins of the Labour Party*, Oxford, 1964, chapter ten.
2   E. Shaw, *Discipline and Discord*, Manchester, 1988, pp. 1–2.
3   *Labour Party News*, March–April 1989, pp. 20–1.
4   P. Seyd, *Rise & Fall*, Basingstoke, 1987, pp. 40–1.
5   *Independent*, 12 September 1989.
6   *Guardian*, 5 September 1990; 5 May 1992.
7   Jenkins quoted in Shaw, *Discipline and Discord*, p. 361. For the decline of working-class involvement see P. Whiteley, *The Labour Party in Crisis*, London, 1983, pp. 53–80 and B. Hindess, *The Decline of Working Class Politics*, London, 1971.
8   P. Seyd & P. Whiteley, *Labour's Grass Roots*, Oxford, 1992.
9   See M. Crick, *Militant*, London, 1984.
10  Shaw, *Discipline and Discord*, p. 248
11  P. Seyd, 'Why the red rose must tend its grassroots and branches', *Guardian*, 16 June 1992.
12  A. Geddes, J. Lovenduski & P. Norris, 'Candidate selection', *Contemporary Record*, 4 April 1991, p. 20.
13  *Guardian*, 13 August 1992.
14  *Guardian*, 27 July 1991; Sunday Times, 12 July 1992
15  R. Kelly & S. Foster, 'Power in the Labour party', *Politics Review*, September, 1991, p. 29; *Guardian*, 17 May 1989.
16  Ball, *British Political Parties*, p. 207; Shaw, *Discipline and Discord*, chapter nine.
17  Kelly & Foster, 'Power in the Labour party', p. 29.
18  C. Crouch, 'The peculiar relationship: the party and the unions', in D. Kavanagh (ed.), *The Politics of the Labour Party*, London, 1982, pp. 176–7.
19  *Guardian*, 26 April 1990.
20  L. Minkin, *Contentious Alliance*, Edinburgh, 1992.

# The Labour Party: organisation

21  See *Guardian*, 24 June 1992; 13 August 1992.
22  Shaw, *Discipline and Discord*, pp. 218–90.
23  Shaw, *Discipline and Discord*, pp. 280–5.
24  P. Mandelson, 'Marketing Labour', *Contemporary Record*, 4, winter 1988, pp. 11–13; see also C. Hughes & P. Wintour, *Labour Rebuilt*, London, 1990 for a fascinating account of the transformation of the Labour Party under Kinnock's leadership.
25  See *Guardian*, 7 June 1991.
26  Seyd, *Rise & Fall*, pp. 77–83.
27  Seyd, *Rise & Fall*, pp. 163–70.
28  Kelly & Foster, 'Power in the Labour party', p. 27.
29  R. T. McKenzie, *Political Parties*, London, 1955.
30  L. Minkin, *Labour Conference*, Manchester, 1978, p. 321.
31  I. McLean, 'Party organisation' in C. Cook & I. Taylor (eds.), *The Labour Party*, London, 1980, p. 44.
32  H. Pelling, *A Short History of the Labour Party*, London, 1965.
33  Minkin, *Labour Conference*, p. vii.
34  Minkin, *Labour Conference*, p. 316.
35  Minkin, *Labour Conference*, p. 359.
36  S. E. Finer, 'The organisation of the Labour and Conservative parties' in M. Burch *et al.* (eds), *Three Political Systems*, Manchester, 1985, p. 45.
37  See Minkin, *Labour Conference*, pp. 278–89.
38  P. Whitehead, *Writing on the Wall*, London, 1985, pp. 189–90.
39  M. & D. Kogan, *The Battle for the Labour Party*, London, 1982, pp. 23–4.
40  Kogan, *Battle for the Labour Party*, pp. 27–9.
41  Seyd, *Rise & Fall*, p. 115.
42  Crouch, 'Peculiar relationship', p. 180; Minkin, *Labour Conference*, p. 322; p. 343.
43  A. Fenley, 'Labour and the trade unions', in Cook & Taylor, *Labour Party*, pp. 75–8.
44  Crouch, 'Peculiar relationship', pp. 81–2. See also Kogan, *Battle for the Labour Party*, pp. 54–5.
45  Seyd, *Rise & Fall*, pp. 320–1.
46  Shaw, *Discipline and Discord*, pp. 26–152.
47  Shaw, *Discipline and Discord*, pp. 153–253.
48  Minkin, *Labour Conference*, p. 321.
49  See Shaw, *Discipline and Discord*, pp. 254–83.
50  McKenzie, *Political Parties*, pp. 485–516. It should also be noted that McKenzie regarded intra-party democracy itself as undesirable since, in his view, it is incompatible with Parliamentary democracy. See R. McKenzie, 'Power in the Labour party: the issue of "intra-party democracy" ', in Kavanagh, *Politics of the Labour Party*, pp. 191–201.

51  Kogan, *Battle for the Labour Party*, p. 79.
52  Seyd, *Rise & Fall*, p. 135.
53  Kogan, *Battle for the Labour Party*, p. 146.
54  Kogan, *Battle for the Labour Party*, p. 150.
55  Seyd, *Rise & Fall*, pp. 129–33.
56  *Guardian*, 1 October 1991.
57  *Democracy and Policy Making for the 1990s*, Statement by the National Executive Committee of the Labour Party, London, 1990. One of the main proponents of this reform was Tom Sawyer, deputy General Secretary of NUPE and chairman of the NEC's Home Policy Committee. Sawyer proposed the creation of the policy review initially. See his 'After the policy review', *Labour Party News*, July–August 1989, p. 7.
58  See E. Shaw, 'A better way to make policy', *New Socialist*, December 1989–January 1990, pp. 30–3.
59  R. Garner, 'Modernisation and the policy review: the Labour Party since the 1987 election', *Talking Politics*, 3, 1989.
60  P. Wintour, 'On the way to a Labour party forum', *Guardian*, 26 April 1990.
61  Wintour, 'Labour party forum'.

# 8

# THE CENTRE OF BRITISH PARTY POLITICS

Prior to 1981, an examination of the centre ground of British party politics would have been concerned exclusively with the Liberal Party. Outflanked by Labour early in the present century, the last Liberal Government folded in 1915 and the last Liberal Prime Minister (David Lloyd George), heading a Conservative-dominated coalition government, left office in 1922. Between 1945 and 1981, despite hanging on to life tenaciously and, indeed, threatening a major revival at times, the party was very much on the periphery of British politics. This seems reason enough for providing a more limited treatment of the centre than that proferred for both Labour and the Conservatives in this book. Such a treatment, however – relatively truncated though it may be – is important.

In the first place, an analysis of the realignment of the party system involving the replacement of the Liberals by Labour tells us a great deal about twentieth-century British politics. Secondly, the Liberal Party – during both its heyday and its period of decline – pioneered many of the ideas that later became part of the British political mainstream. Furthermore, the Liberal revival in the 1970s, boosted by the creation of their Alliance with the newly formed Social Democratic Party in 1981, seemed, for a while at least, to have broken the back of the two-party system, with Labour's future as a major party looking decidely shaky in the early 1980s. The fact that the two-party system has survived this onslaught should not disguise the fact that the challenge of the centre parties has left its mark, not least on the Labour Party. In addition, a political force which has been able to attract, for nearly twenty years, an average of six million votes (20 per cent of those who voted) at general elections, and whose failure to become a party of government can be put down to the workings of a grossly unfair electoral system, deserves not to be neglected.

## Liberalism, social democracy and British party politics

The social democratic split from the Labour party and the brighter prospects for the centre in the 1970s and 1980s can be fully explained only by examining the Liberal Party's decline and Labour's rise in the early part of this century. Thus, to begin with, a historical approach needs to be adopted.

### *Classical liberalism*

The Liberal party emerged from a meeting of Peelites, Whigs and Radicals on 6 June 1859[1] and, from 1868 (with the election of Gladstone's first Government) until the outbreak of war in 1914, alternated in power with the Conservatives. Although always a coalition of diverse interests – representing such causes as Irish Home Rule, free trade, nonconformity and temperance – the party was, above all, the vehicle of the new middle class of manufacturers and merchants created by the Industrial Revolution. In addition, although – as Chapter 4 has shown – this was disputed by the Conservatives (and later by Labour), the party also regarded itself as the natural home of the industrial working class.

Not surprisingly, given that the wealth and power of the new industrial middle class rested upon it, the party's ideology (described variously as Gladstonian, Manchester, Economic, Victorian or Classical Liberalism) was based around a belief in the efficacy of *laissez faire*. The state's role should be limited to the creation and maintenance of the free market both internally and between nations. Thus, interference by the state to, for example, alleviate poverty should be minimal since this would hinder the process of wealth creation by diverting resources required for investment. By allowing the unfettered play of market forces, the greater prosperity generated would benefit the working class in terms of higher wages for those in work and more employment for those idle.[2] This economic analysis was reinforced by an individualistic philosophy. Individuals were responsible for their own actions and those who did not benefit from the new industrial age had only themselves to blame. The poverty and squalor in Britain's cities was blamed particularly on the corrupting influence of drink which prevented men (and women) from seeking work and wasted already limited resources. Thus, the temperance movement, an important group within the Liberal Party, made great efforts to 'liberate' the poor from the clutches of 'evil' (mainly Conservative-supporting) landlords.[3] Self-help and thrift, therefore, were the answers to urban deprivation, not a change in the state's role.

The free market was not only the most economically efficient method of production, it also promoted individual liberty, a central tenet of liberalism. The seminal work here was J. S. Mill's *On Liberty*, published in 1859. Mill, in what is still regarded as a central text by Liberals today, provides the classic case for individual freedom. 'The sole end', he argues:

for which mankind are warranted, individually or collectively, in interfering with the liberty of action of any of their number, is self protection. That the only purpose for which power can be rightfully exercised over any member of a civilised community, against his will, is to prevent harm to others.[4]

Thus, the state or society has no right to intervene in what Mill describes as 'self-regarding' actions. Liberty, for Mill, was crucial because it promoted individual self-development. Only if individuals were allowed to find their own way in the world would they become intelligent, self-motivated people able to participate fully in the political and economic life of the community.

### *The New Liberalism*

The roots of the Alliance between the Liberals and the Social Democrats can be traced back to the crisis which enveloped Classical Liberalism towards the end of the nineteenth century. This ideological crisis was the consequence of a variety of factors.

The extent of the poverty and degradation in late Victorian Britain became much more visible as a result of major social surveys by philanthropists such as Booth and Rowntree and it became apparent that much of it was beyond the control of the victims.[5] This was symbolised by the realisation of many opinion formers that unemployment and poverty were not so much the *effect* of excessive drinking but its *cause*. Of course, it was recognised that, for some, personal failure was the key factor but it became widely recognised (not least by many associated with the Liberal Party) that something had to be done for the so-called 'deserving poor' and that public authorities (initially local authorities, but increasingly by central intervention) would be the major agencies. Social compassion was only part of the reason for this change of attitude. There was also a general feeling that Britain could not compete industrially or militarily if many of its population were unhealthy and unfit. This was driven home in stark fashion by the Boer War (1898–1902) when many of those who attempted to enlist for military service were found to be in poor physical condition. Finally, there was a fear of serious social unrest if something was not done to help the plight of the dispossessed. The period from 1880 to 1900 saw the revival of trade union militancy, and organisations such as the Fabian Society and the ILP were created to promote the doctrine of socialism, which emerged as a serious rival to the prevailing liberalism.

The factors described above led to the reformulation of Classical Liberalism. The 'New' or 'Social' Liberalism that resulted derived in particular from the work of intellectuals such as J. A. Hobson and L. T. Hobhouse who were themselves influenced by the Oxford philosopher T. H. Green.[6] They emphasised that individual self-development through the exercise of freedom was the goal of liberalism but that it was necessary for the state to intervene in order to create the conditions for individual self-development. Thus, state action was justified as a mechanism whereby freedom could be enhanced. This reformulation, then, recognised that the conditions of life for many were such that the freedom they 'enjoyed' was a legal entity with no foundation in reality. For the New Liberals, therefore, the two concepts – liberty and equality – were not, as in Classical Liberalism, totally incompatible since, as Hobhouse pointed out, 'the manifest teaching of experience' told that 'liberty without equality is a name of noble sound and squalid result'.[7] P. F. Clarke sums up the significance of the New Liberalism in the following way:

it meant the end of laissez-faire. The death of the old individualism was pronounced – whatever good it might have done in the nineteenth century. The market was now exposed as neither fair nor expedient in its workings; and in particular the entitlement of the poor to the state's active assistance was explicitly claimed.[8]

This ideology, of course, was to provide the basis for what we have described in earlier chapters as the social democratic consensus which dominated British politics for much of the period after the Second World War. Social democracy – as we pointed out in Chapter 6 – had a Marxist connotation in the nineteenth century, however, and (although after the Russian Revolution in 1917 it began to be used to describe those socialists who sought change through existing democratic institutions)[9] the term did not become widely used, at least in Britain, until after 1945. Prior to that, though, Hobhouse, in particular, had claimed the term for the New Liberals. The old Liberalism had achieved political democracy, he argued, which had 'paved the way for what, if the term were not limited to a rather narrow theory, we might call a social democracy' which was the aim of the New Liberals.[10]

It is important to recognise that there was a good deal of ideological compatibility between this reformulated Liberalism and the newly formed Labour Party. As we pointed out in Chapter 6, it would be correct to describe many leading Labour Party socialists as social democrats and there was a good deal of personal contact between them and the exponents of the New Liberalism. MacDonald, for instance, was involved in the *Rainbow Circle*, a society set up in 1893 to propagate the ideas of the New Liberalism whilst many Liberals were pre-war members of the Fabian Society. The pre-war electoral pact (negotiated by Herbert Gladstone, the Liberal Chief Whip, and Ramsay MacDonald, the Secretary of the LRC, in 1903) symbolised the common ground between the parties. The aim of many Liberals was to create a Progressive Alliance whereby the Liberals headed a coalition of the centre-left, absorbing the interests of the trade unions within its ranks.[11] The success of such a strategy was vital for the long term prospects of the Liberals and as long as the Labour Party remained merely a trade union pressure group in Parliament, and the Liberal Party in general was prepared to accept its new role as the leader of radical social reform in Britain, thus attracting working-class votes, it stood a chance of surviving as a major party of government.

## The downfall of the Liberal Party

It is not clear how far the ideas of the New Liberals permeated the Liberal Party in the early part of the twentieth century nor how far the party's electoral performance up to 1914 was based upon an attraction to these ideas. Such questions are inextricably bound up with the historical debate about the decline of the Liberal Party. The speed of this decline has long fascinated historians and the reasons for it have a great bearing on the character of twentieth-century British politics. In the 1906 election, the Liberals were returned with 400 seats, nearly 50 per cent of the votes cast and a majority of 130 over all the other parties combined. Even in the two elections held in 1910, the party, although deprived of an overall majority in the Commons, was still polling well over 40 per cent of the vote. By contrast, the Labour Party before 1914 made little progress at the Parliamentary level increasing their thirty seats gained in 1906 to only forty-two in December 1910. After the 1924 election, however, this pattern had been reversed. Labour was now the major opposition party with 151 seats and over five million votes whilst the Liberals were reduced to a rump of forty seats and about 18 per cent of the vote.

This dramatic decline has been the subject of a concerted debate amongst historians.[12] All agree that politics in Britain at the beginning of this century was becoming increasingly dominated by a cleavage based upon social class and that the Liberal Party's chances of surviving depended upon adapting to this new environment. The extent to which they were able to do so is a matter of dispute. P. F. Clarke, for instance, in his study of liberalism in Lancashire, suggests that the Liberals had adapted to the new class-based society by promoting a radical programme of social reform, based on the ideas of the New Liberals, which was proving attractive to working-class voters.[13]

Clarke places a great deal of importance on the performance of the Liberal Government elected in 1906. The landslide victory achieved by the party in the 1906 election had more to do with traditional Liberal causes than a campaign for social reform. Nevertheless, the reforms carried out by the radical Liberal Governments led by Asquith from 1908 to 1914 (competently aided by Lloyd George and Winston Churchill) – including the introduction of old-age pensions and a national insurance scheme – involved exactly the kind of redistributive state action called for by the New Liberals.[14] For Clarke, then, the Liberal Party was – although not without some serious problems – reasonably healthy before 1914. What finished it off was the First World War which produced severe divisions within the party and the sacrifice of a number of cherished Liberal principles. Continuing with this medical metaphor, Trevor Wilson has argued:

The Liberal party can be compared to an individual who, after a period of robust health and great exertion, experienced symptoms of illness ... Before a thorough diagnosis could be made, he was involved in an encounter with a rampant omnibus (the First World War), which mounted the pavement and ran him over. After lingering painfully, he expired.[15]

Other historians question the strength of the Liberal Party before 1914 and emphasise that the War only hastened a process which was already well under way. They point to the fact that although, superficially, Labour did not appear to be making much progress before 1914, this disguised the underlying strength of the party; in particular, the extent to which trade unions were affiliating to the party (crucially important was the accession of the Miners' Federation in 1909) which symbolised growing class divisions which were always going to benefit Labour.[16] In addition, it is argued that the New Liberalism did not take a firm grip on the Liberal Party at the national or local level. Middle-class

Liberals in constituency parties (with the possible exception of parts of Lancashire which were, in any case, not typical) tended to be hostile to the new creed and to Labour which they saw as a threat to their interests.[17] Finally, the ability of the Liberals to attract working-class support was never really tested before 1914 because of the limited franchise. Labour's electoral success after 1918 was based upon the introduction of universal male suffrage which, had it been introduced earlier, would have spelt trouble for the Liberals.[18]

## The years in the wilderness

Whatever the reason, from the 1920s to the late 1950s, the Liberal Party played an extremely minor role in British politics. After the 1931 election the party split into three distinct factions; the official party (led by Samuel) with thirty-three MPs, the National Liberals (led by Simon) with thirty-five MPs and the four MPs in the Lloyd George faction. This disguises the true extent of the party's malaise since many Liberal candidates faced no opposition from the Conservatives. A better guide is the share of the vote which – at 11 per cent – spelt disaster for the party. The 'Samuelites' and 'Simonites' joined the National Government formed after the election but the former group left after a year. The National Liberals ultimately merged with the Conservative Party.[19] The following twenty-five years saw further declines in the party's fortunes culminating in the abyss of the 1951 election which saw the Liberal share of the vote crumble to 2.5 per cent, large enough to secure the election of only six MPs. At this point the party came close to extinction. Had Clement Davies, the Liberal leader, accepted Winston Churchill's offer of a place in his Cabinet in 1951, the party would probably have formally merged with the Conservatives.[20] As it was, the party soldiered on, achieving a similar poor result in the 1955 election.

The reasons for the insignificance of the Liberal Party during this period have already been explored both earlier in this chapter and elsewhere in this book and therefore do not need much elaboration here. In an era where social class became the key determinant of voting behaviour, a party which had no claims on any particular class was always going to struggle. By the late 1920s, the Liberal Party was reasonably confident of making some kind of comeback. It was united under the leadership of Lloyd George, and had developed a set of radical policies to deal with unemployment, the key political issue of the time. Indeed, the Liberals offered a far more imaginative approach than either of the two major parties. The party published, in 1928, *Britain's Industrial Future*, better known as the *Yellow Book*, which was the result of the Liberal Industrial Enquiry set up in 1925. This was to form the basis of the 1929 manifesto, *We Can Conquer Unemployment*. The proposals 'were firmly placed in the bedrock of Keynesian economics' (Keynes himself being heavily involved in drawing them up)[21] prefiguring much of the economic strategy of the social democratic consensus by advocating a measure of public ownership together with a massive scheme of public works to relieve unemployment. By contrast, the two major parties stuck with the traditional economic policy known as the 'Treasury view' which held that, in the event of depression, governments should maintain a balanced budget, reducing public spending when the income from taxation declined.[22] Despite the radical nature of the Liberal proposals, it was far too late for them to aid a recovery in the party's electoral fortunes. Indeed, arguably, ideology mattered little as compared to the representation of class interests where the Liberals had already been overwhelmed.

Another, related, aspect of the Liberal decline should be mentioned here. The failure to attract support concentrated in certain areas, itself a product of the lack of disproportionate support from a particular class, meant that the Liberals suffered under the rules of the 'first past the post' electoral system. Thus, in the 1924 election, Labour won less than twice as many votes as the Liberals (33.1 per cent to 17.6 per cent) yet won over three times as many seats (151 to forty). Such figures are a familiar feature of British elections and it is hardly surprising that, since 1922, a central plank of Liberal policy programmes has been electoral reform.

Another important factor that contributed to the decline of the

Liberal Party (also explored in more detail elsewhere in this book) was the post-war 'Butskellite' consensus itself. The Liberals were firmly in support of the basic tenets of this consensus: 'as committed as social democracy to the values of community, fraternity and social equality and as determined to use the power of the state to redistribute resources to the disadvantaged'.[23] The problem was that so were the two major parties. As Vernon Bogdanor has pointed out, in 'the era of centrist politics, there was no room for a centre party'.[24] Liberals had played a significant role in the creation of this consensus. It had much in common with the New Liberalism we discussed earlier, which had an important impact on the 1906 Liberal Government. In addition, the Liberals were the first party to advocate, as part of their election programme in 1929, demand management techniques which became commonplace after 1945. Finally, the key architects of the post-war consensus (Keynes and Beveridge) were both Liberals.

It is important to recognise that, in the inter-war years, the similarity between much of what Labour was offering and the political standpoint of the New Liberals was such that many of the latter found it easy to transfer their allegiance to the former.[25] Many remaining Liberals, particularly in the 1920s, recognised the similarities and used them to campaign for a renewal of the pre-war progressive alliance between the two parties. Hobhouse was one who recognised that party was now getting in the way of principle seeing a division between progressives ('true' Liberal and moderate Labour) and conservatives ('old' Liberals and Tories).[26]

Of course, the 'moderate' Labour referred to by Hobhouse consisted of those with what might be called a social democratic outlook. As we saw in Chapter 6, though, Labour also contained a fundamentalist socialist wing whose commitment to public ownership was an article of faith and not, as for the New Liberals, something to be considered case by case. J. A. Hobson summed up the difference between the two doctrines by distinguishing what he called 'practical' socialism from 'theoretic' or 'full' socialism. The former, the employment of collectivism where appropriate, he regarded as consistent with the New Liberalism.

The latter, though, was inappropriate to the New Liberalism since it involved the indiscriminate application of collectivism without reference to its usefulness. Thus, the aim of the practical socialism was:

not to abolish the competitive system, to socialise all instruments of production, distribution and exchange . . . but rather to supply all workers . . . with all the economic conditions requisite to the education and employment of their personal powers for their personal advantage and enjoyment.[27]

In addition, the class based 'labourism' of the trade unions (also described in Chapter 6) sat uneasily with the New Liberal attempt 'to be the party of social reform with a classless base'.[28] Keynes, for instance, remained a Liberal because Labour 'is a class party, and the class is not my class. If I am going to pursue sectional interests at all, I shall pursue my own . . . I can be influenced by what seems to me to be justice and good sense; but the class war will find me on the side of the educated bourgeoisie.'[29] Despite these differences, however, many New Liberals did find their way into the Labour Party in the inter-war years as it became apparent that Labour, and not the Liberals, was the more effective vehicle for the promotion of New Liberal or social democrat ideas. Only when the fundamentalist socialists began to assert themselves did the social democrats begin to question their allegiance to the Labour Party.

## The road to Limehouse

The Limehouse in the title to this section, of course, refers to the area in London of David Owen's residence where, on 25 January 1981, three senior Labour figures (Owen, Shirley Williams and Bill Rodgers) together with a former Labour Cabinet Minister (Roy Jenkins) met to take a key step in the formation of a new Social Democratic party. The resulting *Limehouse Declaration*, which committed them to the formation of the Council for Social Democracy, was followed, on 26 March, by the formal launch of the SDP and, by the autumn, an electoral Alliance with the

Liberals.[30] This was to alter fundamentally the nature of centre party politics in Britain.

### The Liberal revival

This is to get ahead of ourselves. The formation of the SDP, and the greatly improved chances of the centre parties 'breaking the mould' of British politics, were the result of earlier developments which must be considered. In the first place, it is inconceivable that the so-called 'Gang of Four' would have risked forming a new party without some confidence of electoral success. Central to the formation of the SDP, therefore, was the revival of the Liberal Party.

As we saw, the Liberals, by the mid-1950s, were in some disarray. Towards the end of the decade, though, there were signs of a modest recovery. The party, benefiting from Conservative unpopularity, particularly after the Suez fiasco, came close to winning a by-election in Rochdale (February 1958), gained a Conservative seat at Torrington the following month and had made thirty-one net gains in the local elections of the previous year. This improvement was confirmed in the 1959 general election where the party doubled its 1955 share of the vote and fought many more seats.[31] The recovery continued in the 1960s as the Liberals were able to capitalise on Labour divisions and the growing problems of Macmillan's Conservative Government. The party's membership increased from 150,000 in 1959 to 350,000 in 1963, and after Eric Lubbock's sensational by-election victory at Orpington in 1962 (in which a 14,000 Conservative majority was turned into a 9,000 Liberal lead), the Liberals briefly led in the opinion polls. Although, not surprisingly, this level of support was not maintained, the 1964 and 1966 general elections, in which the party polled 11.2 per cent (nine seats) and 8.5 per cent (twelve seats) of the vote respectively, showed that the revival was no flash in the pan.[32]

During the period of Wilson's second Labour Government (1966–70), the Liberal advance was halted and apparently reversed in the 1970 election with the party's share of the vote reduced to 7.5 per cent and the number of seats to six. This was to be the prelude, however, to another major advance during Heath's Conservative Government. Between October 1972 and November 1973, the party won five by-elections, including two (Ripon and the Isle of Ely) on the same day, and in the February 1974 election secured their highest share of the vote (19.3 per cent – fourteen seats) since 1929 and, with other minor parties, deprived either of the two major parties of an overall majority. In retrospect, this was a missed opportunity for the party. As Michael Steed points out, Liberals had avoided discussing what their response would be in the event of a hung Parliament, concentrating instead on the highly optimistic aim of winning an overall majority and were, therefore, totally unprepared for what happened.[33] Jeremy Thorpe, the Liberal leader, took the initiative and accepted Heath's invitation to discuss the situation after the election but was offered only a seat in the Cabinet with no policy commitments attached. The breakdown of these talks, of course, allowed Wilson to form a minority Labour administration.[34] Had the Liberals been united on the strategy to be adopted – for instance, either a national government (Thorpe's favoured option) or a set of agreed policies which would be the basis for negotiation with one of the two major parties – then their chances of participating in government would have been greatly improved. Moreover, even if such negotiations had failed, the party would have been in a much stronger position to fight the October 1974 election since they could have campaigned effectively along the lines that it was the negative attitude of the two major parties which had led to political instability. As it was, the Liberals could not keep the momentum going winning a reduced share of votes (18.3 per cent – thirteen seats) in October.

The period from 1974 to 1979 marked a further decline. The Liberals were severely embarrassed by the Thorpe court case[35] and, even though the party had a sniff of power during the Lib–Lab pact (where the party agreed to maintain Labour in office), precious little was gained in return. David Steel, elected leader in 1976, regarded it as crucial that the Liberals took every opportunity to show they could share in government but the experiment backfired particularly as the party was alienating

Conservative waverers by supporting 'socialism'. In the 1979 election, the party's share of the vote reduced further to 13.8 per cent (eleven seats), still well up on the catastrophic 1950s but seemingly as far away as ever from making the big breakthrough.

The revival of the Liberal Party was the product of a reversal of the factors which had engineered the two-party system in the post-war period. First, as we saw in Chapter 3, the 1970s witnessed the breakdown of the social democratic consensus. Its apparent failure to deliver (both economically and politically) led to the search for alternative solutions and the consequent polarisation of the Labour and Conservative parties. This in turn left an ideological gap in the centre which the Liberals could exploit. Secondly, and relatedly, the decline of class as the key determinant of voting behaviour relaxed the grip the two major parties previously had on their blocks of class support thereby producing a dealigned electorate much more likely to consider voting for a 'classless' party like the Liberals.

Both of these factors were present as early as the late 1950s and formed the basis of Jo Grimond's strategy as Liberal leader. Grimond hoped for a realignment on the left whereby the Liberals would become the major challenger to the Conservatives by absorbing the moderates in the Labour Party. This new radical, but non-socialist, force would take its place in a new two-party system, with a small socialist party relegated to minor party status. As Bogdanor writes, this would have reversed what had happened in the 1920s: 'Instead of Labour, with the aid of left-wing Liberals, replacing the Liberals, the Liberals, with the aid of right-wing Labour, would replace Labour.'[36] This seemed a plausible scenario for a while as the left were beginning to make a challenge to the party's social democratic leadership. In addition, Labour's three successive election defeats in the 1950s seemed to confirm Labour's inability to attract an increasingly prosperous electorate. Thus, in Grimond's view, the old working class, to whom Labour appealed most, would 'disappear with universal education, television, cars and a middle-class wage'.[37] Of course, Grimond's hopes were not fulfilled at the time but in the 1970s and 1980s they were to be reawakened.

## *Labour and the social democrats*

The realignment Grimond had hoped for was to receive a boost in the 1970s with the mounting crisis in the Labour Party. As the decade wore on, the position of the social democrats in the party was becoming increasingly untenable. As we saw in Chapter 6, ideological divisions in the Labour Party had surfaced almost as soon as Attlee's Government lost office in 1951. In the 1950s, the revisionists (or social democrats) and the fundamentalists fought for the right to dictate Labour's future direction. As Peter Clarke remarks: 'In retrospect, the road to Limehouse appears better signposted than anyone noticed at the time.'[38] Indeed, the split could have come earlier. With Gaitskell's failure to persuade his party to remove Clause IV from its Constitution in 1959, and the victory for the unilateralists in 1960, the social democrats (including such familiar names as Brian Walden, Dick Taverne, Denis Howell and William Rodgers) organised around the *Campaign for Democratic Socialism*.[39] By the time Wilson became Prime Minister in 1964, however, the social democrats had regained control and, devoid of purpose for the time being, the CDS was dissolved in 1963.

During the 1970s, though, conference votes began to swing the left's way and the social democrats were again forced to fight their corner. The social democrats organised in several factions operating within the Labour Party. Some Labour councillors formed the *Social Democratic Alliance* in 1975, the social democrats in Parliament created the *Manifesto Group* in 1974 and in 1977 the *Campaign for Labour Victory* was launched to gather support from the party in the country. All of those who were to be prominent in the formation of the SDP (including Williams, Rodgers and Owen) were active in this latter faction.[40]

A crucial, but often neglected, issue in the conflict within the party was Britain's position in Europe. The Labour conference had voted by a large margin in 1975 to end Britain's membership of the European Community, despite the opposition of the social democrats. Wilson, faced by a serious split in his Cabinet, called a referendum to decide the issue. During the campaign, many Labour social democrats for the first time came into contact and worked closely with those of similar views in other parties.[41] It is interesting to note, in addition, that so important was the issue for the social democrats that Dick Taverne (a former Labour MP and founder member of the SDP) has claimed that he, together with Bill Rodgers and Roy Jenkins, seriously considered forming a social democratic party in 1971 during the passage of the European Communities Bill, which Labour MPs were ordered, on a three-line whip, to oppose.[42] The issue of Europe was also the cause of the split between Taverne and his anti-EEC CLP in Lincoln. Taverne's deselection as Labour candidate in 1972 and his subsequent victories as an 'independent social democrat' in the 1972 by-election and February 1974 general election exemplified both the splits within the Labour Party and the ability of 'social democracy' to attract electoral support.[43]

Most social democrats in the 1970s thought, though, that Labour could still be 'saved' from the left. It was only after the 1979 election that they became gradually more disillusioned about this prospect and more enthusiastic about breaking away. An important intervention was made by Roy Jenkins, who, in his Dimbleby lecture 'Home Thoughts from Abroad' (delivered in November 1979) advocated a realignment of British politics. In Hugh Stephenson's words the lecture 'proved to be the single most important event in placing on the agenda for serious discussion the idea of some new party or grouping in the middle ground of British politics'.[44] In the lecture, Jenkins, who had resigned from the Labour Government in 1976 to become President of the European Commission, decried the growing extremism of the two major parties (Jenkins himself had let his Labour Party membership lapse and had not voted for the party in the 1979 election) and called for electoral reform to represent more accurately the moderate centrist views of the bulk of the electorate. To achieve this a strengthening of the 'radical centre' was required.[45]

At the time, Jenkins was not firmly committed to forming a new party. Indeed, he strongly considered joining the Liberals. The impetus for a new party came firstly from David Steel who persuaded Jenkins that a new party, separate from the Liberals, would stand a better chance – in alliance with the Liberals – of achieving the realignment both sought.[46] Even then, a new party would never have got off the ground without the defection of the 'Gang of Three' from Labour. Since the 1979 election, things, for them, had gone from bad to worse. The resignation of Jim Callaghan and his replacement by Michael Foot (rather than Denis Healey, their prefered candidate), who proved unable to halt the tide of the left, was a severe blow. The final straw, though, was the decision of the special conference at Wembley in January 1981 to introduce the electoral college for the election of a future Labour leader (see Chapter 6). A key power had been taken out of the hands of the PLP and the influence this gave to the left in the trade unions and the CLPs was unacceptable to the social democrats. The *Limehouse Declaration* was issued the following day.

### The rise and fall of the Liberal-SDP Alliance

In retrospect, the Alliance between the Liberals and the SDP – enthusiastically endorsed by the Liberal Party assembly at Llandudno in September 1981 – was a failure in that the 'mould' of British politics was not, ultimately, broken. For a time, though, it appeared likely to succeed. The positive response to the creation of the CSD was so great that the formation of a new party was put beyond doubt. In addition to Owen and Rodgers (the only two of the Gang of Four to be in Parliament at the time) nine Labour MPs immediately announced their intention of joining the breakaway, and, by the middle of 1982, the Parliamentary strength of the SDP had increased to thirty. This included further defections by Labour MPs (and Christopher Brocklebank-Fowler, the only Tory MP to join the SDP) and by-election gains.

The response from the electorate was even more sensational. An advertisement in the Guardian asking for support and donations for the CSD produced, within a month, 80,000 letters and £175,000 in donations.[47] Furthermore, opinion polls suggested that an alliance between a social democratic party and the Liberals would win the votes of a majority of the electorate.[48] These polls were translated into real votes in a number of by-elections. In July, a safe Labour seat at Warrington was turned into a marginal by

Roy Jenkins and this was followed by victory for candidates of the newly created Alliance at Croydon in October (Bill Pitt), Crosby in November (where Shirley Williams won with a 34 per cent swing from the Conservatives) and Glasgow Hillhead in March 1982 (Jenkins winning in more fertile territory).

This unprecedented surge of support, however, was not maintained. The outbreak of the Falklands War in April 1982, coupled with an improvement in the economic environment and a more united Labour Party, burst the Alliance bubble. The SDP turned inward, focusing on a leadership contest between Jenkins and Owen, won – although by a smaller margin (26,300 to 20,900) than had been expected – by the former. Despite the downturn (and it is difficult to believe anyone really thought that the level of support achieved in the heady early days would be maintained) the Alliance came within a whisker (27.6 per cent to 25.4 per cent) in the 1983 election of pushing Labour into third place in terms of votes won. This was a larger share than any Liberal performance since 1923. In terms of seats, however, the Alliance won only twenty-three (seventeen of these going to the Liberals) and most of those MPs who had defected to the SDP lost their seats (including Rodgers and Williams). In the final analysis it was the electoral system which, by granting Labour ten times more seats than the Alliance (despite the closeness of the votes), put paid to their hopes of holding the balance of power. With Labour recovering rapidly under Kinnock's leadership after the *débâcle* of the 1983 campaign it seemed that the Alliance had lost their chance and this was confirmed by the 1987 result which saw their share of the vote drop to 23 per cent.

## The impact of the Alliance

Despite the failure of the Alliance to break the Parliamentary hold of the two major parties, it would be incorrect to conclude that it had no impact on British politics. In the first place, even in 1987 the Alliance share of the vote was higher than any Liberal performance since 1929 and only about seven points behind Labour. There is little doubt that the SDP, containing within it those who had held high government office, gave the Alliance the kind of credibility which the Liberals alone had lacked. Furthermore, the very fact that the votes won by the Alliance were not converted accurately into seats brought the issue of electoral reform firmly on to the political agenda. The electorate could not fail to notice, in particular, the unfairness of the 1983 result.

Secondly, the Alliance has had a large impact on the Labour Party. The formation of the SDP raised the prospect of a viable attack on Labour strongholds, something which the Liberals (with one or two exceptions such as Leeds and Liverpool) had been unable to do. The Grimond strategy of a realignment on the left now seemed more likely to succeed. This strategy had failed in the past because the electoral strength of the party had been con-centrated in Conservative areas. Liberal revivals, therefore – in the early 1960s and between 1970 and 1974 – had occurred largely as a result of discontent with Conservative governments. The effect was to benefit the Labour Party (the opposite of what the Grimond strategy intended) as in February 1974.

In the event, the Alliance dented Labour without themselves being the prime beneficiaries. Like the Liberals before them, the electoral strength of the Alliance was in – primarily southern – Conservative seats. Indeed, survey evidence suggested that, as Ivor Crewe remarks:

SDP supporters place not only their party but themselves in the centre; they are, in fact, fractionally to its right. Typically SDP supporters do not see themselves as moderate but left of centre-voters abandoned by a leftwards-drifting Labour Party. They see themselves as 'middle-of-the-roaders'.[49]

Despite this, in 1983 and 1987 the Alliance was able to split the anti-Conservative vote in a number of Labour-held seats but the effect of this was to produce large Conservative majorities. The Conservative share of the vote actually fell between 1979 and 1983 and yet the party made a net gain of 101 seats in the latter election. Indeed, no Conservative victory had been achieved with such a small proportion of the vote since 1922, when Labour and the Liberals were competing for supremacy. Ironically, of course, had the Alliance done better in Conservative-held seats (as it was they came second in about two-thirds), a hung parliament at the very least could have resulted. The fact that the Conservatives won in 1983 with such a large majority and Labour's vote had dwindled to danger point arguably had the effect of bringing Labour 'to its senses'. Paradoxically, then, this partial success of the Alliance helped to bring about its demise.

### David Owen and the demise of the SDP

Immediately after the 1987 election, David Steel called for the formal merger of the two parties or 'democratic fusion' as he called it. For many in the Alliance, this seemed the natural step. In most constituencies, SDP and Liberal activists worked closely and amicably together with joint selection of candidates taking place in seventy-eight constituencies.[50] Furthermore, the joint leadership of Owen (who had become the unopposed leader of the SDP upon Jenkins's resignation in 1983) and Steel had proved to be a hindrance. Owen, though, was opposed to any such move and, despite his party's eventual approval for merger and the launch of the new Social and Liberal Democratic Party in March 1988, an Owenite rump (including the MPs John Cartwright and Rosie Barnes) continued with the SDP. At first, the SDP threatened to be a serious thorn in the side of the new merged party, pushing the SLD, for instance, into third place in the Richmond by-election in February 1989. The resources of Owen's party were, however, severely strained and, after a poor showing in the local elections in May 1989 – where the party ended up with only fifteen of the 3,509 seats in England and Wales – and a fall in membership to around 10,000, it was announced that the SDP would no longer be a national party, engaging instead in 'selective campaigning'.[51] Finally, after finishing seventh (behind even Screaming Lord Sutch's Monster Raving Loony Party!) in the Bootle by-election in 1990, it was decided to wind up the party's affairs.[52]

It is worth considering Owen's reasons for refusing to contemplate the merger of the two parties since they go to the heart of the problems faced by the Alliance. In the first place, the creation of a merged party was not, for Owen, part of his long-term strategy. In contrast to Grimond and Steel's 'realignment' strategy (whereby a new centre party would replace Labour in a new two-party system) Owen envisaged the Alliance as a short-term device to achieve electoral reform, after which the two parties could go their separate ways competing in a viable multi-party system. It is questionable, therefore, whether Owen would – under any circumstances – have entertained the idea of a merger.

Added to Owen's general doubts, though, were his negative feelings towards the particular merger being considered. First, he feared that the SDP *would be submerged in a merged party*. This view was largely correct. The Liberals had more MPs, a bigger, and much more politically experienced, membership and were an old and established party with a clearer identity than the SDP. This would not have mattered so much had Owen not thought that the two parties had *significant policy differences*. A key area here was defence. The Liberals had a strong unilateralist wing, the party's assembly consistently voting against the siting of American cruise missiles and the replacement of Polaris by Trident as Britain's independent nuclear deterrent. This was totally unacceptable to Owen, who had left the Labour Party partly because of its conversion to unilateralism. A joint commission of the two parties came to the compromise position that Polaris would be retained for ten years until a decision about its future could be taken, with Trident being cancelled in the meantime. This was immediately attacked by Owen as a 'fudge' and, particularly given that the 1987 manifesto broadly took the commission's position, Owen was far from happy with the situation.[53] By 1987, too, Owen had moved to the right on economic policy, symbolised by his reluctance to rule out a coalition with Thatcherism after the election. His idea of the 'social market', which put greater emphasis on the need for wealth *creation* than wealth *distribution*, put him at odds with the bulk of the Liberal Party in addition to Jenkins and his followers in the SDP who were more sceptical about the market and more interested in the traditional social democratic concern with equality (Jenkins having been a leading Croslandite in the 1950s and 1960s – see Chapter 6).[54]

The Owenite faction believed also that the Liberal Party organisation was too fragmented, decentralised and undisciplined

H

to be a serious competitor for power. Much of this, too, was true. At the national level there was a great overlap of functions between the various organs of the Liberal Party, making it extremely difficult for the leadership to gain control and for effective and speedy decision-making. The party was federal in nature, giving a good deal of autonomy to the regional and national parties and there was little central intervention in the selection of candidates. The Liberals were also the first of the mainstream parties to involve their extra-Parliamentary party in the election of the leader, adopting a complicated system of weighted votes in 1976 before introducing a OMOV system in 1981.[55] Liberal conferences were often as rowdy and disorganised as the Labour Party at its worst. This was graphically illustrated in the 1986 defence debate when it was far from clear who was entitled to vote.[56]

The organisation of the Liberal Party reflected its lack of Parliamentary success. For a considerable time, the focus of much Liberal activity had been based upon building up support at the local level. This 'community politics' strategy, developed in the late 1960s, involved 'electioneering tactics which concentrated on local issues, intensive leaflet distribution and the involvement of Liberal candidates and councillors in day-to-day popular griev-ances.'[57] For those Liberals brought up on such a strategy (which proved to be very successful in areas such as Liverpool and Leeds – both of which elected Liberal MPs) a suspicion of centralised control developed. The party's tendency towards a lack of discipline reflected, too, the fact that the Liberals had not (for some time) had to portray themselves as a party of government. It should also, finally, be noted that the party contained many radicals, often associated with fringe causes, who were ideologically indisposed in *any* circumstances to accept centrally imposed direction.[58]

In contrast, the factors which led to decentralisation in the Liberal Party were not present in the SDP. As Mick Moran points out: 'Central control is the natural product of the way the Party was born', as an 'initiative by politicians with an established reputation.'[59] As such, the leadership could retain control, through both institutional devices and the inexperience of rank and file members, the majority of whom had never been active in a party before. The Council for Social Democracy, consisting mainly of the party's rank and file, was in theory the sovereign body of the body. In practice, however, the CSD had no power to initiate policy but could only reject proposals put before it in the form of White Papers by the party's National Committee, a body dominated by MPs. Furthermore, the Parliamentary party was not obliged to accept decisions made by the CSD. Finally, although the leader was elected by a ballot of the whole membership, once elected he was difficult to remove. Only if the leader was not also the Prime Minister, and if a motion calling for an election was passed by more than half the Parliamentary party within a month of the beginning of a new session, could a challenge be provoked.[60]

There were obviously important differences between the Liberals and the Social Democrats. Nevertheless, they can be exaggerated. The policy differences were relatively minor and there have been few problems in ironing them out in the merged party. What united them was far more important – a commitment to the mixed economy, to constitutional change (involving proportional representation, a bill of rights and devolution) and opposition to the class-based fundamentalist socialism of the Labour left. Likewise, the organisation of the new party has, as we shall see below, taken on some of the centralised practices of the SDP. The fact that the bulk of the SDP had few problems with merger demonstrated that what united the two parties was more important than what divided them. Owen's decision, then, should be seen partly in terms of his own personal characteristics – his dislike for compromise and co-operation – partly in terms of a certain organisational loyalty to the party he and others had put so much work into creating and partly because of his divergent long-term political strategy. What is clear is that his decision to oppose merger was to have serious consequences for the prospects of the centre.

## The Liberal Democrats

The SLD (now known by the shortened title of Liberal Democrats after a ballot of the party's membership in October 1989) was launched on 3 March 1988, after the merger terms were accepted by the memberships of both parties (by 87.9 per cent in the case of the Liberals and 65.3 per cent in the case of the SDP). A leadership election was set for July, and, after David Steel announced he would not be standing, the contest was between two other Liberals – Paddy Ashdown and Alan Beith – the former winning with 72 per cent of the vote.

### *Party organisation*

The organisation of the Liberal Democrats is an attempt to reconcile the centralised structure of the SDP with the decentralised, pluralistic Liberal party.[61] Thus, the Liberal Democratic Party has a federal structure with a certain amount of autonomy given to the English regions and Scotland and Wales which have their own conferences and policy committees. The twice-yearly national conference, made up of representatives from every constituency, is in theory the sovereign body of the party having 'the power to determine the definitive policy of the party having implications for Great Britain or the United Kingdom as a whole'.

In practice, though, the power of the conference is limited. In the first place, the majority of policy proposals are put before conference in the form of Green and White papers by the party's Federal Policy Committee. Final decisions can be made only once the Committee has considered any amendments made by conference to the Green papers. Conference then has the opportunity to consider the revised proposals. This is clearly a more democratic procedure than the one that operated in the SDP where decisions made by the CSD applied only if agreed to by the Policy Committee. But it does prevent the conference from reaching decisions quickly, and gives the Policy Committee the chance to argue against a decision that they dislike. This is particularly important given that the Parliamentary party (in the form of the leader, the President, four MPs and one peer) are well represented on the Committee and only thirteen members (out of twenty-seven) are elected by the conference – the other members being three councillors and two Scottish and two Welsh representatives.

In addition, although members of the conference are able to propose motions on policy issues for debate, the Policy Committee has the power to insist that a final decision be deferred to give more time for consultation and thought and, in addition, it has the responsibility – in consultation with the Parliamentary party – for drawing up the election manifesto. Finally, Article 8 of the constitution gives the Federal Executive of the party (responsible for the party's organisation and consisting of fourteen elected members and, *ex officio*, the President, three Vice-Presidents, the leader, three MPs, one peer and two councillors) the power to initiate a ballot of the whole membership on any issue which it considers to be important. One can see that the leadership, well represented on the Executive, could utilise this device to overturn a conference decision with which they disagreed.

The constitution puts into practice the principle of OMOV for the election of leader and President (a post in 1993 held by Charles Kennedy), the selection of Parliamentary candidates and the election of conference representatives. The process for electing a leader owes more to the Liberals than to the SDP. The latter's leader was, as we have seen, relatively secure if he held the support of most MPs. In the new party, a leadership election, conducted by single transferable vote (a form of proportional representation), is held two years after each general election or if a majority of the party's MPs or seventy-five local parties demand it.

The two parts of the constitution which caused most controversy were the party's new name and the preamble. Initially the constitution stipulated that the party's title was to be the New Liberal and Social Democratic Party shortened to the Alliance. This was unacceptable to many in both parties and was changed to the SLD, the shortened version – Liberal Democrats – being adopted in 1989. The preamble to the constitution includes a commitment, insisted upon by SDP negotiators, that Britain should play a full and constructive role in NATO. For many radical Liberals this was unacceptable, being a current policy rather than an enduring statement of values. The SDP negotiators, with the shadow of Owen's submersion charge hanging over their heads, knew full well that such a commitment, enshrined in the constitution, would be difficult for Liberals to alter given the need for two-thirds support from conference representatives.

## A return to the wilderness?

Since its formation, the Liberal Democratic Party has faced an uphill struggle. Initially after the party's formation, its poll ratings slumped into single figures and in the 1989 European elections it seemed that the Greens had replaced it as the natural receptacle of the protest vote. The scale of this downturn in the centre party's fortunes proved to be short-term, the product of the acrimonious merger debate (which was little short of a disaster for a political force which based its appeal on deriding the 'old style' confrontational politics practised by the two major parties)[62] and the inexperience of Paddy Ashdown who found it difficult to establish a high public profile. An important consequence of the merger has been the loss of members. In February 1988, 155,000 members of the two parties participated in the merger ballot yet in July 1990 the Liberal Democrats claimed a membership of only 82,400.[63]

Gradually the Liberal Democrats began to recover. The party won three seats in by-elections from the Conservatives (Eastbourne in October 1990, Ribble Valley in March 1991 and Kincardine and Deeside in the autumn of 1991), polled over 20 per cent of the vote in the 1991 local elections, winning control of fifteen new councils and, in the run-up to the 1992 election, were back well into double figures in the opinion polls. Such was the recovery that in 1992 the Liberal Democrats helped to make a hung Parliament (for the first time since 1945) the *assumption* among most commentators during an election campaign thereby forcing the two major parties to adjust their campaign strategies. In particular, Labour spent much of the week before polling day debating the merits of proportional representation which was regarded by some in the party (most notably Peter Mandelson) as a serious error since it diverted Labour from their strongest campaign themes such as the state of the health service.

In the context of the immediate post-merger problems, the six million votes (17.8 per cent) and twenty seats secured by the party in the 1992 election represented, if not a triumph, then certainly not the disaster that looked, for a time, on the cards. Seen in a longer-term perspective, and particularly in the light of the hopes and aspirations of the early 1980s, the 1992 result was, of course, a big disappointment. For the second consecutive election, the gap between Labour and their opponents in the centre (in terms of vote share) widened. Whilst securing a higher share of the vote than in 1979, the Liberal Democrat performance was similar to the pre-Alliance Liberals with electoral strength limited to tradi-tional Liberal heartlands such as the south-west.

The election revealed how sensitive the Liberal Democrats (and their predecessors in the centre ground) are to the politics of the two major parties. As Labour (and the Conservatives although, arguably, to a lesser extent – see Chapter 3) have moved back to the centre ground it has proved increasingly difficult for the Liberal Democrats to carve out a distinctive position for themselves. This lack of a distinctive doctrine, in addition to the absence of an appeal to any particular interest within society, is the age-old problem for centre parties. The Liberals had traditionally been the vehicle for those who wanted to protest against either or both of the two major parties but they failed to attract enough positive support based on Liberal principles.[64]

The Liberal Democrats, in an attempt to come up with a distinct political identity, have flirted with the idea of 'citizenship'. This 'new' thinking has been particularly associated with David Marquand, a professor of politics, former Labour MP and founder member of the SDP. The notion of citizenship involves giving individuals a stake in society through the granting of formal rights and increased opportunities for participating in the political system – such constitutional reforms being seen as an essential device for effective economic policy making.[65] As Marquand argues: 'At its heart lies the proposition that the city, the polis, belongs to and is fashioned by its citizens: that they must not hand over their obligation to honour and defend it to some charismatic leader or remote bureaucracy.'[66] The Liberal Democratic stress upon reforms to the political system as a prerequisite of economic improvement highlights a fundamental difference from left-wing thinking inspired by Marx which regards the economic sphere as supreme. In addition, the emphasis upon participation and community is aimed at carving a distinctive space for the Liberal Democrats between the top-down corporate collectivism which failed to 'mobilise consent' for government policy in the 1970s and the 'selfish' individualism of the market approach.

This 'populist' approach was emphasised by a policy paper *Our Different Vision* published by the party in February 1989 and has also been taken on board by Ashdown in his book *Citizens' Britain*.[67] The ideals of citizenship, though, have proved to be insufficiently distinctive to enthuse Liberal Democrat activists, let alone voters (not least because the citizenship label – if not the content – has been 'stolen' by the Conservatives). In the 1992 election, traditional economic issues predominated and, even though in this area the Liberal Democrats did offer an alternative approach (by promising to create an extra 600,000 jobs through a 'prudent' increase in borrowing in addition to a one penny increase in income tax, the proceeds of which would be used to spend on education), it never became a pivotal part of the campaign.

It would be wrong, though, to assume that the party system remains virtually the same as in the decade before the creation of the Alliance. As Chapter 2 of this book shows, Labour's fourth successive election defeat is unprecedented in post-war British politics and, inevitably, this provoked post-election discussions about the possibility of electoral pacts between the two opposition parties. This is a, superficially, attractive answer to the problems of the centre-left parties since it makes arithmetical sense. It is doubtful, however, if such a pact would produce the desired outcome not least because it assumes that most (or even a majority) of those inclined to vote Liberal Democrat naturally prefer Labour to the Conservatives – an assumption that was discredited in the 1992 campaign when it seems that Liberal Democrat support drifted away in the final few days in the face of evidence that a centre party vote would produce a Labour Government. In any case, Labour did just well enough in 1992 to shelve serious consideration of deals with the Liberal Democrats. If the Conservatives were to win yet again in the second half of the 1990s (a distinct possibility) then a return to the 'progressivism' of an earlier time would become a more likely proposition.

## Conclusion

One of the key aims of this chapter has been to show that the development of the centre parties has been, and continues to be, inextricably linked with the two major parties, and particularly with Labour. Ideologically, the Liberals have been, throughout the twentieth century, in the mainstream of British political life. Unfortunately for them they have, at key times, been excluded from government both because the other parties have gravitated towards their position in the centre of the political spectrum and because of their lack of a solid class base. This does not mean, however, that the centre parties have not been influential. Events have shown that they serve as a permanent reminder to both Labour and the Conservatives that if they stray too far from this mainstream they risk severe electoral consequences. This has ensured, in particular, that Labour retains a commitment to the ideals which persuaded many Liberals to transfer their allegiance in the early 1900s and which still, despite the partial realignment of the early 1980s, keep social Liberals and social democrats apart.

## Notes

1  J. Vincent, *The Formation of the British Liberal Party 1857–68*, London, 1966.
2  H. V. Emy, *Liberals, Radicals and Social Politics 1892–1914*, Cambridge, 1972, chapter one.
3  B. Harrison, *Drink and the Victorians*, London, 1971.
4  J. S. Mill, *On Liberty*, London, 1972.

5   M. Pugh, *The Making of Modern British Politics 1867–1939*, Oxford, 1982, p. 112.

6   See L. T. Hobhouse, *Liberalism*, Oxford, 1964 (originally published in 1911) and J. A. Hobson, *The Crisis of Liberalism*, Brighton, 1974 (originally published in 1909). See also M. Freeden, *The New Liberalism: An Ideology of Social Reform*, Oxford, 1978.

7   Quoted in R. Behrens, 'The centre: social democracy and liberalism', in L. Tivey and A. Wright (eds), *Party Ideology in Britain*, London, 1989, p. 81.

8   P. Clarke, 'Liberals and social democrats in historical perspective', in V. Bogdanor (ed.), *Liberal Party Politics*, Oxford, 1983, p. 31.

9   Behrens, 'The centre', p. 75.

10  Clarke, 'Liberals and social democrats', p. 28. See also his book, *Liberals and Social Democrats*, Cambridge, 1978.

11  K. O. Morgan, *The Age of Lloyd George*, London, 1971, pp. 32–5.

12  For a summary of the debate see P. Adelman, *The Rise of the Labour Party*, Harlow, 1972, pp. 83–90; A. R. Ball, *British Political Parties*, London, 1987, pp. 82–4; K. Laybourn, *The Labour Party 1881–1951*, Gloucester, 1988, pp. 1–12.

13  P. F. Clarke, *Lancashire and the New Liberalism*, Cambridge, 1971.

14  Morgan, *Lloyd George*, chapter two; Emy, *Social Politics*, chapters five to seven.

15  T. Wilson, *The Downfall of the Liberal Party*, London, 1966, p. 18.

16  H. Pelling, *Popular Politics and Society in Late Victorian Britain*, London, 1968; P. Thompson, *Socialists, Liberals and Labour*, London, 1967.

17  Ball, *British Political Parties*, pp. 81–2.

18  H. Matthew, R. McKibbin & J. Kay, 'The franchise factor in the rise of the Labour party', *English Historical Review*, XCI, 1976, pp. 723–52.

19  Morgan, *Lloyd George*, pp. 104–5.

20  R. Douglas, *History of the Liberal Party*, London, 1971, pp. 262–6.

21  Ball, *British Political Parties*, p. 80.

22  Skidelsky, *Politicians and the Slump*, pp. 31–51.

23  David Marquand, quoted in Behrens, 'The centre', p. 92.

24  Bogdanor, *Liberal Party*, p. 8.

25  See C. A. Cline, *Recruits to Labour: The British Labour Party 1914–31*, Syracuse, 1963.

26  Clarke, 'Liberals and social democrats', p. 36.

27  Hobson, *Crisis*, pp. 133–4.

28  Ball, *British Political Parties*, p. 81.

29  Quoted in Clarke, 'Liberals and social democrats', p. 35.

30  I. Bradley, *Breaking the Mould? The Birth and Prospects of the Social Democratic Party*, Oxford, 1981, pp. 89–98.

31    W. Wallace, 'Survival and revival' in Bogdanor, *Liberal Party*, pp. 47–8.

32    Wallace, 'Survival and revival', pp. 50–9.

33    M. Steed, 'The Liberal Party', in H. M. Drucker (ed), *Multi-Party Britain*, p. 102.

34    Wallace, 'Survival and revival', pp. 67–9.

35    See L. Chester, M. Linklater & D. May, *Jeremy Thorpe: A Secret Life*, London, 1979.

36    Bogdanor, *Liberal Party*, p. 276.

37    Quoted in Bradley, *Breaking the Mould?*, p. 51.

38    Clarke, 'Liberals and social democrats', p. 40.

39    Bradley, *Breaking the Mould?*, pp. 46–7.

40    Bradley, *Breaking the Mould?*, pp. 58–63.

41    Bradley, *Breaking the Mould?*, pp. 31–9.

42    Bradley, *Breaking the Mould?*, pp. 53–4.

43    Williams & Williams, *Labour's Decline*, pp. 102–3. Taverne launched a national Campaign for Social Democracy, which put up four candidates in the February 1974 election.

44    H. Stephenson, *Claret and Chips: The Rise of the SDP*, London, 1982, p. 20.

45    Stephenson, *Claret and Chips*, pp. 20–2.

46    Stephenson, *Claret and Chips*, p. 29.

47    Stephenson, *Claret and Chips*, p. 50.

48    Bradley, *Breaking the Mould?*, pp. 90–1.

49    I. Crewe, 'Is Britain's two-party system really about to crumble? The Social Democratic–Liberal alliance and the prospects for re-alignment', *Electoral Studies*, 1, 1982, pp. 301–2.

50    S. Ingle, 'Liberals and Social Democrats: end of a chapter or end of the book?', *Talking Politics*, winter, 1988–9, p. 48.

51    *Sunday Times*, 14 May 1989.

52    *Sunday Times*, 3 June 1990.

53    Behrens, 'The centre', pp. 88–9; see Williams & Williams, *Labour's Decline*, who emphasise the importance of defence in the Labour split and in Owen's opposition to the merger.

54    Behrens, 'The centre', pp. 89–91.

55    D. Kavanagh, 'Organisation and power in the Liberal party', in Bogdanor, *Liberal Party*, pp. 123–42.

56    Ingle, 'Liberals and social democrats', p. 48.

57    Steed, 'The Liberal Party', p. 101. See also S. Mole, 'Community politics', in Bogdanor, *Liberal Party*, pp. 258–74.

58    A number of radical Liberals opposed merger precisely because the SDP was too centralised. Thus, Claire Brooks, a well-known Liberal activist, commented that the SDP constitution is 'oligarchical, centralist, authoritarian, deliberately disguised to pre-

serve power in the hands of an elite'. *Guardian*, 18 September 1987.

59  M. Moran, *Politics & Society in Britain*, London, 1985, p. 97.

60  H. Drucker, ' "All the kings horses and all the king's men": The Social Democratic party in Britain' in W. E. Paterson & A. H. Thomas (eds), *The Future of Social Democracy: Problems and Prospects of Social Democratic Parties in Western Europe*, Oxford, 1986, pp. 108–26.

61  Details of the Liberal Democrat's constitution can be found in the *Guardian*, 18 December 1989. See also B. Jones et. al., *Politics UK*, Hemel Hempstead, 1991, pp. 261–2.

62  R. Garner, 'The road to merger: the Social Democrats and the Liberals since the 1987 election', *Politics Association Resources Bank*, Manchester, 1989. We now know that the Alliance suffered from debilitating personality clashes right from its inception. See the revelations, for instance, in R. Jenkins, *A Life at the Centre*, London, 1992 & D. Owen, *Time to Declare*, London, 1992.

63  *Guardian*, 17 July 1990.

64  J. Curtice, 'Liberal voters and the Alliance: realignment or protest?', in Bogdanor, *Liberal Party*, pp. 105–6.

65  D. Marquand, *The Unprincipled Society*, London, 1988.

66  D. Marquand, 'So what's the big idea about citizenship?', *Guardian*, 16 August 1990.

67  P. Ashdown, *Citizens' Britain: A Radical Agenda for the 1990s*, London, 1989.

# 9

# POLITICAL PARTIES AND ELECTORAL BEHAVIOUR

No study of political parties would be complete without an analysis of the behaviour of voters. A central characteristic of liberal democracies such as Britain is that political power is granted not to those who can muster enough physical force or to those who claim a 'divine right' to govern others but to those who receive the consent of the people through the ballot box. The result is a seemingly perpetual competition for votes. This electoral competition, of course, is now dominated by political parties. It is parties who put up candidates in each constituency, who put forward programmes of policies to the voters and who are rewarded with seats in the Commons. Likewise, with very few exceptions, it is party labels which dictate the choice of voters in the polling booths. The 'how' and 'why' of individual voting choices is therefore of crucial importance to the parties themselves in addition to political commentators.

Psephology, or the study of voting behaviour, has a high profile within the academic discipline of political science. This, of course, reflects the importance of the subject matter and the considerable public interest that surrounds it. For most people, interest in politics is restricted to the party battle during election campaigns and this mass spectator sport has enabled election night academic pundits such as David Butler, the late Robert McKenzie and – more recently – Ivor Crewe and Tony King to become minor television celebrities. Psephology also has a high profile because, unlike many other areas of political studies, it

227

deals with a large amount of quantitative material. With the aid of – often complex – statistical techniques, psephologists can develop hypotheses which seek to explain past, and predict future, trends in electoral behaviour. Such an ability, however constrained by the unpredictability of human beings, enables students of politics to utilise the methods – and approach the predictive capacity – of natural scientists and thus claim some of the prestige which is attached to 'science' in the western world.

## Models of voting behaviour

The first task for a student of voting behaviour is to discover how people voted or intend to vote. At a superficial level this is an easy task since election results are readily available. We know, for instance, how many people voted Labour and how many Conservative in past general elections. By itself, however, this so called *aggregate* level information is not that useful. If we are to start developing theories to explain with any accuracy *why* people vote the way they do (the second task) we need to know how particular individuals voted and whether their vote has changed over time. Thus, psephologists make great use of surveys in which a sample of voters can be questioned about their voting habits, political opinions and social characteristics.[1] With this information, it is possible to look for patterns of behaviour which may have some explanatory validity.

There is considerable dispute amongst psephologists as to what motivates electoral choice. Various theories or models of voting behaviour have been put forward. At the extremes are two – the party identification model and the rational choice model.

### *The party identification model*

This approach (often described as the 'Michigan' model since it was developed at that city's university in the 1950s)[2] was, at least until recently, the conventional wisdom in accounts of British voting behaviour.[3] The model holds that voters develop a long-term psychological attachment to political parties at an early age. This attachment is learnt through the socialisation process

228

initially involving parents and later reinforced by peer group influence. Voting for that party becomes a habit – an emotional response – rather than a choice based on political factors such as the party's policies or performance in office. Indeed, the party identification is used to avoid such a choice which the voter is unwilling to make or incapable of making. Voters may have views on political issues but these are determined by the previously existing party identification so, if necessary, voters will change their views to fit in with their party identification. Thus, according to the theory, a Labour Party identifier would become, say, a supporter of unilateral nuclear disarmament if the party adopted that position. Of course, if voters have such an attachment to parties then rapid electoral change would be difficult to account for. The model gets round this by distinguishing between short-term factors and the long-term identification. On occasions, voters may be influenced by the former to the extent that at a particular election they may vote for another party. In the long-term, however, they will return to their original attachment.

### The rational choice model

As the name suggests, the voters in this model are imputed with some level of rationality. Thus: 'The theory assumes that the voter recognises his own self-interest, evaluates alternative candidates on the basis of which will best serve this self-interest, and casts his vote for the candidate most favourably evaluated.'[4] The purest form of the rational choice model can be described as the *issue voting model*. One of the earliest versions of this was provided in the late 1950s by Anthony Downs in his book *An Economic Theory of Democracy*. For Downs, voters can be equated with consumers in the market economy buying, with their votes, a policy package which they think will provide them with the greatest satisfaction. Similarly, just as producers in a market economy are forced to make only things that consumers want to buy, political parties will offer policies which they estimate will maximise votes. As Downs explains: 'politicians in our model never seek office as a means of carrying out particular policies; their only goal is to reap the rewards of holding office *per se*.'[5] Put simply, parties will, then, adjust their policies in order to win votes.

A range of criticisms can be made of this model.[6] We will deal briefly with three here. In the first place, the model finds it difficult to explain why so many actually bother to vote at all. A rational voter would only vote if the benefits of so doing outweighed the costs (measured in terms of finding out what the parties stand for and making the effort to vote on the day). Since most seats in Britain are safe, the chances of one vote affecting the result are minuscule and even if a marginal seat was decided in this way, the chances of that seat determining which party forms the government are also small.[7]

Secondly, the issue voting model takes the policy preferences of voters as given. This overlooks the possibility that these preferences may themselves have been 'created' by powerful forces in society, and not least by the government itself.[8] This is the basis of the radical model of voting behaviour associated in particular with Dunleavy and Husbands. They note how Mrs Thatcher's Governments were able to maximise support for the Conservatives not by adjusting their policies to meet the demands of voters but by creating an environment favourable to radical Thatcherite policies. Thus, the manipulation of news (i.e. the adjustments to the unemployment figures and the growing government advertising budget), the sale of council houses, the privatisation programme and the selling of shares have all, it is argued, produced a more pro-Thatcherite electorate. Dunleavy and Husbands argue that this 'increasingly transparent exploitation of state power for party ends, which is implicit in the new Conservative rejection of consensus' has become so all-embracing that fair and geunine competition between the parties is threatened and consequently democracy is 'at the crossroads'.[9] The third criticism of the issue voting model is that voters just do not in reality have the sophistication that Downs wants to impute to them. Surveys have shown that the level of interest in, and information about, politics is low although – as one would expect – there is considerable variety within this broad generalisation.[10] Such evidence may come as a surprise to those – such as political activists and journalists – who take an active interest in politics but for most people it remains a peripheral concern. Whether or not this is a desirable state of affairs is another matter.[11]

### Rationality and voting behaviour

It would be wrong to reject out of hand either of these theories. For one thing, not all voters, of course, have the same motivation and therefore different theories may be required to explain different behaviour. In addition, a theory may be more applicable to one era than another. The party identification model, for instance, is far more able to deal with a period of electoral stability than one of electoral volatility. As we shall see below, for instance, the model was the orthodoxy in Britain during the 1950s and 1960s but, during the 1970s and 1980s, it went out of fashion as voting behaviour became more unpredictable. In these circumstances, greater emphasis was placed upon the impact of political issues and events which, it was suggested, persuaded voters to change their alignments more regularly. It should also be noted though that, even now, a large proportion of all voters choose the same party time after time and the party identification model seems best able to explain their behaviour.

The problem with the pure version of the party identification model is that it surely exaggerates the extent to which voting decisions – and particularly those which involve a switch from one party to another – involve no political judgement.[12] We can readily accept that most voters do not have the ability or inclination to behave in the sophisticated way Downs suggests, but it is possible to conceive of electoral behaviour being somehow related to what parties offer and what governments do. As Denver points out, there is a tendency for psephologists to take a very narrow view of what rational voting is. If voters are not aware of or do not have an opinion on 'transitory matters to be found in the small print of party manifestos or talked about by parties during election campaigns' then rational voting does not exist.[13] Yet voters may have, to a greater or lesser extent, a series of long-standing goals (equality, a free health service or whatever) and a reasonable idea of which party would further their self-interests, however defined. This may not add up to the calculating utility maximiser identified

231

by Downs but it does involve at least some element of political choice.

Furthermore, it has been argued that elections are often about the overall competence of political parties rather than just the detail of policy. Many objectives – such as low unemployment and inflation – are widely shared and so, to judge between the parties, voters will often consider their general capacity to govern – for instance, the ability and experience of the leaders – as much as their different methods of dealing with issues such as unemployment. Thus, Miller in his analysis of the 1983 election argued that:

The issues were not inherently against Labour. Instead, disunity and incompetence in the Labour leadership destroyed Labour's credibility on its own natural issues and allowed its opponents to put their issues on the agenda ... Labour was not ready for government in 1983 and the electorate knew it.[14]

A related approach, described by Harrop and Miller as a 'helpful bridge' between the two models is the concept of *retrospective* voting. Here, voters do not have to evaluate party policies but simply judge the performance of governments thereby developing a party identification as a result of a 'running tally of retrospective evaluations rather than as an emotional attachment'.[15] Ivor Crewe suggests such an evaluation was the key explanation for the Conservative victory in 1987. If the electorate had voted according to their issue preferences Labour would have won since the party was ahead in three of the four most salient issues (defence being the exception). What determined the result, according to Crewe, was the electorate's general feeling of prosperity – a prosperity which the Conservatives had 'created' and were trusted to maintain.[16]

### Britain's changing voting behaviour

It is customary to divide post-1945 British voting behaviour into two distinct periods. The first, from the end of the Second World War to the end of the 1960s, has been characterised as an era where most voters were strongly *aligned* with one or other of the two major parties and where social class was far and away the most important determinant of electoral choice. By contrast, the second, from the 1970s onwards, has been characterised as an era of *dealignment* as the strong ties that bound voters and parties together have loosened and social class has declined from its pre-eminent position as a predictor of voting behaviour.

### Partisan alignment and dealignment

Following Denver, the term *partisan alignment* refers to 'a situation in which voters align themselves with a party by thinking of themselves as supporters of it, by having a party identification'.[17] Thus, in the era of alignment, most voters identified – with a varying degree of intensity – with one or other of the two main parties. In 1964, for instance, no less than 81 per cent of the electorate identified with Labour or the Conservatives. Of these, 51 per cent (of Labour supporters) and 48 per cent (of Conservative supporters) identified 'very strongly' with their respective parties.[18] Not surprisingly, this strong party identification produced a large degree of electoral stability. As we saw in Chapter 2, the two parties dominated general elections in this period, the percentage of their combined vote never falling below the high 80s. In addition, the overall swing (a measure of the net change in the two-party vote from one election to the next) was small, averaging about 2 per cent in the six general elections between 1950 and 1966 with the highest being 3.1 per cent (in 1964) and the lowest 0.9 per cent (in 1951).

Since the 1970s, however, there has been a *partisan dealignment*. Fewer voters now identify with the two parties. By 1979, those identifying with either of the two parties had fallen to 74 per cent whilst, more significantly, the percentage of 'very strong' identifiers had dropped to 29 per cent (for Labour) and 24 per cent (for the Conservatives).[19] This fall continued in the 1980s. Between 1964 and 1970 an average of 40 per cent of the electorate regarded themselves as 'very strong' identifiers whereas by 1987 only 16 per cent did so (rising to 19 per cent if we include all parties).[20] The result of this, as previous chapters have indicated, was a decline in the two-party share of the vote. In the six elections since February 1974, the average two-party share was 75 per cent, with a high of about 81 per cent in 1979 and a low of 70 per cent in 1983 (see table 2.1).

It is regularly pointed out that another consequence of partisan dealignment is increased electoral volatility – the phenomenon of rapidly changeable voter preferences. Certainly, from the 1970s onwards, there has been a tendency for greater swings in by-elections (resulting in many more defeats for the governing party) and opinion poll ratings. We saw in Chapter 8, for instance, how the newly formed SDP swept to remarkably high levels before slipping back equally dramatically during and after the Falklands War. Swings between elections too have increased, with those recorded in 1970, 1979 and 1983 (4.7 per cent, 5.2 per cent and 4.2 per cent) representing the highest in the post-war period. We need, however, to treat these statistics with care. They all deal with the *net* movement in the vote – the combined result of all vote switching. What is more important is the *overall* movement – the measure of the actual proportion of voters who switch from one party to another. Although net volatility increased during the 1970s and early 1980s, studies of the British electorate have concluded that overall volatility has not substantially increased. It still remains the case that, as panel surveys (which involve the same group of voters over a series of elections) have shown, about two-thirds of the electorate vote for the same party, or abstain, from one election to the next.[21] As table 9.1 shows, there was no significant drop in the percentage of those voting for the same

*Table 9.1* Rates of individual voters' constancy and change between each pair of consecutive elections 1959–79 and 1983–87

|  | 1959–64 | 1964–66 | 1966–70 | 1970–Feb. 1974 | Feb–Oct 1974 | Oct 1974–1979 | 1983–87 |
|---|---|---|---|---|---|---|---|
| % constant | 64 | 74 | 66 | 58 | 69 | 62 | 61 |
| % changing | 36 | 26 | 34 | 42 | 31 | 38 | 39 |

Sources B. Sarlvik & I. Crewe, *Decade of Dealignment*, Cambridge, 1983, p. 62; A. Heath et al., 'Partisan dealignment revisited' in D. Denver & G. Hands (eds), *Issues and Controversies in British Electoral Behaviour*, Hemel Hempstead, 1992, pp. 166–7.

party across two elections between 1959 and the supposedly volatile 1970s and 1980s.

The discrepancy between the level of net and overall movement, is caused partly by the fact that, as Moran points out, voters are now more likely to switch from a major party to a minor one rather than – as before – between the two major parties. The latter produced a small net swing (because vote switching tended to cancel itself out) at the same time disguising the extent of the overall movement which was comparable with the period of dealignment.[22] In addition, electoral change is not produced just by voters switching from one party to another. It is also a consequence of changes in the electorate itself, caused by deaths, young voters registering for the first time, immigration and emigration. Thus, for example, fully 28 per cent of the Conservative vote at the 1987 election was made up of first-time voters too young to vote in 1983.[23]

## Class alignment and dealignment

During the era of alignment, by far the most important factor in determining how individuals voted was their social class position. There was, then, a *class alignment*. In a much-quoted passage, P. G. Pulzer wrote during this period that: 'Class is the basis of British party politics; all else is embellishment and detail'.[24] Thus, if you knew a person's class there was a good chance that you could predict how he or she was going to vote. The working class tended to vote Labour and the middle class tended to vote Conservative. Of course, this was never a perfect correlation. Since the working class has traditionally formed a majority of the electorate, such a correlation would have produced permanent Labour governments. Instead, a substantial proportion of the working class (usually about 30 per cent) voted Conservative and, although (in the past at least) far less important in numerical terms, a slightly smaller proportion of the middle class (about 20 per cent) voted Labour. Nevertheless, so clear and stable was this pattern of voting that psephologists spent a great deal of time and effort in trying to explain the behaviour of the so-called 'deviant' voters – those who voted differently from the majority of their class.[25]

Before providing some statistical evidence of the class alignment, it is necessary to define what is meant by 'class'. Such an exercise is nortoriously difficult and, as we shall see below, has recently been the subject of intense debate between psephologists. The most famous definition was provided by Karl Marx, but his distinction between the bourgeoisie (the owners of the means of production – the mines, factories etc.) and the proletariat (those who sell their labour to earn a living) takes too little account of the complexities of the modern social structure to be of much use to students of voting behaviour. Various more discriminating factors could be taken into account such as income or status but the criterion usually adopted is that of occupation. Here, it is common to divide occupations into groups represented by different letters as illustrated by table 9.2 with ABC1 regarded as the non-manual middle class and C2DE regarded as the manual working class.

*Table 9.2*  Occupational class categories, with % of electorate

| | |
|---|---|
| A. Higher managerial, administrative or professional | 19 |
| B. Intermediate managerial, administrative or professional | |
| C1. Supervisory, clerical; junior managerial, administrative or profes-sional | 24 |
| C2. Skilled manual workers | 27 |
| D. Semi-skilled and unskilled manual workers | 30 |
| E. State pensioners, casual workers | |

Source  P. G. Pulzer, *Political Representation and Elections in Britain*, London, 1975, p. 104.

Table 9.3 demonstrates the strength of the class alignment from 1959 to 1970. It can be illustrated in three ways. First, by the overall share of the vote gained by each party in the middle- and working-class occupational groups. Here, Labour's support in the working class and the Conservatives' support in the middle class did not fall below 60 per cent and was often higher. Indeed, over the whole period between 1945 and 1970, Conservative support amongst non-manual workers is even more pronounced since between 1945 and 1958 – a period which included two Conservative election victories – over three-quarters of social classes ABC1 voted for their 'natural' class party. Secondly, by using the so-called *Alford index* (named after the political scientist who invented it) a class 'index' or 'score' for Labour voting can be calculated. This works by comparing the proportions of each class that supports the Labour party.[26] The higher the percentage score, the stronger the class alignment and vice versa. Thus, up to 1970, the Alford index remained around 40 per cent. Thirdly, we can calculate a score for absolute class voting – the proportion of all voters who choose their 'natural' class party. Here again, we find that manual Labour voters and non-manual Conservative voters made up about two-thirds of those who voted.

The dominating role of class was such that other social characteristics played a minor role in explaining voting behaviour. In terms of *age* and *gender*, there was a slight tendency for older voters and female voters to prefer the Conservatives but this pattern largely disappeared in the 1980s (although a so-called 'gender gap' was apparent in the 1987 and 1992 elections. In the latter, Labour had a 13 per cent lead among women aged between eighteen and twenty-four whereas the Conservatives led by 4 per cent amongst men in the same age group; the Conservative lead over Labour, on the other hand, was much higher amongst women than men in the age groups thirty-five onwards). Similarly, *religion* (although a crucial characteristic in the nineteenth century) is now so peripheral (except of course in Northern Ireland) that it is not usually included in survey questions. *Ethnic origin* is a strong determinant of voting, with the majority of Asians and West Indians voting Labour, but this is numerically significant only in a handful of constituencies. In terms of *region*, there was always a slight variation partly accounted for by the simple fact that there have always been more working-class voters in the north of England and Scotland. What was significant in the period of alignment, though, was that swings at general elections were remarkably uniform across the country, thus enabling

Table 9.3    Measures of class voting 1959–92 (%)

|  | 1959 | | 1964 | | 1966 | | 1970 | | Feb. 1974 | | Oct. 1974 | |
| --- | --- | --- | --- | --- | --- | --- | --- | --- | --- | --- | --- | --- |
|  | Manual | Non-manual | Manual | Non-manual | Manual | Non-manual | Manual | Non-manual | Manual | Non-manual | Manual | Non-manual |
| Con. | 34 | 69 | 28 | 62 | 25 | 60 | 33 | 64 | 24 | 53 | 24 | 51 |
| Lab. | 62 | 22 | 64 | 22 | 69 | 26 | 58 | 25 | 57 | 22 | 57 | 25 |
| Lib. | 4 | 8 | 8 | 16 | 6 | 14 | 9 | 11 | 19 | 25 | 20 | 24 |
| Alford index[a] | 40 | | 42 | | 43 | | 33 | | 35 | | 32 | |
| Absolute class voting[b] | 65 | | 63 | | 66 | | 60 | | 55 | | 54 | |

|  | 1979 | | 1983 | | 1987 | | 1992 | |
| --- | --- | --- | --- | --- | --- | --- | --- | --- |
|  | Manual | Non-manual | Manual | Non-manual | Manual | Non-manual | Manual | Non-manual |
| Con. | 35 | 60 | 35 | 55 | 35 | 54 | 34 | 54 |
| Lab. | 50 | 23 | 42 | 17 | 45 | 20 | 46 | 23 |
| Lib.[c]/Lib. Dem. | 15 | 17 | 22 | 28 | 21 | 27 | 16 | 21 |
| Alford index | 27 | | 25 | | 25 | | 23 | |
| Absolute class voting | 55 | | 48 | | 49 | | 50 | |

Notes
[a] The Alford index is calculated by subtracting Labour's share of the non-manual vote from its share of the vote among manual workers.
[b] Absolute class voting is the proportion of voters supporting their 'natural' class party.
[c] In 1983 and 1987 the Liberals fought with the SDP as the Alliance.

Sources  D. Denver, *Elections and Voting Behaviour in Britain*, Hemel Hempstead, 1989, pp. 54–5; B. Sarlvik & I. Crewe, *Decade of Dealignment*, Cambridge, 1983, p. 87; *Sunday Times*, 12 April 1992.

psephologists to predict an election outcome on the basis of a few constituency results.[27]

It is important to recognise that the class/party link is only a pattern of voting behaviour and, as such, does not tell us *why* there should be such a link. Indeed, the class pattern of voting can be 'explained' by both of the models of voting behaviour we discussed earlier. According to the party identification model, from an early age individuals inherit voting patterns from their parents and these are reinforced by peer groups. Since this socialisation takes place within a class context, it is not surprising that voting takes on a class character. As Dunleavy and Husbands point out, occupational class positions are a good guide to how people vote: 'not because class is an "issue" or a "problem" that is consciously perceived by voters, but because knowing someone's occupational class is the best summary index that we have of the kind of contexts in which he or she passes his or her daily life.'[28] For adherents of a more 'rationally' based model of voting behaviour, a class pattern exists because the vast majority of voters tend to define themselves in class terms and are inclined to view their personal interests – in the social and economic sense – as synonymous with those of a particular class. In political terms, this class consciousness is translated into support for either of the two class-based parties (whose clear class origins and historical perspectives have been documented in previous chapters).

Clearly, both perspectives are based upon the existence of a homogenous working class. The causes of this phenomenon relate to the nature of the British economy, which for most of this century was dominated by 'heavy' industry (coal, steel, shipbuilding, manufacturing etc.) and units dealing in the mass production of goods. Marxists now often refer to this period as the 'Fordist era', taking their cue from Gramsci's observation that modern capitalism reflected the 'mode' of production pioneered by the Henry Ford motor company – one involving a series of standardised factories, engaged in standardised production on a huge scale and employing a large unskilled and semi-skilled workforce with similar jobs, wages and conditions.[29]

The consequences for the British workforce and, by implication, British politics, were profound. The bulk of the electorate after 1918 (when the Representation of the People Act finally removed the property franchise) were employed in such industries as manual workers, and thereby had similar incomes and 'life-styles' – reinforced by the fact that most of them lived in the same, tightly-knit, urbanised communities. These factors produced a strong sense of class consciousness among manual workers and a sense of being socially, economically and culturally different from those who did not share their living and working conditions. This class division was to prove far more potent than any regional division and was generally accepted and echoed by those in non-manual or middle-class occupations. Put simply, the atti-tudes and socio-economic interests of a working-class voter in Manchester would have much less in common with a middle-class voter in Manchester than with a working-class voter in Southampton.

Since 1970, it has become gradually more difficult to predict individuals' voting intentions from their occupational class. This *class dealignment* can be clearly seen if we look again at table 9.3. In 1966, 69 per cent of manual workers voted Labour but by 1987 only 45 per cent did so (rising to 46 per cent in 1992). The severest decline has occurred in the C2 category of skilled manual workers where, by 1987, the party's share had fallen to 34 per cent (compared to an average of 60 per cent between 1945 and the late 1950s) rising to only 40 per cent in 1992. On the basis of these figures Ivor Crewe could state in 1987 that 'Labour's claim to be the party of the working class' was 'sociologically, if not ideologically, threadbare'.[30] It is also important to recognise that the Conservatives have lost support from middle-class voters, polling barely 50 per cent of the ABC1 classes in 1983, 1987 and 1992. As a consequence, in these three elections both the Alford index and the level of absolute class voting were significantly lower than previously.

Of course, Labour has suffered most from class dealignment. Although the Conservative share of middle-class votes has declined, the party has more than made up for this by capturing working-class votes from Labour. Thus, in 1987, fully 43 per cent of C2 voters chose to vote for Mrs Thatcher's party and the Conservative vote among manual workers as a whole has remained remarkably consistent over the last four elections at a level higher than the 1960s and 1970s.[31] In addition, it was the Alliance – and not Labour – who were the main beneficiaries of the decline in the Conservatives' vote share amongst non-manual workers. Finally, it should be remembered that we are talking here about the proportion of each party's support in particular social groups and not the number of voters. A key explanation for Labour's decline, although not to be confused with class dealignment itself, is that social changes have increased the number of non-manual voters so that a declining share of the middle-class vote for the Conservatives is not equivalent to a reduction in the number of actual votes cast for the party since there are now more middle-class voters to go round.

### Heath, Jowell, Curtice and class voting

Not all psephologists accept that class dealignment has taken place. Heath, Jowell and Curtice in their studies of the 1983 and 1987 elections dispute this conventional assertion.[32] Their arguments depend largely upon the validity of complex statistical techniques which makes it difficult for the layperson to assess their contribution. What is offered here is a simplified (albeit useful, we hope) account of their case.[33]

Heath and his colleagues base their revisionist claim that class voting has not declined on two main grounds. In the first place, they argue that the usual A–E occupational scale is inadequate since it fails to take into account the real class interests of voters. Three main changes are made. First, married women are assigned to a class according to their own occupation (if they have one) rather than, as is traditionally the case, their husbands'. This has the effect of removing from the working class the many women, married to manual workers, who themselves have non-manual occupations. Secondly, the authors distinguish between levels of responsibility in the workplace, removing from the working class all those with supervisory functions in their employment. Thirdly, self-employed manual workers are removed from the working class and allocated to a new 'petit bourgeoisie' group. Table 9.4 shows the rearranged class categories and how they voted in 1983 and 1987. Two points, in particular, should be noted. First, sharper voting patterns than those produced by the traditional occupational scale emerge. Almost a majority of the working class voted Labour and a very strong pattern of Conservative voting, particularly in 1983, occurs in the petit bourgeoisie and, to a lesser extent, in the salariat. Secondly, the newly defined working class is smaller and has declined, shrinking from 47 per cent of the electorate in 1964 to 34 per cent in 1983. The conclusion drawn from this is that Labour's problems stem not so much from a weakening of class loyalties as a contraction in the numbers of working-class voters. This, they argue, accounts for about half of Labour's lost support since 1964.

*Table 9.4*   Heath, Jowell and Curtice's class categories

| % *of electorate* | | *Con.%* | | *Lab.%* | | *All.%* | |
| | | 1983 | 1987 | 1983 | 1987 | 1983 | 1987 |
|---|---|---|---|---|---|---|---|
| 8 | Petit bourgeoisie | 71 | 65 | 12 | 16 | 17 | 20 |
| 27 | Salariat | 54 | 56 | 14 | 15 | 31 | 29 |
| 7 | Foremen/technicians | 48 | 39 | 26 | 36 | 25 | 24 |
| 24 | Routine non-manual | 46 | 52 | 25 | 26 | 27 | 23 |
| 34 | Working class | 30 | 31 | 49 | 48 | 20 | 21 |

Sources A. Heath et al., *How Britain Votes*, Oxford, 1985, p. 33; A. Heath et al., *Understanding Political Change*, Oxford, 1991, p. 69.

The second major argument put forward by Heath, Jowell and Curtice is that psephologists have confused the decline of the Labour Party – caused partly, as we have seen, by a shrinking working class and by an ineffective political performance particularly between 1979 and 1983 – with a decline in class voting. This confusion comes about, it is argued, because an incorrect measure of class voting is utilised. Thus, what is important is not the *absolute* measure of class voting (the proportion voting for their 'natural' class party) but the *relative* level of class voting (the difference between the parties' share of the vote in the middle class and the working class). What matters, therefore, is whether

Labour's support in the working class has changed relative to its support from other classes. If one uses this method then it becomes apparent that Labour's support has declined across the board in all of the authors' class categories. The Conservatives did become more popular amongst working-class voters between 1979 and 1983 but this was because of short-term factors – Labour's divisions, poor campaign, unpopular leader etc. – rather than any long-term decline in class voting. The implication, then, is that in a more 'normal' election, the working-class voters who deserted Labour in 1983 would return.

Heath, Jowell and Curtice provide an interesting challenge to the conventional view but, as Denver points out, it 'emerges relatively unscathed' from their assault.[34] In the first place, their redrawing of class categories has been criticised. It has the effect of 'minoritising' the working class. Given the fact that 60 per cent of the electorate in 1983 regarded themselves as working class it is a little strange that many of them are excluded from the working class described by Heath *et al.*[35] It is as though they have artificially contracted the working class in order to recreate a class alignment that was declining because the working class was fragmenting.[36] Furthermore, barely half of this smaller working class voted Labour in 1983, and in 1987 and 1992, when many of the short-term problems faced by Labour had disappeared, the party's support amongst working class voters did not markedly increase.

Secondly, even if we accept their use of relative levels of class voting, it has been argued that the ratio between Labour's support in the working class and the middle class *has* declined. Although not as extensive as the dealignment produced by absolute levels of class voting, this is quite consistent with class dealignment.[37] In addition, the Conservatives' middle-class vote share *has* declined so it is incorrect to say that the changes simply reflect Labour's decline. Heath, Jowell and Curtice do not show this because they ignore the fact that it was the Alliance, rather than Labour, who were the beneficiaries so it does not show up on the relative level of class voting calculated for Labour. This is tantamount to describing a middle-class Alliance vote as a class vote (which

Heath *et al.* do). Yet, surely, the Alliance was, and the Liberal Democrats are, the archetypal non-class political formation.[38]

### Explaining dealignment

It is a much easier task to describe dealignment than to explain why it has taken place. Although a partisan alignment can exist independently of a class alignment, in the British context the two are obviously related. Nevertheless, for the sake of simplicity, it is probably wise to consider partisan and class dealignment separately.

### Explaining partisan dealignment

A simple explanation for partisan dealignment is that the two main parties have just become more unpopular, with Labour taking the brunt of this dissatisfaction. Thus, many voters were disillusioned – not surprisingly perhaps – with their governing record in the 1970s and began to look elsewhere. Similarly, the breakdown of the social democratic consensus and the polarisation of the two major parties proved unpopular with many voters who occupy a 'middle-ground' position. This vacation of the centre ground therefore created a space which the centre parties were able to exploit.[39] This simple 'unpopularity' theory is backed up by Crewe who discovered that over the past twenty years or so there have been significant changes in issue preferences. This was particularly bad news for Labour since Crewe's analysis revealed: 'a quite exceptional movement of opinion away from Labour's traditional positions amongst Labour supporters . . . There has been a spectacular decline in support for the "collectivist trinity" of public ownership, trade union power and social welfare.'[40] Given that Conservative policies remained relatively popular, this would seem to explain why Labour has suffered more than the Conservatives from dealignment.

A related change here is the argument that voters have become increasingly sophisticated. Thus, they no longer choose between parties on the basis of a long-standing identification but are far more instrumental, examining party policies and records in office. This growing sophistication is itself put down to the impact of greater educational opportunities and the massive increase in television coverage of politics over the last twenty years or so. This has enabled ordinary voters to become more informed about and interested in politics.[41] Evidence for this is provided by Mark Franklin among others. Franklin stresses the growth of issue voting which, he argues, increased substantially between 1964 and 1983. Many voters, he suggests, no longer blindly identified with a particular party and their issue preferences became independent variables determining the choice of party.[42] The problem here is that, as Franklin himself admits, party identification still accounts for most voters whose knowledge of political issues is slight. In addition, it is very difficult to prove that issue preferences determine party choice since the direction of causation is problematic. It could be that party identification determines issues preferences so, for example, falling support for Labour's policies could be the result of falling party identification rather than the other way round.[43]

### Explaining class dealignment

Class dealignment would seem to be a political reflection of the vast amount of social and economic change that has occurred in recent years. In the first place, *social mobility* has increased markedly over the past thirty years. This is a product of the rise in non-manual occupations (43 per cent of the voters were non-manual workers in 1987, only 35 per cent were in 1959). Many of those who belong to the new enlarged middle class have working-class backgrounds and may retain their Labour voting habits. Linked to this is the fact that the growth of the middle class since 1945 mirrors to a large extent the growth of the public sector of the economy, encouraging a wide range of new white-collar employment in state education, the civil service, the NHS, the nationalised industries and local authorities. The ideals underpinning these new areas of employment (emphasising social need and state-led provision rather than commercial gain) served to foster a centre-left outlook among their workers which was rather at odds with traditional, middle-class attitudes to politics and society. This is illustrated by table 9.5 which demonstrates that in the 1987 election Conservative support was far weaker in the public sector middle class than in the private sector middle class.

*Table 9.5*   Public and private sector voting in the middle class (%)

| | Public sector | | private sector | |
| | 1987 | 1983–87 | 1987 | 1983–87 |
| --- | --- | --- | --- | --- |
| Con. | 44 | −4 | 65 | +1 |
| Lab. | 24 | – | 13 | – |
| All. | 32 | +4 | 22 | −1 |

Source I. Crewe, 'A new class of politics', *Guardian*, 15 June 1987.

The manual working class has changed even more fundamentally. Over the past twenty years or so, the *previously homogenous working class has fragmented*. This has been a product of the changing nature of the British economy. The dominance of heavy 'Fordist' industry, so vital to the development of class consciousness, has gradually given way to new forms of economic production, characterised by smaller units employing a smaller, more diverse, more skilled workforce where trade union membership, for example, seems less relevant (union membership has fallen by about three million since 1979 alone and now represents only 23 per cent of the British electorate).

This development has had a crucial effect upon the class consciousness of the workforce and therefore the character of the British electorate. As units of production have become more diverse, so have the wages and conditions of manual workers (reflected in the growing divisions within the trade union movement, for example the fragmentation of the National Union of Mineworkers after 1984 and the expulsion of the Electricians Union from the TUC in 1988). The living standards of some manual workers have changed to the extent that they have taken on the trappings of the traditional middle-class lifestyle, a change often referred to as *embourgeoisement*. A growing number are homeowners (65 per cent in 1988, 20 per cent in 1959), live in suburban areas (36 per cent in 1985, 20 per cent in 1959), own shares (20 per cent in 1987, 6 per cent in 1979) and take foreign holidays. Thus, the homogeneity of income and lifestyle which formed the basis of class consciousness among manual workers has been corroded with the result that divisions within the working class are, perhaps, now more revealing than those between manual and non-manual workers.[44]

These new divisions within the working class are powerfully reflected in contemporary voting behaviour. As table 9.6 shows, it is possible to divide the working class into two distinct groups. The 'old' or traditional working class has tended to remain strongly Labour but the 'new', more affluent, working class has veered towards the Conservatives. In the 1987 election, the Conservatives had substantial leads over Labour amongst working-class voters living in the south, owning their own homes and not belonging to a union, and were only narrowly behind Labour amongst working-class voters employed in the private sector. In 1992, Labour narrowed the gap amongst southern and owner-occupier working-class voters but a significant difference between the voting behaviour of the new and traditional working class remains.

## Dealignment or realignment?

Since class has declined as a key determinant of voting behaviour psephologists have sought to identify a replacement. If a new cleavage – or cleavages – emerge which have the same force as class used to have, we can usefully talk about a *realignment*.

## Sectoral cleavages

One view is that a cleavage based on occupational class has been replaced by one based on sectors of employment and consumption.[45] Here, it is argued that the growth of the state since 1945 has created new divisions in society which cut across occupational class. Thus, those who are employed in the public sector and who are reliant upon publicly provided services (housing, transport, state benefits) tend to vote Labour whatever their class whereas those who work in the private sector and provide for themselves in

247

*Table 9.6*   The fragmentation of working-class voting behaviour (%)

| The new working class | | | | | | |
|---|---|---|---|---|---|---|
| | Lives in south | | Owner-occupier | | Non-union | Works in private sector |
| | 1987 | 1992 | 1987 | 1992 | 1987 | 1987 |
| Con. | 46 | 38 | 44 | 40 | 40 | 38 |
| Lab. | 28 | 36 | 32 | 39 | 38 | 39 |
| All.[a] | 26 | 22 | 24 | 18 | 22 | 23 |

| The traditional working class | | | | | | |
|---|---|---|---|---|---|---|
| | Lives in Scotland/ north | | Council tenant | | Union member | Works in public sector |
| | 1987 | 1992 | 1987 | 1992 | 1987 | 1987 |
| Con. | 29 | 29 | 25 | 24 | 30 | 32 |
| Lab. | 57 | 56 | 57 | 58 | 48 | 49 |
| All.[a] | 15 | 13 | 18 | 12 | 22 | 19 |

*Note*
[a]  1992 figures refer to the Liberal Democrats

Sources I. Crewe, 'A new class of politics', *Guardian*, 15 June 1987; *Sunday Times*, 12 April 1992.

areas such as housing and transport are more likely to vote Conservative whatever their class. This is backed up, to a certain extent, by the figures from the 1987 election illustrated in tables 9.5 and 9.6. Labour received much more support from publicly employed council tenants than from privately employed owner-occupiers within the working class whilst the Conservatives were much stronger among middle-class voters who work in the private sector.

Two cautionary remarks should be made, though. First, the correlation is not that strong (with the exception of housing which is now at least as good a predictor of voting behaviour as occupational class).[46] For example, in patterns of employment, class, rather than sector, was still more important. Labour still led (although very narrowly) in the private sector working class as did the Conservatives in the public sector middle class. Secondly, it is by no means certain that sectoral cleavages actually explain the way people vote. For instance, does working in the public sector cause middle-class voters to be more likely to vote Labour or are Labour-inclined middle-class voters more likely to work in the public sector? Similarly, do working-class home owners tend to vote Conservative because they perceive that party as more likely to further the interests of owner occupiers or because they are affluent and live in the south?[47]

### *Regional voting*

Regional variations in voting behaviour have been apparent for a considerable time but they have intensified in recent years with both a north–south and an urban–suburban divide becoming increasingly apparent. In 1987, for instance, there was a national swing to Labour of just over 1 per cent. In the north of England and Wales, however, there was a 4.5 per cent swing to Labour, in Scotland the swing was 6 per cent to Labour but in the south east there was a small swing to the Conservatives. The Conservative share of the two-party vote was nearly 20 per cent below what it would have been if Scotland had moved in line with Britain as a whole in the period 1955 to 1987.[48] Similarly in 1992, Labour won twice as many seats from the Tories as they would have done if the average swing had been uniform across the whole country because the party tended to perform better (although not well enough) in their key target seats. The use of the overall swing, then, as an accurate guide to individual constituency results is no longer applicable and the psephologist's task is made that much harder. This regional pattern has also, of course, affected Parliamentary representation. After the 1987 election, fewer than 25 per cent of Conservative MPs represented constituencies in Scotland, Wales and the north of England. More importantly, Labour won only three seats in the South of England, outside London.

The 1992 election did little to rectify this regional imbalance. Labour did lose some ground in Scotland to the Conservatives in terms of both seats and votes whilst the reverse happened in London (where Labour made 25 per cent of its gains) and the south east. Nevertheless, regional disparities are still far more pronounced than they were in the 1950s and, indeed, even the 1970s. As table 9.7 reveals, the Conservatives held thirty-six seats in Scotland and seventy-five seats in the north of England after the 1955 election but by 1992 the figures were eleven and forty-seven. Similarly, Labour held forty seats in the south of England (including East Anglia) after the 1955 election whereas in 1992 they held only ten, itself a major improvement on the three seats the party had when the election was called. Of course, these regional patterns reflect Labour's decline both because the Conservatives are stronger in the north than Labour is in the south and because there are now more seats in the south.

It is by no means clear why these regional patterns have emerged. Certainly, territorial loyalties (seen, in particular, in support for the nationalist parties in Scotland and Wales) play only a small role. Another theory is that of the 'neighbourhood factor'. Here, there is a tendency for individuals to vote for the party which dominates in the area in which they live. Thus, middle-class voters in working-class dominated Labour strongholds are more likely to vote Labour than in middle-class Conservative seats and vice versa. Why this occurs is not known, although there is some evidence for a 'contagion' effect whereby voters take on board the traits of the dominant class.[49] A more likely explanation for regional voting patterns is that social and economic trends have affected regions differently. Crucially important is that the 'new' more prosperous working class tends to be heavily concentrated in the south whilst the 'traditional' working class employed in the remaining heavy manufacturing industries and living in council houses tends to be concentrated in the north.[52]

## Labour, voting behaviour and the 1992 election

Of course, the changes in voting behaviour which we have identifed have, however they are interpreted, had a devastating impact on the Labour Party whose electoral decline in the last two decades has been startling. It is nearly twenty years now since Labour last won an election and more than twenty years since the party gained over 40 per cent of the vote in a UK general election

*Table 9.7* Geographical distribution of parties' seats in selected post-1945 general elections

|  | Con. | Lab. | Lib.[a] | Nats.[b] |
|---|---|---|---|---|
| **1955** |  |  |  |  |
| London | 15 | 27 | – | n/a |
| S. England[c] | 163 | 42 | – | n/a |
| Midlands | 39 | 57 | – | n/a |
| N. England | 75 | 90 | 2 | n/a |
| Wales | 6 | 27 | 3 | – |
| Scotland | 36 | 34 | 1 | – |
| **1970** |  |  |  |  |
| London | 9 | 33 | – | n/a |
| S. England | 169 | 34 | 2 | n/a |
| Midlands | 51 | 45 | – | n/a |
| N. England | 63 | 104 | – | n/a |
| Wales | 7 | 27 | 1 | 1 |
| Scotland | 23 | 44 | 3 | 1 |
| **Oct. 1974** |  |  |  |  |
| London | 41 | 51 | – | n/a |
| S. England | 128 | 29 | 5 | n/a |
| Midlands | 40 | 58 | – | n/a |
| N. England | 44 | 117 | 3 | n/a |
| Wales | 8 | 23 | 2 | 3 |
| Scotland | 16 | 41 | 3 | 11 |
| **1987** |  |  |  |  |
| London | 58 | 23 | 3 | n/a |
| S. England | 170 | 3 | 3 | n/a |
| Midlands | 67 | 33 | – | n/a |
| N. England | 55 | 68 | 3 | n/a |
| Wales | 8 | 24 | 3 | 3 |
| Scotland | 10 | 48 | 9 | 3 |
| **1992** |  |  |  |  |
| London | 48 | 35 | 1 | n/a |
| S. England | 161 | 10 | 6 | n/a |
| Midlands | 57 | 43 | – | n/a |
| N. England | 47 | 77 | 2 | n/a |
| Wales | 6 | 27 | 1 | 4 |
| Scotland | 11 | 49 | 9 | 3 |

*Notes*
[a] The Liberal total of seats becomes that of the Liberal–SDP Alliance in 1983 and 1987 and the Liberal Democrats in 1992.
[b] 'Nats' usually denote the SNP in Scotland and Plaid Cymru in Wales.
[c] The figures for Southern England include East Anglia.

whereas between 1945 and 1970 the party did not once fail to achieve this level of support. In 1983, Labour's share of the vote was their lowest since 1918 and even though the 34.4 per cent gained in the 1992 election represented an improvement (on both 1983 and 1987) it still ranks as the seventh worst result for the party in the twenty-one elections fought since 1918.

Clearly, the roots of this decline lie in the changing nature of British society. In addition to the fragmentation of the working class, Labour's problems are compounded by two other factors. In the first place, the 'new' working class – which has progressively turned its back on Labour – is likely to grow as the effects of economic change and Conservative policies bite deeper. Secondly, the manual working class (the section of the electorate from which Labour has traditionally drawn the bulk of its support) is declining as the proportion of the electorate employed in non-manual occupations increases. Put simply, Labour is now receiving a declining share of a declining class.[51] The party's malaise was summed up by Crewe after the 1987 election. Labour, he wrote, has:

come to represent a declining segment of the working class – the traditional working class of the council estates, the public sector, industrial Scotland and the North, and the old industrial unions – while failing to attract the affluent and expanding working class of the new estates and new service economy of the South.[52]

The impact of these changes was really fully appreciated only after the 1992 election since they had, to a certain extent, been disguised in the 1980s. Labour could comfort themselves in 1983 and 1987 with the thought that defeat could be explained by a variety of short-term factors – a poor leader, disunity and extreme policies in 1983; unilateralism and an economic boom in 1987 – which would not recur. In 1992, however, Labour went into the election with a cautious programme of policies, with an experienced leader and in the midst of a steep recession which many blamed on the Government. Yet despite all of this, Labour only received 34 per cent of the vote, a mere 3 per cent or so increase on 1987 and still over 7 per cent behind the Conservatives.

It is in this context that many political commentators began to express real doubts about Labour's prospects of ever again winning a general election on its own. The analyses offered from a variety of quarters have been remarkably uniform.[53] They centre on the view that social and economic change has put too many voters permanently beyond Labour's grasp. More specifically, the changes have produced an electorate to which Labour's collectivist and egalitarian philosophy (which finds its practical expression in state-led social provision funded by redistributive taxation) no longer holds any appeal. Instead, voters in the 'New England' – detached from traditional working-class communities where solidarity, collectivism and Labour voting once went hand in hand – have become imbued with individualistic values and the desire to succeed through personal initiative and effort rather than reliance on the state.

It is this new culture, of course, which Mrs Thatcher (through allowing ordinary people to buy their council houses, buy into privatised industries and keep more of their earned income) was able both to promote and to encourage. By contrast, Labour is regarded with suspicion by this new culture, as the party which threatens individual achievements and seeks – in the words of Bryan Gould – to 'cap the aspirations' of those who seek to better themselves (hence the unpopularity of Labour's tax proposals which, although hitting only those who earn over £22,000 a year, were seen as a disincentive to those who aspired to earn that amount). As Vernon Bogdanor, then, pointed out:

For voters in the new England, a Labour vote reflects the background from which they have come, a background of organised trade unionism and collective provision. A Conservative vote, by contrast, expresses an aspiration, an aspiration to a world in which they can make decisions for themselves, free from the paternalism of trade union leaders or local councillors.[54]

What should we make of this 'inevitable decline of Labour' thesis? In the first place, it might be argued that it underestimates Labour's performance in the 1992 election. After all, the party had to achieve an unprecedented 8 per cent swing to secure the barest of overall majorities. As it was, Labour has apparently 'seen off' the challenge of the centre party. In particular, whereas the Alliance was second in 261 seats after the 1987 election, the Liberal Democrats finished second in only 154 in 1992. In addition, Labour recovered ground in the south, winning more seats than at any time since 1974 and there are in 1993 seventeen seats where the Conservative lead over Labour is less than a thousand votes. Finally, the gap of 8 per cent between the two major parties is misleading in the sense that, because the swing to Labour was greater in their target seats than it was overall, the party was relatively close to depriving the Tories of an overall majority. Indeed, had just 3,899 people in twelve constituencies voted in a different way, a hung parliament would have been the outcome.[55]

All of this is not to belittle the problems faced by Labour and the social and economic changes, in particular, which have reduced Labour's natural constituency of voters. But to claim that these changes automatically spell inevitable electoral defeat for Labour is to adopt a determinist position which takes little account of the actors involved. Thus, it can readily be agreed that society has changed and that a state-dominated collectivism which seeks to uniformly protect, control and direct people is no longer appropriate. But Labour has already moved a long way from this post-war ideal, seeking to adapt itself to a more mobile and affluent working class and this process of adaptation has not been completed. This, after all, was what Kinnock's leadership was all about (see Chapters 6 and 7). Furthermore, the emphasis on the individualistic values of the 'new England' does not sit well with surveys which deny that Thatcherite values have hit a widespread chord amongst British voters. A majority of voters, for instance, say they would prefer increased spending on public services rather than tax cuts (see Chapters 3 and 4) and even in 1992 an exit poll by Mori revealed that fully 60% favoured the distribution of income from the better off to the less well off.[56] Mrs Thatcher's demise was itself, it should be remembered, the product of Labour's large lead in the opinion polls which seemed to demonstrate the popularity of a moderate social democratic party in British politics.

In this context, it would perhaps be wise to consider the conclusion of John Curtice who argued that 'nothing about Labour's defeat seems to have been inevitable. It was the product of political difficulties and mistakes at least as much as sociological or economic determinism.'[57] Thus, the key factor according to Curtice was not so much that Labour's tax policies frightened voters but that the Conservatives managed to persuade enough of the electorate that they were more competent managers of the economy than Labour and as such offered the prospect of both lower levels of taxation *and* higher public spending. If this is correct then the Government's pre-election borrowing may have been crucial. But here lies a problem for the Conservatives, since, when the deflationary consequences of the increased PSBR become apparent, necessitating public spending cuts, the electorate may turn against the Government.

## Conclusion

In conclusion, the period since 1970 has witnessed profound changes in voting behaviour which in turn have had equally profound consequences for the British party system. We should not exaggerate the extent to which occupational class has declined as a determinant of voting behaviour. In addition, the class dealignment that has taken place should not be cited as the only explanation for Labour's decline – the single most important development in recent British party politics – since a reduction in the size of the manual working-class has also played a significant role. Social class still remains the single most important indicator of voting choice in Britain. Despite the influence of other cleavages, Labour was still ahead amongst working-class voters and the Conservatives by far the most popular party amongst middle-class voters in the last three elections. Knowing an individual's class is, however, nowhere near as effective a predictor of voting behaviour as it was in the 1950s and 1960s. Today we need more information such as region, sector of employment, and housing tenure. The problem for Labour is that their strength lies in a social landscape (the industrial working class, trade unionism, the public sector, council tenants etc.) which is becoming electorally insignificant. The party's prospects of depriving the

Conservatives of another term in office depend upon the extent to which they can break even further out of their heartlands which no longer provide an election-winning coalition of support. The unpredictability of voting behaviour should make us wary of betting against a future Labour election victory despite the favourable odds.

## Notes

1  D. Denver, *Elections and Voting Behaviour*, pp. 4–5.
2  A. Campbell, P. Converse, W. Miller & D. Stokes, *The American Voter*, New York, 1960.
3  The classic account of its application to British politics is D. Butler & D. Stokes, *Political Change in Britain*, London, 1974.
4  M. Harrop & W. L. Miller, *Elections*, p. 145.
5  A. Downs, *Economic Theory of Democracy*, New York, 1957, p. 28. For a modern application of this theory to British politics see H. T. Himmelweit, P. Humphreys & M. Jaeger, *How Voters Decide*, Milton Keynes, 1981.
6  For a full assessment see B. Barry, *Sociologists, Economists and Democracy*, London, 1970.
7  For further discussion of this point see I. McLean, *Elections*, London, 1980, pp. 37–8.
8  P. Dunleavy & H. Ward, 'Exogenous voter preferences and parties with state power: some internal problems of economic theories of party competition', *British Journal of Political Science*, II, 1981, pp. 351–79.
9  P. Dunleavy & C. T. Husbands, *British Democracy at the Crossroads*, London, 1985, p. 215. For an assessment see W. Miller, 'Voting and the electorate', in P. Dunleavy, A. Gamble & G. Peele (eds), *Developments in British Politics 3*, London, 1990, pp. 55–61.
10  Harrop & Miller, *Elections*, chapter five.
11  W. H. Morris Jones, 'In defence of apathy', *Political Studies*, II, 1954, pp. 25–37.
12  Note that, as Harrop and Miller, *Elections*, p. 161 point out: 'Most advocates of the party identification model now accept that party identification *reflects* as well as *shapes* voting choices. In what proportions we are not told!'
13  Denver, *Elections and Voting Behaviour*, p. 86.
14  Quoted in M. Harrop, 'Voting and the electorate', in H. Drucker et al., *Developments in British Politics 2*, London, 1986, p. 52.
15  Harrop and Miller, *Elections*, pp. 148–9.
16  I. Crewe, 'Tories prosper from a paradox', *Guardian*, 16 June 1987.

17 Denver, *Elections and Voting Behaviour*, p. 29.
18 B. Sarlvik and I. Crewe, *Decade*, pp. 333–8.
19 Sarlvik and Crewe, *Decade*, p. 337.
20 Denver, *Elections and Voting Behaviour*, p. 47.
21 Harrop, 'Voting and the electorate', pp. 34–5. See also A. Heath, R. Jowell & J. Curtice, *Understanding Political Change*, Oxford, 1991, pp. 10–31.
22 Moran, *Politics and Society*, pp. 74–5.
23 D. Kavanagh, *British Politics: Continuities and Change*, Oxford, 1990, p. 110.
24 P. G. Pulzer, *Political Representation and Elections in Britain*, London, 1975, p. 102.
25 See Denver, *Elections and Voting Behaviour*, pp. 39–43.
26 See D. Robertson, *Class and the British Electorate*, Oxford, 1984, pp. 18–29.
27 Denver, *Elections and Voting Behaviour*, pp. 33–5; 65–6.
28 Dunleavy & Husbands, *British Democracy*, p. 4.
29 See S. Hall & M. Jacques, *New Times: The Changing Face of Politics in the 1990s*, London, 1989.
30 I. Crewe, 'A new class of politics', *Guardian*, 15 June 1987.
31 Crewe, 'New class'.
32 A. Heath, R. Jowell & J. Curtice, *How Britain Votes*, Oxford, 1985; Heath et al., *Political Change*, pp. 62–84.
33 See D. Denver & G. Hands (eds), *Issues and Controversies in British Electoral Behaviour*, Hemel Hempstead, 1992, pp. 51–126 which reproduces a number of key articles in the debate.
34 Denver, *Elections and Voting Behaviour*, p. 65.
35 Denver, *Elections and Voting Behaviour*, p. 63.
36 I. Crewe, 'On the death and resurrection of class voting: Some comments on How Britain Votes', in Denver & Hands, *British Electoral Behaviour*, pp. 85–96.
37 Harrop, 'Voting and the electorate', p. 40.
38 Miller, 'Voting and the electorate', pp. 48–9.
39 Dunleavy & Husbands, *British Democracy*, p. 17.
40 Quoted in Harrop, 'Voting and the electorate', p. 51.
41 Denver, *Elections and Voting Behaviour*, pp. 49–50.
42 M. Franklin, *The Decline of Class Voting in Britain*, Oxford, 1985.
43 Denver, *Elections and Voting Behaviour*, p. 76.
44 G. Marshall, 'What is happening to the working class?', *Social Studies Review*, January 1987, pp. 37–40. For a full statistical analysis of social change and its relationship to voting behaviour see M. Harrop and A. Shaw, *Can Labour Win?*, pp. 113–39.
45 Dunleavy & Husbands, *British Democracy*.
46 Harrop & Miller, *Elections*, pp. 195–7.

47 Harrop, 'Voting and the electorate', pp. 44–5.
48 D. Butler & D. Kavanagh, *The British General Election of 1987*, London, 1988, p. 331.
49 Harrop and Miller, *Elections*, pp. 207–9.
50 See R. J. Johnston & C. J. Pattie, 'The changing electoral geography of Great Britain', in Denver & Hands, *British Electoral Behaviour*, pp. 316–21.
51 I. Crewe, 'Can Labour rise again?', *Social Studies Review*, September 1985, pp. 13–9.
52 Crewe, 'New class'.
53 See V. Bogdanor, 'Britain's quiet revolution', *Sunday Independent*, 12 April 1992; M. Ignatieff, 'How the glitz turned to ashes', *Observer*, 12 April 1992; B. Crick, 'In defence of compromise', *Guardian*, 13 April 1992; M. Jacques, 'The party that nobody wants', *Guardian*, 20 June 1992; G. Mackenzie, 'Fatal flaws in the machine', *Times Higher Education Supplement*, 31 July 1992.
54 Bogdanor, 'Quiet revolution'.
55 *Sunday Times*, 12 April 1992.
56 *Guardian*, 13 April 1992.
57 J. Curtice, 'Labour's slide to defeat', *Guardian*, 13 April 1992.

# 10

# ARE PARTIES MAKING A DIFFERENCE?

Any discussion concerning the effectiveness of political parties must first recall the functions they are supposed to perform. This is itself a matter for debate as the aims of political parties are invariably shaped by the perceived nature of the party concerned and the society in which it exists; those belonging to Marxist (or 'vanguard') parties will obviously view the nature of party activity in a rather different light to those belonging to, say, the Conservative Party. This problem is compounded by the fact that, in Britain, parties are still voluntary bodies without any clear constitutional role – unlike in Sweden, for example, where the main parties are much more closely integrated into the political system through such mechanisms as extensive state funding.[1]

Mindful of these difficulties, the opening chapter of this book ventured to suggest that one of the prime functions of British political parties was to condense and articulate various public demands and attitudes in order to offer the electorate a clear, structured choice of policies at a general election. This suggestion was consistent with most other mainstream analyses of British parties in the post-war era – notably McKenzie's acclaimed study of 1955, which defined parties as groups of persons trying to win control of state power by presenting the electorate with a set of ideas designed to attract more popular support than those of their principal rivals.[2]

This view of political parties as 'agents of choice' depends heavily, however, upon two imperatives. First of all, there must be a genuine choice available between those parties which contend seriously for government; that choice is plainly undermined if there is little substantial difference between the parties' diagnoses and prescriptions. Secondly, and perhaps more pertinently, a party elected to government with a 'mandate' for a particular set of policies must be able to implement them so as to make a clear impact upon the way we are governed and the society in which we live. If it is evident that parties in office are either unwilling or unable to translate election promises into reality, this renders meaningless any notion that parties confront voters with a signal opportunity to alter the tenor and direction of society.

## A negligible impact?

Perhaps the most distinguished challenge made during the 1980s to the idea that parties are inclined to offer radically alternative policies to their opponents at elections, and then carry through those policies in office, came from Professor Richard Rose.[3] To those who wish to believe that elections, manifestos, campaigns and intra-party democracy actually matter, Rose's study – *Do Parties Make a Diference?* – makes dismal reading. Rose endeavours to make two central points: that party manifestos have more in common than their protagonists care to acknowledge and that, in any case, manifesto-based policies play a surprisingly small role once the party has been elected to government.

A sizeable chunk of this book has already lent support to Rose's thesis by describing how much of British politics during the post-war years has been characterised by a broad consensus between the parties. As Chapter 3 recorded, for almost thirty years the two main parties in Britain agreed on a Keynesian approach to the economy, extensive state provision of welfare, a judicious blend of private and public ownership in industry, the incorporation of major economic interest groups into government decision-making, and the utility of the Atlantic Alliance. As Cook and McKie wrote of the 1964 general election, the contest was 'less between competing philosophies, much more about which set of managers was likely to get better results.'[4] More recently, it has been suggested that a new social market consensus has emerged, stemming partly from Labour's acceptance of many of the changes wrought during the 1980s and partly from adjustments in the Tory Party following Mrs Thatcher's resignation.[5]

For Rose (echoing the analysis of Anthony Downs fifteen years earlier), this tendency to agree behind the adversarial rhetoric was the ineluctable consequence of how 'serious' parties function in democratic societies. Parties are primarily in the business of attaining power, which in a modern democracy involves reflecting the opinions of substantial portions of electors, and especially those 'floating' voters not firmly aligned to any one party. The search by all the major parties for such voters' support, which almost by definition tends to be 'middle of the road', tends to mitigate the differences between them and produce a centripetal effect upon party political debate. If there are fundamental differences between the major parties, the implication has to be that at least one of them is failing to reflect properly the concerns of the middle-ground voter, a condition that can lead to either ignominious defeat for the 'guilty' party or widespread disenchantment with the party system altogether if the failure is more general (the latter condition was possibly exemplified in the 1974 elections when no single party managed to attain 40 per cent of the votes cast). Rose argued that it was no coincidence that the 1945–79 period, in which both major parties governed for roughly seventeen years, was also a period when policy differences between the parties were generally peripheral. Conversely, the two elections where there did seem to be substantial and essential differences about social and economic policy – 1945 and 1983 – were occasions when one of the two parties plunged to a catastrophic defeat. Likewise, Rose would find it entirely predictable that Labour's recovery as a likely party of government after 1987 was accompanied by a willingness to abandon many of the distinctive policies on which it had fought and lost previous elections and adopt many of the ideas associated with a government that had been twice re-elected. The moral seems to be clear: if there is to be more than one potential party of government, then the policy differences between these parties cannot be extensive.

Rose did not dispute the existence of inter-party bickering based upon the contents of election manifestos (which after all form the basis of most election campaigns). Instead, he pointed out that the bulk of manifesto pledges (assuming there would be more than one 'viable' party) were non-partisan; statements, in other words, which could not be seriously contested by other parties – 'we shall aim to secure more job and training opportunities for school-leavers', 'we attach great importance to the maintenance of law and order', 'we intend to enhance the quality of life for all our citizens', and so on.[6] Many of the differences between the manifestos stem from what Rose terms 'talking past' each other: one party devoting more space to defence than the other, promising (as in 1951) to build even more council houses than their opponents. In short, Rose considers manifesto differences to be deliberately exaggerated by their proponents, with arguments being mainly derived from detail and emphasis rather than ideological contradictions.

In developing this argument, Rose was not sailing into entirely uncharted waters. McKenzie contested that the 'adversary' nature of party debate merely concealed the large measure of agreement between the parties. Indeed, McKenzie argued that the oligarchic structure of both major parties (the central theme of his analysis) was itself necessary to ensure that the parties were not as far from the middle ground as their militant activists might wish – an argument which recalled Michels's 'iron law of oligarchy' formulated at the beginning of the century.[7] Such an argument has crucial importance for students of British political parties, for it implies that changes in the direction of politics in a democratic society spring mainly from shifts in public opinion which parties respond to rather than instigate. Unless they are indifferent to electoral success, changes in party policy merely reflect changes in public perceptions, which themselves spring mainly from factors other than the propaganda of political parties. Thus, if a party is elected on a radical, 'alternative' manifesto (as in 1945 and 1979) it is probably because it has effectively gauged shifts in public opinion stemming from circumstances beyond the parties' control. As Hennessy wrote of the Attlee Government's record:

A huge advantage was the highly disciplined condition of the British people. Almost 6 years of total war had left no citizen untouched by its rigours, whether in the form of the siege economy on the home front or by military service abroad. The population was used to receiving orders and to strict regulation [which] helped create an atmosphere in which carefully conceived and centrally directed schemes of national improvement became a norm and not a pipedream.[8]

Other forces which might produce such a change in public mood would include changes in the nature of employment and the distribution of the population. In addition, of course, the success or failure of previous party policies in government must be considered (which might also have played a part in the aforementioned changes in employment and population). The key question, however, is to what extent was the impact and nature of these policies determined by the calculations of the party in power?

The growing interdependence of the British economy (the health of which determines the feasibility of most other government schemes) has led many to argue that government economic policy is largely at the mercy of external pressures: the policies of the governing party – if they are to be effective – must recognise these pressures rather than seek to defy them. Thus the difference that parties can make in government is limited; as one observer of economic policy since 1945 asserted:

The major source of Britain's difficulties is to be located among the non-state actors . . . the efficacy [of governments] cannot be great when industrial firms, bankers, trade unions who are directly involved in economic acivity . . . are unable to invest, produce and sell efficiently . . . Politicians in power prate and posture, taking the credit and the blame for the diverse fortunes that ensue from the interplay of international market forces, without usually being responsible for either the good or the bad results.[9]

This line of argument is complemented by Rose's research. Unlike Anthony King, who claimed only 'a random relationship' between what a party said in its manifesto and what it did in office, Rose discovered that most manifesto pledges were actually implemented.[10] More recently, a study by Rallings confirmed this by recording that 75 per cent of pledges from successful election manifestos were effected between 1945 and 1987.[11] Rose's point, however, was that manifesto-based policies account for less than a fifth of actions carried out by governments – the vast majority being taken on an *ad hoc* basis in response to unforeseen events which left the government usually little choice as to the policies it adopted.[12] Support for this argument comes from David Butler, who lists the following as the most decisive events in the post-war era prior to 1979: the financial crises of 1947 and 1949, the Korean War, Suez, the attempts to enter Europe in 1962, 1967 and 1972, the retreat from Empire and east of Suez, the oil price rises of 1973 and the intervention of the IMF in 1976. Most of these, he argues, 'would have occurred whichever party had been in power and most would have evoked a broadly similar reaction'.[13] Pulzer reaches a similar conclusion when assessing what he considers to be the key moments in post-war economic history: 1957 (first sterling crisis), 1961 (first incomes policy), 1962–63 (stabilisation through growth), 1967 (devaluation) and 1972 (Heath's U-Turn). All, he claims, were unaffected by the previous election result.[14]

These general observations (that changes in party policy outside government, if to be electorally effective, are the product of wider changes in society largely beyond governments' control, and that parties in office are limited in the impact they can make) have been corroborated by a series of detailed studies concerning the record of successive post-war British administrations. It has even been argued that the changes which took place under the Labour Governments of 1945–51 – arguably the most radical and effective ministries of the twentieth century – had their roots not in Labour Party policy itself, but in the events of the inter-war years (which vitiated the intellectual basis of *laissez-faire* economics) and, even more significantly, the agreements reached by the wartime coalition which, in response to external pressures, extended the ethos of state control into most areas of society, while sanctioning the *Beveridge Report* on welfare provision and the Keynesian White Paper on Employment. Pulzer has suggested that the Conservative manifesto of 1945 – 'nationalisation and foreign policy apart' – was not grossly dissimilar to Labour's and that 'if the post-war consensus started anywhere, it was in 1942–43'.[15] Crosland lent support to this theory as early as 1956, when he recalled that the objectives of 1945–51 'did not spring from a doctrinal vacuum, or from acts of pure cerebration', but rather from 'a particular kind of society which existed by 1945'.[16]

A number of leftist academics have insisted that, given the hopes raised by Labour's landslide vitory and the propitious political climate in which Attlee became Prime Minister (see Hennessy quotation above), it is remarkable how *little* his Governments achieved. According to Ralph Miliband, the Attlee ministries will be remembered chiefly for being 'cautious and unradical in the scope of the nationalisation programme, unwilling to envisage real industrial democracy, susceptible to the views of the Chiefs of Staff, economically and militarily dependent on the United States and espousing consolidation rather than socialist advance'.[17] Coates has likewise denounced the Attlee Government for having 'simply created a mixed economy in which the bulk of industry still lay in private hands, and the six years ... only marginally altered the distribution of social power, privilege, wealth, income, opportunity and security'.[18] Put another way, Miliband and Coates believe that the conduct of British government after 1945 would not have been very different had Churchill not been defeated, and use the record of the Attlee Governments to bolster their Marxist convictions that political authority must always be subordinate to the economic power of the dominant capitalist class; all that parties in government can do is to manage the economy in the interests of those who own and control society's wealth.

These arguments were reinforced by the performance of Labour Governments in the 1960s and 1970s – all of which were apparently committed to the creation of a more 'fair' and 'equal' society and all of which have been subjected to intense criticism by many of those who subscribe to such objectives. It will be recalled from earlier chapters that the changes in Labour Party organisation between 1979 and 1981, accompanied by a leftward drift in policy, derived from a widespread feeling among grass roots party members that the egalitarian hopes raised when Labour took power in 1964 and 1974 had not been fulfilled. The very titles of various publications concerning these administrations are telling in this respect: *Labour in Power?*, a study of the 1974–79 Labour Government by David Coates; *Office Without Power*, the ministerial diaries of Tony Benn; *Breach of Promise: Labour in Power 1964–1970* by Clive Ponting.[19] As one author recalled recently in an attempt to rescue the reputation of Harold Wilson, these Governments have been almost universally vilified for their 'failure' to realise manifesto ideals.[20] A stark example of this argument rests with the Department of Economic Affairs, set up in 1964 to stabilise and quicken economic growth. It initially looked forward to a 25 per cent increase in the Gross Domestic Product by 1970, yet the actual rate of increase turned out to be no more than 14 per cent, with the DEA being effectively shut down after two years.[21] Even more 'scandalous' is the recollection that the Labour Government elected in 1974, promising expansionary economics and a 'fundamental and irreversible shift in the balance of wealth and power' ended up introducing a version of monetarism and severe cuts in government spending. Neither can the desolate record of these Governments be attributed to a paucity of individual talent. As K. O. Morgan points out, these Governments were blessed with the *glitterati* of the social democratic intelligentsia – Wilson, Healey, Crosland, Crossman, Jenkins, Shore, Williams *et al.*[22] One such member of these Governments offered an explanation of their disappointing record which illustrates perfectly the problems of party government identified by Rose and others:

These governments overestimated their ability to shape and manage the complex drives of a mature economy. They wrongly assumed that governments could produce remedies for all its problems ... It is significant that the Wilson government's National Plan ultimately was derided by the Cabinet itself. The real world obstinately refused to conform to the principles of an election manifesto.[23]

For Tony Benn, who served in all the aforementioned Labour Governments, the explanation for their 'failure' lies not only in the exigencies of international finance-capitalism. Institutional restraints in Britain are seen as equally formidable adversaries for Labour Governments seeking to transform society: of these he cites the City, Whitehall, the military chiefs, the security forces and 'above all' the mass media, which together with the EEC, NATO, the IMF and the multinationals conspire to frustrate the ambitions of any socialist administration.[24] These agencies ensure that there is 'absolute freedom to put up alternative candidates to run the system if, but only if, accompanied by secret assurances that the essential nature of the system will not be changed'.[25] Benn, however, is not as fatalistic as Rose or Marxists like Miliband; he believes that Labour Governments could make a radical impact providing that Labour's internal structure gave rank and file members more control over the behaviour of their 'perfidious' Parliamentary leaders. Richard Crossman, who had also criticised the Attlee Governments for simply producing 'welfare capitalism' was also far from deterministic about the opportunities open to Labour Governments seriously intent upon radical change.[26] He argued that the major obstacle for reforming administrations was the intransigence of the senior civil service, but conceded that its power was facilitated largely by the lack of detailed policy preparation undertaken by parties in opposition (it may be recalled that Labour took office in 1945 with a long-standing commitment to nationalise the coal industry without any plans for how this could actually be carried out).[27]

It should not be thought that only Labour Governments are used to exemplify the restrictions attending those parties in which hopes for major reforms are invested. The 1951 general election was considered by many at the time to be one of the most important since Britain became a democracy, presenting the electorate with a stark choice between a Labour Government hoping to consolidate the new social democratic state and a Conservative Party vowing to 'set the people free' of state controls and regulations.[28] It may be noted, in deference to Rose's thesis, that the libertarian tone of the 1951 Tory manifesto sprang not from Conservative policy research (which, between 1945–50 had a strong flavour of statist intervention under the influence of R. A. Butler) but from a significant change in the public mood. As *The*

*Times* remarked in 1950: 'There is a real and mounting distaste for restrictions, whether needed or not, and a resentment of bureaucratic meddling.'[29] Yet, as Seldon's study of the 1951–55 Tory Government reveals, it was 'remarkable above all for its consensus approach in most areas of policy and for its continuity with policies pursued by the Attlee government.'[30] Denationalisation was minimal, the new NHS left untouched, and several areas dear to the Tory rank and file (trade union reform, immigration, pruning welfare expenditure) evaded. The process of 'decontrol' and 'derationing', for which the Government became so popular, was only a continuation of Harold Wilson's 'Bonfire of Controls' initiated in 1949. Chancellor Butler's plan to make sterling convertible in 1952 was abandoned in the face of acute difficulties posed by international finance, whereupon Butler confessed to 'reverting to normal Keynesian economics'.[31] Although the Conservatives were re-elected in both 1955 and 1959 on a general sense of economic well-being, most historians of the period agree that this was mainly caused not by prudent government policy but by a general upturn in world trade following the post-war recession, an improvement accelerated by the outbreak of the Korean War in 1950.[32]

Perhaps the most spectacular illustration of the gap between governmental aspiration and achievement is offered by the Conservative Government of 1970–74. The Tories came to power with no lack of reforming ambition, expounding the need for a 'quiet revolution' that would challenge the collectivist mode of the 1950s and 1960s and forge a more individualistic, market-based society. There would be less state intervention in industry, a rejection of the prices and incomes policies attempted since the early 1960s, a more 'selective' system of welfare, less public expenditure and direct taxation and reform of the trade unions. Crossman's views notwithstanding, it was also armed with five years of detailed policy preparation and is generally considered the most prepared government to assume office this century. One of the Conservatives' main pledges in the 1970 election, moreover, was that under the next Tory Government 'the gap between politicians' promises and governments' peformances will be closed'.[33]

Blake has maintained that the Conservative victory in 1970 owed everything to the perceived incompetence of the Wilson Government rather than any positive endorsement of Heath's 'new ethos'.[34] This was underlined within two years as public impatience grew with the mounting cost of Heath's policies in respect of unemployment and bankruptcies. The 'U-Turn' of 1971–72, leading to reflation, striking increases in public spending, statutory incomes policies and an Industry Act betokening an unprecedented level of state intervention – in short, a return to the economic ideas of the 1960s – was largely a response to the threat of electoral disaster. This episode bears out in startling fashion Rose's contention that parties can pursue radical changes only in so far as they are consonant with political expediency which, in turn, is determined by the climate of public opinion. The increased difficulties faced by the Government as a result of the Arab–Israeli War, and the subsequent oil crisis of 1973, also support Rose's point about governments being slaves to international economic realities. The outcome of all these problems was that the Heath Government vainly sought re-election in 1974 'in defence of policies it had explicitly repudiated when elected over three and a half years earlier'.[35]

During the mid-to-late 1970s, Anthony King's theory of 'overload' was also being used to diminish the potential effectiveness of parties in government.[36] It became voguish to assert that the expansion of governmental functions and responsibilities in the post-war years weakened the chances of a party converting its proposals into reality, thereby contributing to the 'crisis of ungovernability' then thought to be afflicting British politics. King's thesis involved two central themes. First, that the growth of statism had encouraged parties to pledge initiatives in such a wide range of areas that the likelihood of the manifesto being wholly implemented naturally receded; in trying to accomplish so much, parties in office invariably overstretched themselves and eventually accomplished very little, save even more public scepticism with the political system (what Roy Jenkins later termed 'manifestoitis'). Secondly, the intrusion of government into so many realms of society led it to rely heavily upon the co-operation of innumerable interest groups and private institutions if government schemes were to be effective; the failure of incomes policies and other aspects of economic planning in the 1970s showed that such co-operation was by no means certain, thus imposing further limitations upon the scope of governing parties. The belief that the state's field of activity should be curtailed (or 'rolled back') so as to restore the effectiveness and credibility of government was to form an important part in the revision of Tory policy after 1974.

## A question of finance?

The idea that parties were 'underachieving' was upheld by two reports, published in the 1970s and early 1980s, claiming to represent an objective assessment of British political parties. The first of these was produced in 1976 by the *Houghton Committee on Financial Aid to Political Parties* (Cmnd. 6601), the second being the *Hansard Report* of 1981 entitled *Paying for Politics*. Both agreed that the formulation of alternative sets of policies, to be duly implemented in government with the electorate's support, was one of the prime functions of political parties. Both reports also suggested that this function was being jeopardised by the way in which the main parties were currently financed. Furthermore, their means of income were also thought to be at odds with the parties' other principal tasks which were said to include political recruitment, political participation, political education and the representation of society's multifarious interests. The problem of finance was thought to be two-dimensional: the parties were seen to have insufficient revenue to perform the tasks 'upon which democracy depends' (to quote Houghton) and, largely as a result of this, the two main parties were worryingly reliant upon 'institutional' donations from trade unions and business. Evidence in support of these allegations has been available in recent years. Conservative Central Office accounts showed a deficit of over £5 million in 1991, while in October 1989 Labour's overdraft stood at £1.2 million.[37] In addition, Pinto-Duschinsky has calculated that trade unions contributed three-quarters of Labour Party income betwen 1983 and 1987, with business donations (in a

270

non-election, or 'routine' year) about 60 per cent of central Conservative income.[38]

According to Houghton and Hansard, this state of affairs did much to explain the low public esteem in which the parties were held. The parties' dependence upon institutional funding was thought to make them too eager to echo narrow sectarian interests rather than public opinion generally – a view arguably corroborated in 1989 when the Tory Government diluted its plans to 'liberalise' public houses after intense pressure from its backers among the large breweries. Meanwhile the shortage of funds overall made it difficult to attract a wider span of members, 'educate' the public through the most up-to-date methods of communication and (of particular importance to this chapter) carry out the requisite amount of policy research needed to guarantee the implementation of party policy in office.

Both reports believed that the solution to the problem of party finance, and therefore the efficiency of British political parties, was greater assistance from the state. It must be emphasised that state funding already exists to a sizeable extent: all Parliamentary candidates receive free use of halls for election meetings and free postage for an item of mail to each elector. In 1987, the estimated value of these subsidies totalled £13.2 million each for the Conservative, Labour and Alliance parties.[39] Since 1975, the availability of 'Short Money' (named after Edward Short, the Leader of the House, who unveiled the scheme) has also meant greater assistance for Parliamentary opposition parties with the cost of research and secretarial facilities. Nevertheless, Houghton and Hansard considered these apparently generous subsidies inadequate and proposed more direct state funding to the extra-Parliamentary parties. Houghton proposed a method similar to that used in Sweden, where parties receive state subsidies according to the number of seats and votes won at the previous general election, whereas Hansard advocated a scheme adopted in Canada, whereby state aid was increased in line with the number of new party members recruited (thus absolving their scheme from the complaint levelled at the Houghton proposal, namely that it would prop up parties that made no effort to attract a mass

271

membership). By adopting either of these proposals for greater state aid, the reports hoped that parties would acquire more revenue, diminish their reliance upon institutional support, become genuinely populist in character and thus play a more effective role in influencing the evolution of politics and society.

From our examination of some of the considerable constraints from international trade and finance alone, it is not at all obvious that such a reform would alleviate the difficulties faced by parties seeking to be programmatic in government. As previously explained, the Heath Government represents one of the most conspicuous examples of governments failing to adhere to the ideals of an election manifesto, yet it was probably the most prepared and researched government of the post-war period. The role of external think tanks (like the Adam Smith Institute and Institute of Economic Affairs), and their importance to the Thatcher Governments, also raises the question of whether a governing party needs to rely upon internal party machinery to be effective in policy implementation.

Neither is the correlation between the parties' institutional backers and the policies of the party in government as clear-cut as the two reports suggest. The 'Winter of Discontent', which emasculated the Labour Government of the late 1970s, arose from government actions failing rather than fulfilling the aspirations of organised labour – it is not just Marxist critics who believe that the Callaghan ministry deferred far more to the wishes of the IMF than of the TUC.[40] Likewise, the relationship between the first Thatcher Government and the CBI (which incorporates the Tory sponsors) came under severe strain as a result of the deflationary policies adopted in the early 1980s. Parties in office, especially Labour, cannot hope to survive or be re-elected simply by reflecting the views of their benefactors, a point recognised by Neil Kinnock and others in Labour's review of policy and organisation prior to the 1992 election (which consciously aimed to distance the party from the trade union movement). There may, indeed, be some relationship between the policies of the parties in government and the interests of the institutions which support them, but as Ewing remarked in a detailed study of party finance: 'It would be wrong to say that Conservatives are pro-business simply because they are financed by business, or that Labour is pro-union because that is where the bulk of its money comes from. The relationship is much more subtle than that.'[41]

## From Thatcher to Major: was Rose wrong?

So far, this chapter has concentrated on those arguments suggesting that parties are limited in the impact they can make upon politics and government. Yet there is a body of academic opinion that is not as dismissive. Since 1974, there has been a burgeoning interest in electoral reform and proportional representaion. Much of this obviously stems from the lack of proportionality usually extant between a party's share of the votes at a general election and its subsequent share of Parliamentary seats. Yet support for proportional representation also comes from a conviction that coalition governments (the most likely consequence of PR) would provide much-needed continuity in British Government and mitigate the 'adversary' system of politics which has allegedly bedevilled this country since 1945. This argument was cogently stated by S. E. Finer in 1975 in a study which claimed that alternating single-party governments, as allowed by the present electoral system, not only exaggerated national differences while concealing the strong desire for consensus but also encouraged chronic ruptures in government policy that were inimical to economic success.[42] West Germany and many of the Scandinavian countries were used to substantiate the idea that PR led to greater continuity in policy which, in turn, led to greater economic and industrial achievement. This argument was endorsed in 1979 by another Hansard report (*Politics and Industry: The Great Mismatch*), which claimed that the present electoral system precluded the sort of long-term planning required by industrialists, who were concerned lest the next election produce a sudden and drastic change of policy – what Roy Jenkins later termed 'the ideological big dipper'.[43] Some of the examples used to strengthen this argument were the fate of the iron and steel industry (nationalised, denationalised and renationalised), the record of incomes policies (established, dismantled and reformed) and the legal status of the trade unions. This discontinuity, Hansard argued, was bad enough; when executed by parties flagrantly bereft of majority support, it was nothing short of outrageous.

All this implies that parties in government have not merely the *capacity* to make an impact, but *too much* capacity which needs to be curbed by electoral reform. This rationale has been fortified by the record of the Thatcher Governments, all of which lacked majority support – or even respectable levels of support in many parts of the country (such as Scotland). Indeed, it may be said that the behaviour of the Thatcher Governments not only amplifies the case for electoral reform but also undermines the Rose thesis about the limitations of party government. A series of dramatically entitled studies attest to the widespread belief among political observers that the Tory Governments of the 1980s made a difference that would have been inconceivable in 1979: *Mrs Thatcher's Revolution, Thatcherism and British Politics: The End of Consensus?*, *The Thatcher Years: A Decade of Revolution in British Politics*, *The Thatcher Phenomenon*.[44]

Kavanagh maintains that the Thatcher Governments deal a mortal blow to the theory that, no matter how determined and programmatic a party in office intends to be, its objectives are always diluted by the vicissitudes of administration. In support of this claim, Kavanagh recalls that in 1978, an essay by Rhodes Boyson clarified the six major tasks confronting a future Tory Government if Britain were to be revived in the way he and the Tory leadership envisaged. These were the reduction of income taxes and a top rate of 60 per cent, a substantial increase in police numbers and pay, ending exchange controls and allowing the pound to find its 'natural' level, ending the statutory monopoly of nationalised industries, a 5 per cent cut in annual government spending over five years and, finally, state welfare to be replaced by a scheme of payments and vouchers. Kavanagh argued that all but the last two objectives had been fulfilled by 1985 – an extraordinary achievement given the ambitious nature of the objec-

tives.[45] Kavanagh also believes that the 'adversary thesis' pro-
mulgated by Finer has been vindicated in a number of key areas,
citing trade union reform, rejection of formal incomes policy and
'tripartite' decision-making, stress upon the containment of
inflation even when unemployment was rising rapidly, privatisation and local government reform as 'significant dis-
continuities'.[46] He suggests that Mrs Thatcher's premiership has
changed the terrain of British politics to such an extent that many
of the changes will prove irreversible, a view shared by Gamble
who notes that the 'traditional post-war argument about different
kinds of interventionism has been replaced by a much broader
debate'.[47]

Riddell's survey of the Thatcher decade lends further support:
'The political agenda has changed. The focus has shifted from the
problems of producers and trade union obstruction to the freeing
of the market and the extension of consumer choice.'[48] For
Riddell, the vital element in the 'Thatcher revolution' has been
the determination of the premier in surmounting the difficulties
that threatened to deflect her Governments from the chosen path
(in a way that would have been considered commonplace by
Rose):

Mrs Thatcher's distinctive contribution has probably been to ensure that
critical events – the 1981 budget, the Falklands War in 1982 and the
miners' strike of 1984–85 – that might have fatally weakened her government were overcome. She has forced the pace of change and extended
her free-market counter-revolution further than alternative Tory leaders
might have done.[49]

Hugo Young echoes the view that her decision to persist with
deflation in July 1981 was crucial to the future of the Government.
Far from being inevitable, as Rose might suggest, Young insists
that it demanded 'extraordinary political will' in the face of contrary advice from large sections of the Cabinet and numerous
outside bodies of 'experts'.[50] Vincent agrees that 1981, 'the pivotal year of Thatcherism', marked a 'new determination by
government to govern'.[51] This willingness to defy pressures from
both external and internal sources to retreat from bold manifesto
themes was not applauded only by the radical right; left-wingers

like Benn inferred that Thatcherism showed what could be achieved by a Labour Government that had the courage of its convictions and was prepared to pursue doggedly 'its own brand of radical class politics'.[52]

Although most authors acknowledge that British politics and society have changed a good deal since 1979, there is a 'revisionist' school which argues that many of those changes would have occurred regardless of Mrs Thatcher's three election victories. As Pimlott observed: 'Clearly Britain is very different now from what it was in 1979; but it was very diferent in 1959 from what it was in 1949 after a decade of so-called consensus politics.'[53] The Thatcher Governments, as Rose emphasised in his updated version of *Do Parties Make a Difference?* (1984), sailed with, rather than against, many of the tides affecting society and the economy. Mrs Thatcher's task of revoking the social democratic ethos was made infinitely easier by the fact that it had been widely discredited already by events of the 1970s – the principal reason, perforce, for her accession to power; the rejection of Keynesian expansion as a cure for incomes policy and tripartism was fatefully undermined in 1978–79, even the idea of selling council houses was inspected by the Callaghan Government. As Vincent concedes, 'Many of the decisions that shaped government in the 1980s had already been made under Labour.'[54]

It is undeniable that the emergence of a 'white collar society' in the 1980s was influenced as much by the long-term decline of heavy industry and the long-term trend towards a skill-based service economy as by the policies promoted by the Thatcher Governments themselves (who were often responding to, rather than instigating such changes). Riddell has expressed doubts about whether even the spread of share and home ownership is a phenomenon for which the Thatcher Governments may claim total responsibility.

By far the greatest influence has been the death of that generation of first-time homeowners from the 1950s and 1960s. Their homes have been inherited by children in their thirties and forties, often already owning their own homes and who therefore receive a big increase in available capital. The sale of council houses, cuts in income and capital taxes and the inducements to buy shares in the main privatisation floatations have . . . extended an existing trend rather than created a new one.[55]

In a similar vein, John Kelly has written an extensive study of trade unions in the 1980s which concludes that although the Tory trade union laws of 1980, 1982, 1984 and 1988 did alter the political status of organised labour in Britain, much more pressing factors (which, to a large extent made those laws possible) were the rise of unemployment and the decline of those industrial areas which provided trade unionism with its traditional strongholds.[56] Pimlott concurs: 'Any government would have found itself in a very much stronger position in the 1980s when dealing with unions than was true in the 1970s.'[57]

The argument that government economic policies can only reflect international economic trends also appears germane to any study of the Thatcher Governments; as Young conceded, 'the anti-Keynesian posture of British Conservatism has been the global norm for most of the decade'.[58] There was a shift towards right-wing governments during the 1980s in West Germany, the USA, Canada, Netherlands, Belgium and Japan, with the hegemony of social democracy also being disturbed in Sweden, Denmark and Norway. Even more significant was the adoption of tax cuts, deflation and deregulation by supposedly socialist governments in France, Spain, Australia and New Zealand – a point developed in a study by Oliver Letwin – *Privatising the World* – which demonstrated that the Tories' privatisation programme only mirrored a general disenchantment with state-run industry.[59]

Despite Kavanagh's admiration for the programmatic success of the Thatcher Governments, neither are they entirely immune to the general argument that governments fail to secure many of their basic objectives on account of electoral, institutional and international restraints. Of particular importance here has been the initial emphasis upon monetary control, the core doctrine of government economic policy at the start of the 1980s. Between 1981 and 1984, the money supply rose by 50 per cent, against a target of 16–30 per cent, and continued to rise at around 20 per cent a year.[60] By early 1986, the Government was considered guilty, by many of its ideological gurus at the Centre for Policy Studies, of 'a potentially reckless monetary binge and a reflationary feast of backdoor Keynesianism' (hence its pamphlet *Whither Monetarism?*). It was also interesting that the Government chose to meet the inflationary surge of the late 1980s not with renewed emphasis upon stringent monetary control but with the traditional Keynesian panacea of high interest rates. Thus, the claim that Conservative economic policy in the 1980s embodied 'the resolute approach' deserves qualification, as does the boast that it fostered an 'economic miracle'; although economic growth rose significantly after 1979, by 1989 it had reverted only to the rates of 1969 when many were already deriding Britain as 'the sick man of Europe'.

Much of the explanation for the waverings of economic policy in the 1980s is to be found in the issue of public attitudes, which offers an intriguing note on which to finish any assessment of Thatcherism's impact. A critical element in the Rose thesis was a belief that a 'radical' party could be elected only if its proposals were resonant of shifting public attitudes. This may have been applicable in 1979: Sarlvik and Crewe found that during the 1970s there was a growing public hostility towards the trade unions and nationalisation and a growing interest in lower taxation, a return to 'traditional' moral values and greater individual choice.[61] The Thatcher Governments intended to capitalise on this trend by promoting a 'cultural revolution' in which 'the dependency culture would be replaced by the enterprise culture'.[62] Surveys conducted in the mid-to-late 1980s revealed that this 'crusade' (to use Crewe's term) had failed. The public was seen to favour the extension of public services to further tax cuts, more public ownership rather than more privatisation and a country which emphasised 'the social and collective provision of welfare' to one in which 'individuals are encouraged to look after themselves'.[63] As Crewe commented in 1989, 'the figures suggest that after ten years of Thatcherism the public remains wedded to the collectivist, welfare ethic of social democracy'.[64]

Such data would seem to confirm Rose's claim that the ability of parties to shape public opinion is seriously limited. Yet what Rose, writing in 1980, could not forsee was that governments at odds with public opinion over most key issues could still succeed in getting re-elected – if certain circumstances prevailed. In 1983, these circumstances were obvious, namely Labour's ill-conceived policies and campaign, its uninspiring leader, the 'Falklands factor', the novelty of the Alliance and the subsequent, predictable split in the anti-Conservative vote. In 1987, however, these factors no longer existed to the same extent. Labour fought a slick campaign and seemed more attuned to the principal concerns of the electorate; yet it was still defeated convincingly. Psephologists like Crewe attributed this anomoly to the 'feel good factor' – a belief among enough voters that the present Government had improved their personal economic situation and was better equipped than its opponents to sustain that improvement (see Chapter 9).[65]

It might be added, however, that Kavanagh does not find the issue of public attitudes in the Thatcher era especially significant or surprising, regarding the data as predictable by-products of a government that has held office for a considerable length of time:

In a sense, what you have you take for granted. The responses to many of the questions about values may, in many ways, be a tribute to the success of Thatcherism, i.e., that many of the things she would say she's accomplished have now so much been taken for granted that people can pine for yesterday's collectivist and egalitarian values.[66]

The Thatcher Governments have thus presented a fascinating test-case for the Rose thesis. There can be little doubt that many of the changes they instituted were in harmony with many of the changes already taking place both at home and abroad by the end of the 1970s. Yet despite the gap between much of the rhetoric and the reality, there can also be little doubt that the Tories in office have extended and accelerated these changes far more than their opponents would have dared or wished. The Thatcher era therefore suggests that a party in government can have a marked impact upon the nature of politics and society by defying short-term public opinion. To achieve this objective, it naturally requires a clear, programmatic idea of what it wishes to do, strong, determined leadership, favourable sociological trends, a discredited or depressed opposition and no small measure of specific good fortune (as provided, for example, by Argentina in 1982). With respect to the Attlee Government of 1945–50, it also needs more than one full term in office, a proposition which obviously relates to its economic performance but which also touches once again upon the state of its political opponents.

The period 1979–87 was thought to be a rare one in which the above factors seemed to conflate. Mrs Thatcher's downfall, and her replacement by a more consensual leader, were thought by many commentators to signal a return to 'normality'. Nevertheless, the re-election of the Major Government in 1992 has important consequences for students of party politics in Britain. The Conservatives' success was achieved in the midst of recession and with opinion polls again indicating that, on the 'vital' issues of health, education and employment, their policies still commanded less confidence than the Opposition's. The fact that the Government still clung to its 1987 share of the vote, and still enjoyed a substantial lead over Labour, suggested that there is still – ultimately – a widespread antipathy to the prospect of a Labour Government. This in itself has critical consequences, not just for the nature of Britain's party system but also for the outlook of a Conservative Party that seems almost impossible to remove from office. This may further encourage the belief, fostered by Mrs Thatcher, that it can endeavour to 're-educate' public opinion – and endure short-term unpopularity – without seriously jeopardising its chances of re-election. Rose's notion that party government would be forced into a consensual mode seems to fit ill alongside an Opposition that may no longer be capable of winning a general election.

### Endpiece: the European dimension

With the onset of the 1990s, any analysis of what parties can hope to achieve must give greater attention to the influence of the European Community. Of course, the implications of Community membership detain not only students of British political parties but those with a wider interest in the nature of Parliamentary government and the British Constitution. Nonetheless, as British Government has always meant party government, in this matter the two are – again – indivisible.

The debate concerning the restraints imposed upon British governments by the European Community is not a phenomenon of the late 1980s and 1990s. It was current during the years leading up to Britain's entry in 1973, underpinned the national referendum on continued membership in 1975 and was a major cause of division inside the Labour Party until the early 1980s. As a result of the European Communities Act 1972, British Government accepts that laws emanating from the Community's institutions are superior to legislation passed by Westminster, that British Governments are duty bound to enforce those laws, that British courts have no authority to question the primacy of EC legislation and that, in the event of any conflict betwen Westminster and the EC, the final verdict rests with the European Court of Justice. The British Government, through the European Council of Ministers, contributes to the formulation of the most politically sensitive decisions and has the power of veto in many areas; yet in practice this is not easy to exercise due to 'the combined effect of the increasing use of majority voting, the political pressures to concede and compromise so as to allow progress to be made, and the practial political difficulties involved in any attempt to use the veto'.[67]

The limitations upon governing parties at Westminster intensified during the 1980s, during which there was a steady increase in EC policy responsibilities. In areas such as control over company mergers and state aid to industry, this took the form of strengthening authority where the EC was already involved, while in areas such as anti-terrorism and consumer protection it has involved enchroaching into areas previously regarded as outside its purview. As Nugent explained: 'There are now few policy areas in which the Community is not involved in at least some way. Indeed, of the policy issues which customarily most concern governments, only defence and law and order remain virtually untouched by the Community's hand.'[68] (Nugent might have added that control over most aspects of defence policy has rested for some time with NATO rather than Westminster.)

Greater EC incursion into national policy-making spheres was one of the important effects of the Single European Act 1986 to which Britain was a signatory. The Act was also poignant in that it permitted greater use of majority voting in the Council of Ministers, thus circumscribing the value of the national veto. According to Nugent, over a hundred decisions are taken annually by majority voting 'and the number is growing as the practice comes increasingly to be regarded as acceptable'.[69] Furthermore, the entry into the EC of Spain and Portugal in 1986 made it impossible for any nation, under the arithmetical rules of majority voting, to block a proposal without the support of at least two other member states. In brief, membership of the EC during the 1980s brought about an erosion of what British parties in office might wish to accomplish.

The trend is likely to intensify further in the 1990s. Britain's entry into the European Exchange Rate Mechanism in 1990 and the creation of a European 'Single Market' in 1992 have increased the pressure for majority voting in the Council of Ministers as well as fuelling demands for greater monetary integration. By the start of the 1990s, a furious debate was raging between and within the major British parties over the merits of European Monetary Union and a single European currency. This was thought by many (such as Nicholas Ridley, whose outburst to the *Spectator* led to his Cabinet resignation in July 1990) to have profound implications for British Parliamentary sovereignty and, eventually, the scope of initiatives left open to parties in government. The arguments for monetary union were seen – not without justification – as part of a larger campaign for European political integration, a drift towards European federalism which would reduce Britain to a regional institution, akin to an individual state within the USA. As Congdon wrote:

It follows that if the power to issue money is transferred from national central banks to a pan-European central bank (or Euro-Fed) ... the power to raise taxes and interest rates would be shared between the Euro-Fed and national parliaments. The fiscal prerogative would no longer be exercised only at the national level.[70]

This would make it increasingly difficult to hold British parties in government wholly responsible for many aspects of economic policy, while the enhanced ability of the EC to raise money from European taxpayers would strengthen enormously its capacity to initiate new schemes and policies affecting EC countries. For Congdon, the issue of monetary union was not just about taxation, savings, inflation, pensions and mortgages (vital though these are to the dynamics of modern voting behaviour), but 'ultimately, nothing more or less than whether Britain is to remain an independent and sovereign state'.[71]

For many on the centre-left of British politics, however, this 'pooling' of sovereignty was to be welcomed as it increased the chances of the aims they held dear being realised – aims which the Labour Party in government had struggled, in vain, to achieve. Indeed, many of these aims were enshrined in EC President Jacques Delors' *Social Charter* (1989), seen by many on the right as confirming their suspicion that the EC represented the 'restoration of social democracy by stealth'.[72] As the *New Statesman and Society* pointed out in 1990, the increasingly interdependent character of the western world precluded any 'progressive' party in government from taking critical decisions without regard to the growth in the volume of international trade, the internationalisation of money markets and the omnipresence of multinational corporations.[73] Economic and political federalism, in short, were necessary precisely because national governments could no longer hope to meet the most important expectations of their voters without compromising and co-operating with other national governments. According to this argument, European federalism would give governing parties in Britain some influence over the international forces that would otherwise deflect their objectives.

This is a rather sobering note on which to finish an examination of political parties in Britain today. Much of this textbook, like most other studies of British government and politics, has been based upon a tacit assumption that having sorted out their policies, strategies and organisation, electorally successful parties may then go on to govern in a way that they and their electors see fit. That assumption, already questionable in the 1980s, may be clearly untenable as the 1990s draw to a close.

## Notes

1  K. Ewing, *The Funding of Political Parties in Britain*, Cambridge, 1987, chapter seven.
2  R. T. McKenzie, *Political Parties*, London, 1955, pp. 2–7.
3  R. Rose, *Do Parties Make a Difference?*, London, 1980.
4  D. McKie & C. Cook (eds), *The Decade of Disillusion*, London, 1972.
5  D. Kavanagh, *Thatcherism*, Oxford, 1987, pp. 297–304.
6  Rose, *Do Parties Make a Difference?*, p. 169.
7  R. Michels, *Political Parties*, New York, 1954.
8  P. Hennessy & A. Seldon (eds), *Ruling Performance*, Oxford, 1987, pp. 32–3.
9  J. Hayward, quoted in S. Ingle, *British Party System*, Oxford, 1987, p. 191.
10  A. King, 'Death of the manifesto', *Observer*, 17 February 1974.
11  C. Rallings, 'The influence of election programmes: Britain and Canada 1956–79', in I. Budge, D. Robertson & D. J. Hearl (eds), *Ideology, Strategy and Party Change*, Cambridge, 1987.
12  Rose, *Do Parties Make a Difference?*, p. 72.
13  Hennessy & Seldon, *Ruling Performance*, p. 326.
14  P. Pulzer, 'Do parties matter', *Contemporary Record*, winter, 1988.
15  Pulzer, 'Do parties matter'.
16  C. A. R. Crosland, *Future of Socialism*, London, 1953, p. 61.
17  Quoted in Hennessy & Seldon, *Ruling Performance*, p. 49.
18  D. Coates, *The Labour Party and the Struggle for Socialism*, London, 1975, p. 47.
19  D. Coates, *Labour in Power?*, London, 1980; T. Benn, *Office Without Power*, London, 1989; C. Ponting, *Breach of Promise: Labour in Power 1964–1970*, London, 1989.
20  D. Walker, 'The first Wilson governments', in Hennessy & Seldon, *Ruling Performance*.
21  Hennessy & Seldon, *Ruling Performance*, p. 203.
22  K. O. Morgan, 'The Labour party's record in office', *Contemporary Record*, April 1990.
23  Harold Lever, review of Barbara Castle's diaries, *Listener*, 22 November 1984.
24  Hennessy & Seldon, *Ruling Performance*, p. 307.
25  Hennessy & Seldon, *Ruling Performance*, p. 308.

26  Quoted in R. Eatwell, *The 1945–1951 Labour Governments*, London, 1979, p. 162.

27  R. H. S. Crossman, *Inside View*, London, 1971.

28  See J. Ramsden, 'Adapting to the post-war consensus'.

29  Hennessy & Seldon, *Ruling Performance*, p. 81.

30  Hennessy & Seldon, *Ruling Performance*, p. 67.

31  Hennessy & Seldon, *Ruling Performance*, p. 80.

32  See A. Sked & C. Cook, *Post-War Britain*, London, 1984, pp. 114–41.

33  Hennessy & Seldon, *Ruling Performance*, p. 222.

34  Blake, *Peel to Thatcher*, p. 310.

35  D. Kavanagh quoted in Hennessy & Seldon, *Ruling Performance*, p. 231.

36  A. King (ed.), *Why is Britain Becoming Harder to Govern?*, London, 1976.

37  Conservative Party's Treasurer's Department, *Statement of Accounts 1990–91*, CCO Publications, London; *Guardian*, 30 September 1989.

38  M. Pinto-Duschinsky, 'The funding of political parties since 1945', in A. Seldon (ed.), *UK Political Parties Since 1945*, Hemel Hempstead, 1990, p. 97.

39  Pinto-Duschinsky, 'Funding of political parties', p. 101.

40  See, for example, R. Taylor, 'Who needs the TUC?', *Observer*, 11 February 1979.

41  Ewing, *Funding of Political Parties*, p. 177.

42  S. E. Finer (ed.), *Adversary Politics and Electoral Reform*, London, 1975.

43  R. Jenkins, 'Home thoughts from abroad', in Kennett, *The Rebirth of Britain*.

44  P. Jenkins, *Thatcher's Revolution*, London, 1987, Kavanagh, *Thatcherism*; J. Cole, *Thatcher Years*; London, 1987, H. Young & A. Sloman, *The Thatcher Phenomenon*, London, 1986.

45  Kavanagh, *Thatcherism*, p. 283.

46  Kavanagh, *Thatcherism*, p. 315.

47  Kavanagh, *Thatcherism*, p. 298.

48  P. Riddell, *The Thatcher Decade*, Oxford, 1989, p. 208.

49  Riddell, *Thatcher Decade*, p. 216.

50  H. Young, *One of Us*, London, 1989, p. 544.

51  Hennessy & Seldon, *Ruling Performance*, p. 285.

52  *The Campaign for Labour Party Democracy*, Labour Party Conference pamphlet, October 1982.

53  B. Pimlott, 'The audit of Thatcherism', *Contemporary Record*, Autumn 1989.

54  Hennessy & Seldon, *Ruling Performance*, p. 275.

**55**   Riddell, *Thatcher Decade*, p. 207.
**56**   J. Kelly, *Trade Unions and Socialist Politics*, London, 1988.
**57**   Pimlott, 'Audit'.
**58**   Young, *One of Us*, p. 526.
**59**   O. Letwin, *Privatising the World*, London, 1988.
**60**   Young, *One of Us*, p. 533.
**61**   I. Crewe and B. Sarlvik, *Decade of Dealignment*, Cambridge, 1983, chapter eight.
**62**   I. Crewe, 'The policy agenda', *Contemporary Record*, February 1990.
**63**   From Worcester & Jacobs, *We British*, p. 25.
**64**   Crewe, 'Agenda'.
**65**   I. Crewe, 'Why Mrs. Thatcher won with a landslide', *Social Studies Review*, September 1987.
**66**   Pimlott, 'Audit'.
**67**   N. Nugent, 'The European Community and British independence', *Talking Politics*, autumn 1989, pp. 29–33.
**68**   Nugent, 'European Community'.
**69**   Nugent, 'European Community'.
**70**   T. Congdon, 'The last of England', *Spectator*, 23 June 1990.
**71**   Congdon, 'The last of England'.
**72**   Editorial, *Spectator*, 21 July 1990.
**73**   Editorial, *New Statesman and Society*, 22 June 1990.

# INDEX

numbers in bold indicate main page references

287